AN ILLUSTRATED HISTORY OF
FRANCE

André Maurois

AN ILLUSTRATED HISTORY OF

FRANCE

Translated by Henry L. Binsse

and Gerard Hopkins

THE VIKING PRESS

NEW YORK

CONTENTS

I

The First Beginnings and the Middle Ages

Gaul and France till 1483

In the French province of Périgord, in ages long past, there used to be a sort of prehistoric city, formed by caverns, as thick as rabbit warrens on the edge of a forest. About thirty thousand years ago a people dwelt there; fishing and hunting supplied their needs and, on the stone surface of their caves, they drew, with the ease and charm born of long acquaintance, pictures of reindeer and buffalo. It cannot be said that the history of these men belongs to the history of France, for nations had not yet taken shape. Nevertheless, the thin outer skin of historic times encases many layers of prehistory, and successive generations which seem to have left no trace of their passage through this world other than bits of stone and bronze tools, have in fact bequeathed man a legacy of words, institutions and recipes without which the sequel to their story would have been past conceiving.

There has never been a French race: there were Ligurians inhabiting the Alps, and Iberians in the Pyrenees. Over the Mediterranean came Phoenician sailors, Semitic traders, and, later on, Greek navigators who brought with them the civilization of the East.

Many centuries before Christ a new civilization, the Celtic, filtered into the valleys of the Rhine and the Rhône, and in the fourth century their superiority of armament and their prowess enabled them to conquer an empire, and become the overlords of the native populations in the lands which are now France and Spain. In French veins is mingled the blood of the Iberians and the Ligurians as well as that of the Celts, Romans and many another race. As for the name Gaulois, it was the appellation given by the Romans to the Celts (Galli).

Be it in Gaul or in Britain, Celtic societies were, Caesar tells us, divided into clans. A group of clans formed a tribe, several tribes a nation. The total population of Gaul in Caesar's time was somewhere between five and thirteen millions. The villages, crudely built in the middle of clearings, must have resembled those of the present-day tribes in Central Africa. The climate was colder than in Italy; breeches (or trousers) and a deerskin jacket were worn.

The Gauls worshipped local and rural divinities such as Borvo, god of hot springs, who has bequeathed his name to the royal House of Bourbon, and Diva, goddess of rivers. They also practised a more secret cult, the mysteries of which were taught by the religious fraternity of Druids, part astrologers, part witch-doctors.

Gallic society was barbarous but not savage. The Gauls were capable of heroism but not of discipline or long-continued effort. Factional strife split not only clans and tribes but even families, and tribal hatreds were at times so violent that the aristocracy of one tribe would call in the Romans to help them against others of their own blood.

The Romans could hardly feel scrupulous about seizing a country ravaged by private wars, the frontiers of which lay unprotected. In fact, to conquer Gaul became a legitimate and even praiseworthy undertaking.

In 58 B.C. the proconsul of both Cisalpine and Transalpine Gaul was Julius Caesar, a forty-six-year-old politician, as ambitious as he was able. In his opinion the republican aristocracy was finished, and some day a strong man would seize the reins of Roman power. He wanted to be that man. But to carry out this great scheme, he needed prestige and an army: the proconsulate of the two Gauls could supply him with both. As early as 59, Gallic quarrels had paved the way for intervention. Backed by an army of well-trained veterans and a great superiority in armaments, he had within a few years conquered the whole of Gaul, and arrested German encroachments along the Rhine.

Caesar's harsh treatment of the Gauls ended by making rebellion inevitable. Vercingetorix, son of the chieftain of the Arvernes, assumed leadership of the rebels and for several months, by a campaign of guerrilla and partisan warfare, succeeded in holding in check the best army in the world, but his defeat was inevitable. In September 52,

STATUETTES FROM GAUL: FEMALE AND MALE Both are cast in bronze and were unearthed at Neuvy-en-Sullias (Loiret). *Yves Guillemaut, Jean Suquet.* (*Musée historique de l'Orléanais, Orléans.*)

besieged in Alesia, he was obliged to surrender, and even so the war of independence dragged on for another year or two.

Had Gaul not been Latinized, though, the Roman Empire would quickly have become an Oriental empire. Latin Gaul restored the equilibrium, to the advantage of the West. For Gaul became Latin, and in spite of the harshness of Roman oppression, speedy assimilation took place. Caesar, whose ambition thenceforward looked to Rome itself, wished to leave a pacified Gaul behind him. This he achieved principally by means of the policy of winning to his own purposes the natural leaders of the conquered country. The aristocracy became Romanized. In each town a municipal senate made it possible for the old families to assume titles and honours. At Vienne, Lyons, Lutetia were erected mass-produced Roman cities, each with its theatre and basilica, the latter serving at once as city hall and meeting place. Roman aqueducts brought them their water.

For five centuries Gaul remained a Roman province. At the beginning of the conquest the country prospered greatly. At last the country had roads, frontiers, a military police. Everywhere along the Roman highways sprang up new dwellings, Mediterranean in type, villas adorned with columns and porticoes, marble or terra-cotta statuary. Only a few decades earlier the Gauls had dwelt in huts of mud wattle in the midst of wildernesses. Yet the poorer townspeople and the peasants remained loyal to Celtic traditions.

A new faith now began to spread through the Mediterranean world. It took a hundred years for Christianity to reach Lyons, but the blood of the martyrs helped to sow the seed in men's hearts. Later, the Empire itself became Christian under Constantine; and when subsequently the Empire weakened to a shadow, the Church remained the only organized power as well as an embodiment of justice and culture.

Meanwhile, the numerous German tribes beyond the Rhine were constantly on the move towards the west and the south in search for new lands and pasturage. These Barbarian invasions were in no sense large-scale movements into Gaul and Italy on the part of organized armies, but little by little the bands that occupied a particular territory and belonged to the same tribal group fashioned a kingdom. Thus, in the fifth century the Visigoths occupied Aquitania, the Burgundians the valleys of the Saône and the Rhône, the Alamans Alsace, and the Franks northern Gaul. For a time, the Barbarians and the Gallo-Romans lived side by side, each people speaking its own language, but 'fraternization' was inevitable.

Later, in the face of new invasions, they were to join forces, and in 451 Gauls, Franks and Romans together defeated Attila's Huns in the Battle of the Catalaunian Fields, thus consecrating the unity of the west.

After the fall of the Empire, Gaul became a mosaic of Barbarian kingdoms, soon to be dominated by Clovis, chieftain of the Franks. The Christian faith made certain the continuance of some sort of unity in Gaul, a unity further enforced when Clovis fell under the influence of his Catholic wife and was baptized, thus guaranteeing himself the all-powerful support of the bishops. By slaughtering friends and enemies, by trickery and assassination as much as by prowess in arms, Clovis extended his kingdom to the Pyrenees. But this royal gangster did his country great service.

His descent from a race of heroes, his military leadership and his consecration by the Church gave him sufficient prestige to be able to re-establish, after the collapse of the Empire, the territorial unity of Gaul, soon to be named France (land of the Franks).

The dynasty of the Merovingian kings ruled France for three hundred years, longer than the Valois or the Bourbons.

This age was one of the blackest in history, as are all those when an old order disappears, leaving men at the mercy of their own passions. The Gallo-Romans were no longer governed by an administrati n of the Roman variety. The Barbarians had wrecked the idea of the law, they had wrecked the idea of State finances and the Merovingian kings had squandered the kingdom; they had wrecked the idea of a State justice, and the nobles, like the Church, thenceforth claimed the administration of their own justice. Gregory of Tours paints a frightful picture in which the violence of these half-savage despots was wreaked upon their own sons, their wives and even on ecclesiastical dignitaries. After Dagobert who, prematurely exhausted by his numerous spouses, died *of old age* at the age of thirty-four, the Merovingians fell into utter decay. A society of this sort could not last. After his death, 639, the decay was past mending and no great ruler made any further attempt to arrest it.

A high official called the Mayor of the Palace came to be the real chieftain of the kingdom and the leader of an independent aristocracy. One such mayor, Charles Martel, reigned *de facto* over Austrasia and Neustria for twenty-six years. He had shaped a body of rugged Frankish infantry, with which, near Poitiers, he stopped an Arab raiding party sent from Spain (732). The Pope, recognizing the advantage of a strong army under a loyal Catholic prince, agreed to legitimize a dynastic change and to recognize Charles Martel's son Pepin. He was anointed in the Basilica of Saint Denis, in 754 by Pope Stephen II who proclaimed the new king and his two sons 'Patricians of the Romans' and ordered the Franks never again to choose their sovereigns outside this family. In return for this noteworthy service, Pepin drove the Lombards from the Pope's domains. In Charles, son of Pepin (later surnamed Carolus Magnus, or Charlemagne), the family produced the most illustrious of its leaders. Not that he was a creator. But he had the luck to reign for forty-three years, and to be able to govern by himself; a long reign is a great opportunity, and his character was equal to his good fortune. During these forty-three years Charlemagne waged war. But his campaigns, unlike those of the Merovingian kings, were not civil strife among jealous relatives. He was following out a vast scheme: the defence against the pagans of the former Roman Empire. In this way he extended his kingdom

JULIUS CAESAR As proconsul he conquered Gaul, 58-52 BC; he was assassinated in 44 BC. (*Metropolitan Museum, New York.*)

from the Rhine to the Vistula. He was confirmed in his role of arbiter of Christendom when, on Christmas Day, in the year 800, he was crowned by Leo III in Saint Peter's, Emperor of the Romans under the name of Charles Augustus. At a stroke the Western Empire was revived and the Roman pontiff was ensured the right to make an emperor out of the soldier of the Church. In 814 he died, and his empire did not long survive him: it was carved up as a result of family partitionings. His grandsons, after having long fought each other, came to an agreement on the division of their inheritance at Verdun in 843; as a result of this partition, two of the States of modern Europe — France and Germany — were created. It also opened the road to the long-continued violence between the two countries by creating

THE PONT DU GARD
This aqueduct, 269 metres long and 48 metres high, carried water from the springs at Uzès to Nîmes; here it crosses the Gardon. c. 19 BC. *Photo Molinard.*

1 - St Clotilde prays to St Martin at Tours to avert the war between her sons, 534. f⁰ 23.

2 - Chilperic I, King of the Franks at Soissons, strangles his wife Galeswinthe, c. 567. f⁰ 31.

3 - Sigebert I, King of the Franks at Metz, is murdered at Vitry by agents of Fredegund, 575. f⁰ 33 v⁰.

4 - Tortured for three days, Brunehaut, widow of Sigebert I, is killed at the age of more than eighty, 612. f⁰ 60 v⁰.

5 - Death of Roland, Count of the Breton Marches, at Roncevaux, August 15th, 778. f⁰ 122 v⁰.

6 - Charlemagne crowned Holy Roman Emperor by Leo III, December 25th, 800. f⁰ 97.

Grandes Chroniques de France; ms. fr. 2813. *Photo B. N.*

LA·ROYNE·CLOTILDE   AVRELIEN

THE BAPTISM OF CLOVIS (*Musée de Reims*), *tapestry of the life of St Remy*.

Tapestry included in a series offered by Cardinal Robert de Lenoncourt, Archbishop of Rheims, to his cathedral and to Saint-Remi (1530-1531). King Clovis (c. 483-511) is being baptized by St Remy, Bishop of Rheims; the time and place of the ceremony is open to question but was probably at Christmas, 508, in the Cathedral of Tours, this city being then the religious centre of Gaul. Three legends are woven into this tapestry: the dove bringing from Heaven the Holy Phial, the angel bringing the emblem of the fleurs-de-lys, and the king carrying the emblem of the toads on his banners before his baptism.

PÉPIN THE SHORT He was anointed by the Gallic bishops assembled at Soissons, and then by Pope Stephen II at Saint-Denis, (July 28th, 754). *Sacramentaire de Metz;* ms. lat. 1141, f° 2 v°. *Photo B. N.*

TYMPANUM OF THE DOORWAY OF SAINT-PIERRE DE MOISSAC The vision of Christ in glory with the twenty-four Ancients of the ▶ Apocalypse; completed about 1120 (Tarn-et-Garonne). *Photo Bulloz.*

KING AND QUEEN AT THE END OF THE XIIth CENTURY King Solomon and the Queen of Sheba, originally at Notre-Dame de Corbeil (Seine-et-Oise), now in the Louvre. *Photo Arch. Photographiques.*

between them that Lotharingian corridor which both of these civilizations would continue to claim. Nevertheless, and despite the rapid break-up of his empire, it can be said that Charlemagne had created the West, by reawakening Latin culture there and by giving the West a feeling of its own unity.

After the treaty of 843, the dismemberment of Charlemagne's empire continued. As early as 888, seven different kingdoms could be counted: France, Navarre, Provence, Burgundy, Lorraine, Germany and Italy.

The mass of the people accepted this partitioning and even hoped for it. For one thing, national characters were taking shape, and the union — under a single State — of nations already different was hard to bear. In the second place, the peoples could see that the Empire was incapable of protecting them either from the Norse invaders or from the Saracens. The small landholders and peasants, therefore, asked the local governments to ensure the defence of the land against brigands and pirates. The skeleton of such governments already existed. It was built of counts, marquises and dukes, all the warriors who had been granted domains or given commands. These soldiers, at least, were able to defend the regions they governed against the invaders, with the help of their retainers who, in their turn, gathered their vassals and came to their lord's assistance. Feudalism amounted to an armed band settled permanently on a domain around a chieftain and constantly ready to leave the labour of the fields for battle. The general had portioned the land out to his soldiers but retained the right to recall the soldiers to duty whenever that land was threatened. Thus a class of landowning soldiers began to take shape — the nobility of the following centuries.

The feudal order had its faults and they were bad ones, but at least it was an order. In the tenth and eleventh centuries it afforded a remedy for anarchy and it quieted fears. At the beginning these sovereign lords in their turn derived from the Carolingian King, but by the tenth century the Frankish monarchy was in tatters and it was precisely from this 'paralysis of sovereignty' that feudalism was born.

Moreover, the monarchy was then weakened in France by strife between two houses: the traditional Carolingian and a 'Robertian' (later Capetian) house, sprung from Robert the Strong, Count of Anjou and Blois, one of the greatest landowners in the country lying between the Seine and the Loire, which is the heart of France. The French clergy supported the Robertians against the Carolingians because the latter no longer had enough power to be the Church's

effective protectors. So when in 987 the lords of France met to elect a king, the choice fell on Hugh Capet, founder of the third French dynasty. But the first Capetians had to play a difficult part. Their kingdom was reduced to their family domain. Also, the elected king was dependent upon his electors. He was so weak that such lesser lords as the counts of Corbeil and Melun worried him. And not only were the first Capetians poor, their domain small, their vassals powerful, but linguistic anarchy added to the sovereign's weakness. Norman was spoken at Rouen and at Caen, Celtic in Brittany, the *langue d'oc* in Provence and Aquitaine. Another danger lay in the elective system which, each time a sovereign died, opened to question what had been achieved. The Capetians successfully sought to ward off this threat by having the King's eldest son consecrated during his father's lifetime.

Three major facts dominate the eleventh century. The first is the conquest of England by the Normans under William the Conqueror. Henceforth the presence, on the soil of his kingdom, of a great vassal who was himself a powerful sovereign was a constant threat to the King of France. The problem would be resolved only on the day when the King of France became master of Normandy — or the King of England master of France.

The second important fact is the part played by the Crusades, by means of which the Church endeavoured to put the courage of the feudal warrior at the service of Christendom. The First Crusade was preached by Urban II, a Frenchman, at the Council of Clermont in 1095. Peter the Hermit, astride his mule, wandered all over France enlisting men of the people under the banner of the Cross. This poor men's Crusade was touching and ill-fated. The greater part of its forces perished before reaching Jerusalem. The Crusade of the knights, better organized, was supplied by sea, thanks to the merchants of Italy. Jerusalem was taken in 1099; a kingdom of Jerusalem was set up as a feudal State, the sovereign and barons of which were French. The third important fact of the eleventh century was the rebirth of the cities and the formation in France of a new bourgeois class which leaned on the King and supported him against the unruly barons. Thus, Louis VI, the Fat (1108-37), began to play the part of a righter of wrongs throughout the country. Whether he granted charters, intervened as a mediator between cities and their feudal masters, or installed his own provosts, the King worked hand in hand with the bourgeoisie.

CHARLES II THE BALD AND COUNT VIVIEN (*First*) *Bible of Charles the Bald;* ms. lat. 1, fᵒ 423. *Photo B. N.*

This work was executed c. 846 by the School of Tours. Monks, their hands veiled in the oriental fashion, bring the bible to the king, on whose right is Vivien, Count of Tours and lay Abbot of Tours and Marmoutier. The king is crowned with lilies and the hand of God is over him. In 851 Robert IV the Strong, ancestor of the Capetians, was to succeed Count Vivien in his honours.

ST LOUIS IX, KING OF FRANCE Probable statue of this king (d. 1270) carried out at the beginning of the XIVth century; it is now in the church at Mainneville (Eure). Louis IX was canonized in 1297 by Boniface VIII. (*Photo by Raymond Voinquel from Robert Darène's film 'St Louis, King of France'.*)

His son, Louis VII, was gallant, pious and naively like-able. But his queen, Eleanor of Aquitaine, a woman of overweening temperament, had become enamoured of the Count of Anjou, Henry Plantagenet. She married him and brought him Limousin, Gascony, Périgord and the whole Duchy of Aquitaine. Such were the absurd results of the feudal and personal relationship; the whim of a pretty woman could carve up empires. From his mother, Matilda, Henry already possessed the Duchy of Normandy; from his father, Maine and Anjou. After his marriage he was much more powerful in France than the King of France. When, in 1154, he also became King of England, the Angevin Empire threatened to swallow France.

The son of Louis VII, Philip Augustus, became king at the age of fifteen, inheriting a heart-rending situation. Between the Angevin Empire of the Plantagenets and the German Empire of Louis the German, which likewise included a portion of Italy (in the old tradition that the Emperor was also King of the Lombards), the King of France in the twelfth century looked like a second-class sovereign. Yet Philip Augustus conquered the Emperor and drove the Plantagenets from France. Energetic, ruddy, as healthy and thick-set as a peasant, bushy-haired, violent but cunning, self-centred but reasonable, he was the very opposite of a feudal king. His ideal was not that of a knight but of a patient and crafty politician. Skilfully he played his game. Severe with the powerful, astute in making use of lesser men, he enlisted the support of the cities against the feudality, and from the beginning of his reign he kept in check a coalition of the more important lords. In his struggle against England, he was helped by the rancour of the Church, which had not forgiven Henry II for his murder of Archbishop Thomas à Becket, and by the family quarrels between Henry and his appalling sons. Had they been united, the Plantagenets would easily have conquered him. But they imprudently allowed him to play the sons off against the father, then later, brothers against brothers. With Richard Cœur de Lion, who succeeded Henry II, Philip Augustus was at first on good terms. Together they went on a crusade, then they fell at odds, and upon his return, Philip undertook the conquest of Richard's lands. It was lucky for him that the English king died (1199), leaving him with John Lackland as his opponent — a madman suspected of several murders, whose misdeeds made it possible to place his domains under confiscation. In this way feudal law played into the hands of Philip Augustus, enabling him to recapture, almost without fighting, Normandy, Maine, Anjou, Touraine and Poitou. For France here was a miraculous draught of fishes. The ease with which all these provinces changed hands proves that French unity existed in men's hearts before it existed in deeds. Yet the danger was not exorcized. The King of France's enemies joined forces; the King of England (John Lackland), the Emperor of Germany (Otto IV), Ferrand, Count of Flanders, together with other great lords massed their strength in Flanders. Against this coalition Philip Augustus had the support of the Church and the people. In 1214 at Bouvines, with the help of twenty thousand bourgeois infantrymen — a great novelty — he overcame the reactionary feudal forces and the foreign invaders. This victory consolidated the work of the Capetians. It was greeted by France with that extraordinary joy which goes with the liberation of a country aware of its unity. Everywhere the people danced, clerks sang, churches were hung with tapestries, the streets were strewn with flowers, grasses and leafy branches. For seven days and seven nights the students of Paris revelled with songs and dancing. The King had forgiven even those who had been leagued against him. The national community was born.

Philip Augustus was a modern king, a good organizer, a good diplomat, a good technician. He was not only lord of lords, but a governmental head. He realized the importance of economic matters and helped French merchants to recover their credit abroad. Moreover, he also took under his protection merchants from other countries who came to visit the fairs. To the French monarchy he gave 'the three instruments of rule which it lacked: tractable officials, money and soldiers'.

Philip Augustus was also one of the first lovers of the city. He bestowed great care upon Paris, his capital, paving the two streets adjoining his palace, 'La Cité', streets which before his time had been malodorous mud paths. He set up a police force, the royal watch, made up of twenty men on horse and forty on foot. Facing the Cité on the right bank, the city of Paris was growing up as a business centre; on the left bank was the Latin Quarter, where dwelt the university students. The King built ramparts round this triple agglomeration, and for its defence erected 'Our Tower of the Louvre' to the west of this enclosure. When he went off on a crusade, it was to six Paris merchants that he handed over the keys of his Treasury and the guardianship of the seals. Although a devout man, he well knew how to maintain the rights of the State against the claims of the Church. Pope Innocent III looked upon all kings as his vassals; Philip Augustus never subscribed to this view. He allowed a crusade to be organized against the Albigensian heretics by Simon de Montfort, but he refused to associate himself with it and only intervened, after the defeat of the Albigenses, in order to reunite to the crown the domains of Raymond VII, Count of Toulouse, and those of his vassals, the Viscount of Béziers and the Count of Foix. Thus the Church was responsible for the atrocities of this crusade and the monarchy took the spoils.

If one compares maps of the royal domain in 987 with those of 1223, one realizes that in the course of these two centuries the Duke of Ile-de-France had become the King of France. The Capetians had so closely linked the crown and the national welfare that none but a few jealous great vassals questioned any longer the legitimacy of their power. The notion that the King could be elected by an assembly had been completely forgotten. Philip Augustus was the first of the Capetians who could without recklessness omit having his son consecrated during his own lifetime. Despite this omission, his son, Louis VIII, succeeded to the throne without any difficulty, but died after a very short reign.

Louis IX was endowed by his parents with deep piety and a violent temperament. Every morning he went to Mass and, after his siesta, heard the office of the dead. But despite his religious humility, he did not hesitate to dress himself royally, in a vermilion surcoat edged with ermine. In no sense was he a bigot, but a handsome knight with a laughing countenance who loved to jest with his intimates. And his meetings at the oak tree of Vincennes, under the shadow of which he meted out justice, seated upon a carpet among his companions, have remained famous. In his decisions he never took the rank of pleaders into account and, devout as he was, did not hesitate to defend the rights of his subjects against the Church.

TADDEO GADDI: TRIUMPH OF ST THOMAS AQUINAS A Dominican friar, St Thomas taught in the University of Paris. He remains today the Church's foremost philosopher. (*Spanish Chapel, Santa Maria Novella, Florence.*) *Photo Alinari-Giraudon.*

Saint Louis, a valorous soldier, took part in two crusades: the Seventh in 1248, which lasted six years and was a long series of disasters, and the Eighth in 1270, which ended with the King's death in Tunis from an attack of the plague. To preserve peace among Christians and to fight the infidel was the sum total of his foreign policy. When, in 1270, he died, he bequeathed his son a prestige greater than that which he himself had inherited from his ancestors: he had acquired the prestige of moral authority. Such was his private sanctity as well as his integrity as a king that it was natural that he should have been canonized (in 1297).

It is hard to be the son of a saint. Philip III, the Bold, (1270-1285), was pious, stout-hearted and a typical knight, but France's admiration for his father paralysed him and made him a spiritless sovereign.

The King who, after Philip Augustus and Saint Louis, completes the trinity of great Capetians, was his successor, Philip IV, the Fair (1285-1314). He fell heir to a strong government and he made it stronger. Philip the Fair, 'the most spendthrift of our kings', had only one financial principle, to get hold of money by any and every means. In 1306 all the Jews were arrested and their goods seized. Then came the turn of the Lombard bankers. And finally came devaluation through a debasing of the currency. In the meantime the Anglo-French problem had not been settled, and could not be as long as the King of England remained master of Guienne. Numerous incidents led finally to war. France had Scotland as her ally; England, the Count of Flanders. At Rouen, Philip the Fair caused a squadron to be built to control the Channel. In the end Edward kept Guienne, admitted that he was a vassal of the French throne, married Marguerite (Philip the Fair's sister) and married his son (later Edward II) to Isabel, the daughter of the King of France. This was a serious mistake on Philip's part and was one of the causes of the Hundred Years War, for the claim which Edward III, Isabel's son, was to lay to the crown of France sprang from this marriage. Flanders wavered, as she would continue to do for centuries, between France and England. She was wealthy, proud and independent; the Flemish middle class resisted the pretensions of the counts of Flanders, thus encouraging foreign intrigue. Philip the Fair long struggled against Flanders, with alternate success and failure, for this people of weavers was more than once able to put to flight the knighthood of France, and the Matins of Bruges were as bloody as the Sicilian Vespers. At last, in 1305, a treaty was drawn up. Philip

had acquired Lille, Douai and Orchies, today one of the richest of French provinces.

But the most serious struggle of this reign was that between the King of France and the Papacy. The Capetian monarchy, jealous of its rights, was sooner or later bound to fall out with Rome, and the bull *Unam sanctam*, in 1302, sparked the quarrel, in the course of which the Pope, Boniface VIII, died. His successor likewise died very shortly after his elevation and in 1305 French influence brought about the election of the Archbishop of Bordeaux, Bertrand de Got, who chose the name of Clement V; in 1309 he settled himself in the convent of the Order of Preaching Brothers at Avignon. The popes dwelt there from 1309 to 1377 utterly subject to the influence of the kings of France, and only in 1377 did they return to Rome.

Under Philip the Fair the most painful episode in these quarrels between France and Rome was the suit against the Knights Templars, who had acquired great wealth in France. Nogaret the Terrible, master of the seals, set out to ruin the Templars and succeeded: the Order was stripped and dissolved; its Grand Master, Jacques de Molay, was burned to death; its goods were seized.

In order to win public opinion in all these conflicts, Philip the Fair, in 1308, convoked the States General at Tours. Not only the clergy and the barons but two hundred and fifty cities were represented therein. But whereas in England knights and merchants were willing to sit together in the House of Commons, in France the three estates remained separate, thus making impossible any idea of national representation. The States General did not debate or initiate anything; it listened and gave its approval. Calling its members together merely helped the King to levy taxes and to put an end to complaints against the debased currency. This support was sorely needed, for at that time there was much irritation throughout the country. When Philip the Fair died, he was hated, perhaps unjustly. He had strengthened royal absolutism, fought feudal and ecclesiastical power and substituted the public might for individual interest.

As early as the tenth century there had begun a French renaissance, the ideas and the arts of which were to spread out over all Europe. The diffusion of a culture throughout Europe was, then, all the easier because the Church constituted a sort of community of peoples, imposing Latin upon them as a universal language and bringing about the acceptance by all of beliefs substantially unchallenged. In France as in England or in Germany, as in Spain or in

KNIGHTS OF THE STAR AT THE TABLE OF HONOUR *Grandes chroniques de France;* ms. fr. 2813, f⁰ 394. *Photo B. N.*

By a decree of November 6th, 1351, John II the Good created an élite company of 500 knights, the apex of his structure of royal companies. The Company of Our Lady of the Noble Household had its headquarters at Saint-Ouen and was known as the Order of the Star, after its insignia. Its members, of whom the king was 'prince', had the benefit of a military club, insurance and pension rights. The order disappeared under Charles V.

il ne sont pas paini si come il
doiuent seoir. mais lordre est ou
souller precedent

il ne sont pas paini si come il doiuent
seoir. mais lordre est ou souller precedent

Italy, the Middle Ages were above all an age of faith. The moment cities became wealthy, local pride and unity of faith spurred them on to dedicate their energies and their credit to the construction of churches worthy of God.

It was the Church likewise which had organized education, and as early as the twelfth century Paris was a teaching centre celebrated throughout Europe. Abélard's dream, like that of every learned man, was to teach there, and when he was unable to do so within the city itself, he established himself on the other bank of the Seine. The popes made use of the University of Paris to spread sound doctrine: an object attained more by the interpretation of texts than by unbiased enquiry according to the Socratic method. Saint Thomas Aquinas, however, by showing that it was possible to reconcile Aristotle with the Scriptures, intelligence with faith, opened the road to the modern world.

From as early as the eleventh century there existed in France minstrels or 'inventors' (*trouvères*) who journeyed from castle to castle and from public square to public square reciting historical songs in the vernacular, *chansons de geste* (*gesta* being deeds). These exalted both the warlike and the gentle virtues of chivalry, honour and loyalty as well as courage and skill at arms. Alongside the *chansons de geste* grew up in France the literature of courtly love. It was the Crusades which, because of the lengthy absence of the lord, gave more power to the 'lady'. The only men who remained in the castle were adolescent pages or clerics able to read and write. Among them desire was mingled with respect; the page or the clerk 'sublimated' in love poems that which they dared not declare. Moreover, a wealthier society possesses more leisure; there is more time to make music for the ladies. At the charming petty courts of the Limousin, Périgord, Poitou or Aquitaine, troubadours sang their verses to their own accompaniments. The love they expressed was that of a servant, a respectful, almost a religious love. They had read Ovid's *Art of Love*. 'Courtly marriages' of a rather equivocal nature were celebrated which at least in theory tied bonds only of the heart and the mind, but at which on occasion a priest officiated. Great ladies had a lover when at the same time they had a husband; here were the beginnings of a long tradition. Eleanor of Aquitaine brought these 'courtly' manners to the court of France, then to that of England. 'Courtliness' produced not only songs of love and the *Roman de la Rose*, but a new discipline of customs and manners — a great step forward on the path to civilization.

Because in the Middle Ages religion lay at the centre of every thought, religious architecture and sculpture, conceived as a handmaiden of architecture, were the pre-eminent arts of the period. The Romanesque cathedrals had above all been the achievement of monasteries and princes, but beginning with the twelfth century, the cathedral became the achievement of everyone dwelling in a given town. It was 'the

CORONATION OF CHARLES V AND OF JEANNE DE BOURBON The Peers, including Margaret, Countess of Artois, support the crowns at Rheims, May 19th, 1364.
Grandes Chroniques de France; f° 439. *Photo B. N.*

BAPTISM OF CHARLES II, DAUPHIN DE VIENNOIS The future Charles VI was born on December 3rd, 1368, and was baptized on the 6th in the church of St Paul. At this point Du Guesclin knighted him.
Grandes Chroniques de France; f° 446 v°. *Photo B..N.*

book of a people wihout books'. Upon its walls and portals, revealed truth was blazoned, while upon the columns of its capitals was depicted the morality of daily life or the suffering of the wicked. The cathedrals expressed the faith of a religious era and the local patriotism of the towns and the guilds. These cathedrals, the *chansons de geste*, knighthood, courtesy — all these were new and admirable inventions. The human animal, tamed in the ancient world by the philosophers, had once again been unleashed in all its cruelty after the fall of the Roman Empire. Hence the necessity of imposing upon that animal new rules, a faith, a political system, manners, taste. France furnished in great part the elements of a civilization which set up as the end of life, of the family, of marriage, of trade, of art, not happiness but salvation, and the influence of this civilization has been great on the whole of Christendom.

The art, the customs and the language of the French had acquired characteristics which were French alone. Yet there remained a confusion and a danger. It lay in the strange interdependence of the kingdoms of France and England. Ever since the Norman conquest the English upper class had been Gallicized. English poets wrote in French; Eleanor of Aquitaine had introduced courtly manners into the English royal household; English kings bore themselves before ladies (as Froissart shows) as though they were French knights.

But all this did not justify their being, on French soil, the lords of Guienne and other places. In 1328 the problem became urgent. Charles IV, the Fair, had died without an heir. Two candidates could lay claim to the throne: Edward III of England, son of Isabella of France and grandson of Philip the Fair; and Philip of Valois, grandson of Philip III, the Bold. The latter, although he was only a first cousin of the late king, carried the day because he was 'born in the kingdom'. Later on, in justification of this choice, the lawyers appealed to an ancient law of the Salic Franks under which women could not succeed to the throne or transmit the succession. The truth was that the Salic Franks were merely an excuse; what was wanted was a French king. Thus ended the direct line of the Capetians and began the Valois dynasty. France did not gain by the change. The first Valois above all busied themselves with feudal prestige. Philip VI, of Valois — brilliant, impulsive, ill advised — looked upon war as a tourney, in which the object was not to be the victor, but to show one's courage and follow the rules of the game.

He found confronting him in England a young king, Edward III, who also prided himself on chivalric courtesy, but who acted with the hardest realism. His motto was, 'It is as it is', and he might well have inherited it from his Capetian ancestors. He was wise enough to accept Philip

SCENES FROM THE VALOIS ERA In the course of a riot (left), Etienne Marcel, provost of the merchants of Paris, has the Marshals of Champagne and of Normandy butchered (right) in the presence of the Dauphin; Paris, February 22nd, 1358. *Grandes Chroniques de France;* f° 409 v°. *Photo B. N.*

of Valois' accession to the throne, bide his time and prepare. These preparations concerned both fighting men and armaments. In order to break the charge of the feudal barons' cavalry, Edward III had recourse to catapults and, above all, to bowmen. Edward I had discovered the Welsh long bow, and had decreed that archery should be the sole sport permitted to his subjects. Thus it was easy for Edward III to recruit an infantry, and in 1340 he possessed the most modern armament in all Europe. The basic cause of the war was Edward's firm intention to lay claim to the crown of France. Its immediate cause was the Flanders question, key to English-French relations. England's principal product was wool; Flanders' chief industry, the weaving of cloth. The Count of Flanders, Louis de Nevers, was supported by his suzerain the King of France; the Flemish townsmen showed themselves to be violently pro-English. When, in 1337, Edward III, having completed his military preparations, defied Philip VI, denied his legitimacy, and summoned him to yield the throne of France, the English king was backed by the City of London, which feared that indispensable Flanders would fall under French influence.

Thus the Hundred Years War was a dynastic war, a feudal war, a national war, and above all an *imperialist* war. And, we must add, this war was popular in England because it would lead her armies into a wealthy countryside, western

France, where the soldiers would find abundant spoils.

In Guienne, Edward III already had a bridgehead, but Frenchmen in revolt told him that Normandy was not defended. Hence the landing at La Hogue, with one thousand ships, four thousand knights and ten thousand English and Welsh archers (1346). Normandy had not known war for several generations and allowed herself to be devastated without opposition, but the French army met the British near Abbeville, at Crécy. The battle here is of great importance because it marks one of the great military changes which wholly upset the relationships between classes in Europe. Crécy marked the defeat of the finest feudal cavalry, that of France, by the foot-soldiery of the Welsh bowmen. Philip VI's knights fought bravely. They were defeated because they did not have a proper respect for the new foot-soldiery, and because they were more devoted to individual exploits than to collective discipline. The following year, Edward III having laid siege to Calais, the King of France once again mobilized his knights and sent a message to the King of England, who was altogether too well entrenched, asking him to select a place of battle where the two armies would have equal chances. But Edward III wanted a battle and not a tournament. He refused and took Calais, which England was to keep until the days of Mary Tudor, thus guaranteeing her control of the Channel.

LOUIS II, KING OF SICILY, DUKE OF ANJOU, REACHES PARIS *Chroniques de Froissart;* ms. fr. 2645, f⁰ 321 v⁰. *Photo B. N.*

The nine-year-old king reached Paris in 1386 via Bicêtre. He was met in front of the gate to the rue Saint-Jacques by his uncles the Dukes of Berry and of Burgundy. Notre-Dame can be seen, Sainte-Geneviève on the right and the Temple on the left. Louis II was to be the father-in-law of Charles VII and the husband of Yolande of Aragon.

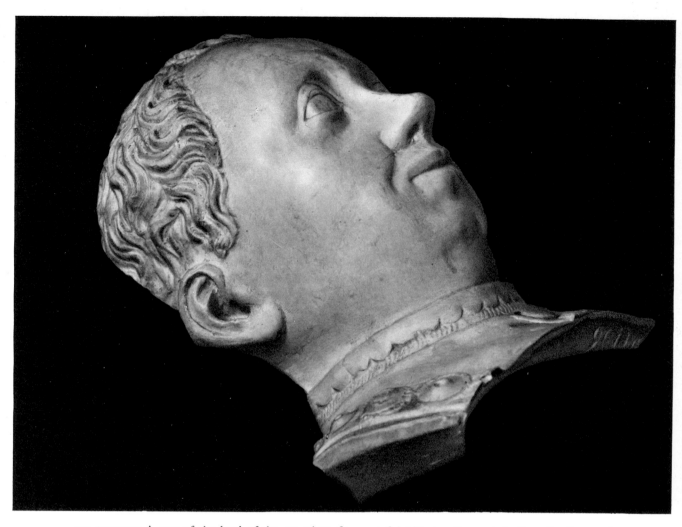

DU GUESCLIN A cast of the head of the recumbent figure at Saint-Denis. Bertrand du Guesclin, Count of Longueville, Constable of France and of Castille, died in 1380 a little before Charles V, who had him buried among the kings. (*Musée de l'Armée.*)

The Pope obtained a truce. When warfare began anew, France had a new king, John II, the Good, a man as mediocre as his predecessor. Edward's eldest son, the Black Prince, undertook to link Bordeaux with Normandy. He won back Languedoc, then in 1356 he moved towards Poitiers where he defeated a French army four times as large as his own. The King of France himself was taken prisoner and his son, the Dauphin Charles, became regent (he was the first heir presumptive to bear this title, Dauphiné having been sold by its Dauphin, Humbert II, to Philip VI in 1349 on condition that the title of Dauphin would be borne in France by the sovereign or by his princely heir). Defeat, exacerbated by the Black Death, which laid waste the countryside, diminished the prestige of the monarchy. For several months there was reason to believe that the French monarchy, under the regency of the Dauphin, Charles the Wise, would be forced to submit to constitutional limitations and that the French, taking advantage of the weakening of the King, were going to force him to accept the principle of taxes by free consent.

At the States General of 1356, two men, Robert le Coq, Bishop of Laon, and Étienne Marcel, Provost of the merchants of Paris, proposed reforms which we should today describe as democratic. For two years the States General endlessly assembled, even without royal convocation, and voted taxes. But Robert le Coq's schemes ended in nothing; it is always a mistake to try to base a national revolution upon a defeat.

In the mind of Étienne Marcel, who was not afraid of new or extreme measures, there remained one solution. Could not the Commune of Paris govern the kingdom, relying, as had happened in Flanders, on a federation of communes? Marcel believed that it could, and founded a party in Paris. Unfortunately he went too far and was lost. He permitted an invasion of the King's residence and allowed the slaughter of two marshals under the Dauphin's very eyes. The latter, 'abashed', quit Paris resolved to find support in the provinces. In the neighbourhood of the capital, peasants rose in rebellion; ever since the beginning of this war they had suffered too much misery, and companies, or

[25]

armed bands, provoked 'alarms' throughout the countryside. In Paris, right-thinking people began to be indignant at seeing English soldiers as allies of the Provost of the merchants, and he was 'hooted at and censured', then assassinated. Charles re-entered his capital and was wise enough to show clemency. At last he signed a peace at Brétigny. The King of England renounced all claims to the throne of France, but besides Guienne he received Poitou, Périgord, Limousin and other provinces. This was a truce, not a solution.

No one knew this better than the Dauphin who, in 1364, became king under the name of Charles V. He was resolved to revise the treaty of Brétigny, but first he had to reorganize the kingdom and rebuild an army. Charles was capable of this task. This small man, frail, pious, learned, was a great sovereign. He entrusted the reorganization of the army to a minor Breton aristocrat, Bertrand Du Guesclin, who had called attention to himself as much in fighting the English as in fighting those 'great companies' of men-at-arms who were pillaging the country areas, and in fighting the Navarrese. Charles soon summoned him back to Paris and made him commander-in-chief. At the same time the King was building a fleet and making ready a modern artillery force. When he died in 1380, he had almost swept the English out of the kingdom, and that with very little fighting.

But there is never a great man who does not make great mistakes. Charles V had a younger brother, Philip the Bold, to whom King John the Good, their father, had given as appanage the Duchy of Burgundy, one of the richest and most beautiful of French provinces. Charles made the error of favouring the marriage between the Duke, his brother, and the heiress of the Count of Flanders, thus uniting under one house all the provinces which covered France's borders to the north and the east: instead of having a brotherly vassal at Dijon, he would henceforth face a hostile sovereign in Brussels. Never did France, still very newly united, run a greater risk of splitting, of drifting into a civil war.

It was France's ill fortune, at the most difficult moment in her relationship with England, to have kings whose legitimacy or authority were open to question. Charles VI was only twelve years old when Charles V died. Any minority brings with it a regency, a tutorship, conflicts; the King's uncles, especially Philip of Burgundy, plundered the kingdom. When the King came of age, he showed good intentions and called back his father's senile advisers. But he had married a sensual and dangerous foreigner, Isabeau of Bavaria. He loved her, made her live in an atmosphere of great festivity, probably had good reason to be jealous, grew worried and tired and, coming of an unstable lineage, lost his reason. To have a mad king is a disaster for a country; to have a king whose derangement is intermittent is the worst kind of disaster, for he can be neither replaced nor respected. Around the unfortunate Charles VI, his uncle, the Duke of Burgundy, and his brother, the Duke of Orleans, struggled for power. John the Fearless, who had become Duke of Burgundy on the death of Philip the Bold (1404), had his cousin of Orleans assassinated (1407). Thus was unleashed one of those passionate, extraordinary and vain civil wars which have so often divided France. An Orleans party and a Burgundy party confronted each other. Bernard of Armagnac took the leadership of the former, for his daughter had married the new duke, Charles of Orleans, while John the Fearless led the 'Burgundians'.

Civil hatreds put a country at the mercy of its enemies. When Henry V of England, in 1415, saw France torn between the Orleans and Burgundy factions and governed in the name of a mad king by a young and friendless dauphin, he cynically revived Edward III's claims to the throne of France. Such demands were too absurd to be met even by a country as unfortunate as France then was. War became inevitable. Like his great-grandfather, he landed in Normandy, this time with a mere thirty thousand men, all told. He seized Harfleur, the great arsenal of the west, then decided to march on Calais. Finding the ford at the Somme defended, Henry V moved higher up the river and met the army of the French nobility at Agincourt. A terrible battle ensued in which France's knighthood found itself shot to pieces by the archers and butchered by the English king's men-at-arms. Ten thousand Frenchmen perished in this battle (1415), one of the bloodiest of the Middle Ages.

Despite this victory, Henry could not have succeeded in seizing France with his tiny army had there not been complicity on the French side. But when, in 1417, the English invaded Normandy and its inhabitants appealed to the King of France, the High Constable of Armagnac replied that he was busy fighting the Burgundians. As for John the Fearless, he urged the people of Rouen to come to an understanding with the English, with whom he had entered into partnership because of the interests of his Flemish subjects. In Paris, an uprising handed the city over to the Burgundians, but not without producing thousands of victims.

JOAN OF ARC DRIVING THE BAWDS AWAY FROM THE ARMY Painted long after the event, which took place in April 1429. *Vigiles de Charles VII;* ms. fr. 5054, f⁰ 60 v⁰. *Photo B. N.*

At the very moment when it still seemed possible to hope for a French-Burgundian reconciliation, Tanneguy du Châtel, friend of the Dauphin, killed John the Fearless on the Montereau Bridge (1419). Paris and the Burgundians now swore *never* to acknowledge the Dauphin. By the Treaty of Troyes (1420), Isabeau, an accomplice of the Burgundians, constrained her demented husband to give their daughter Catherine to Henry V of England in marriage and to make Henry regent of France and, eventually, heir of the kingdom. As for the Dauphin, cut off, banished, disowned, he was reduced to defending himself as best he could between the Seine and the Loire.

And yet the French did not resign themselves to becoming English. When, in 1422, Henry V and Charles VI died within three months, there was no knowing who would in fact be the next king of France — the child Henry VI of England or the Dauphin Charles. Never had the country's situation been more deplorable. France had almost ceased to exist as a free nation. An English regent, the Duke of Bedford, governed in Paris. Charles VII, for his part, who was still called the Dauphin, was deeply pious and irresolute. A tormenting doubt deprived him of courage to struggle for his inheritance: was he truly the heir of the house of

France? The misconduct of his mother, Isabeau, justified this doubt. He had little money, few soldiers. But the will of the French people bore him up. The French, with touching eagerness, wanted a French king. But what could they do? Bedford, master of the north of France, had undertaken the conquest of the centre, and had laid siege to Orleans. Nevertheless, that city defended itself even more heroically because its lord, Charles of Orleans, was a prisoner among the English and because in feudal law an attack against a fief deprived of its lord was a great crime. For this reason the people of Orleans hoped that God's judgment would be in their favour and that they would be delivered. But by whom? Then it was that Joan of Arc appeared.

In March 1429, a young girl who had come from Lorraine to Chinon asked to see the Dauphin. She was 'strong, a little dark of complexion, with uncommon physical powers, but of modest mien and feminine voice'. As a peasant's daughter, she had been a shepherd girl and had led her father's beasts to their pasture. All about her, in the village of Domrémy, everyone spoke of the tragedy which had befallen the kingdom of France. Joan, very devout, had heard celestial voices while she was guarding her flock and had seen appear 'in a great light' the Archangel Michael, Saint

VICTORY OF PATAY On June 18th, 1429, Joan of Arc, the Constable de Richemont, the Duke of Alençon and the Bastard of Orleans defeated at Patay (Loiret) the troops of Talbot and of Scales, who were taken prisoner. *Jean Chartier, Chroniques de Charles VII; ms. fr. fº 2691, 38. Photo B. N.*

Catherine and Saint Margaret, who had exhorted her to go to seek the Dauphin and to deliver Orleans. 'Since God ordered it, it was fitting to do it'. And finally she had succeeded in persuading the nearest captain royal, him of Vaucouleurs, after he had equipped her with a man's armour, to have her conducted to Chinon, where Charles was residing. It was already an astounding thing that a girl from the fields should have convinced this captain, but the story of Joan of Arc is at once the most surprising succession of miracles and the most reasonable succession of political actions. The aims which this Lorraine shepherd girl proposed were practical and urgent. She wished to restore to the Dauphin faith in his birthright — this she could accomplish because he was himself very devout and would believe in voices coming from Heaven; to deliver Orleans, because this symbolic victory would give confidence to the French people; and to have the Dauphin consecrated at Rheims,

because the oil of the holy vial would ensure, in the eyes of all believers, the legitimacy of his power.

Everyone knows how she was introduced into the castle and at once recognized the King who was hiding amidst his lords and saluted him with the title, 'Gentle Dauphin'. He was highly moved when Joan reassured him about his birth: 'I tell thee, on behalf of the Great Lord, that thou art the true heir of France and son of the King . . .' From that moment on, Charles believed in Joan's mission. As for Joan, she had never had the least doubt concerning her voices, and it was in full confidence that she — a paltry girl — called upon the powerful English army to quit France. She won from the Dauphin a small army, entered Orleans and freed the city to the sound of the *Veni Creator*. She had caused a standard to be embroidered for her: the points of the oriflamme bore the words JESUS MARIA and the fleur-de-lys. The fleur-de-lys and Christianity: with a sure instinct

THE LIMBURG BROTHERS: JOHN, DUKE OF BERRY, AT TABLE (*Musée Condé, Chantilly*). *Très riches heures du duc de Berry;* month of January. *Photo Giraudon.*

This son of John II the Good was eminently an art-lover and also a great builder. Towards 1411 the Limburg brothers entered his service and illuminated this manuscript which was still unfinished at the duke's death (1416). He was remarkably ugly. His companion here is no doubt Martin Gouge de Charpaignes, Bishop of Chartres, his Chancellor of the Exchequer. A chamberlain welcomes visitors with the cry 'Approach, approach'.

Joan buttressed herself on the two powers which had wrought France's unity. Did she hate the English? No, she was too good a Christian for that; far from hating them, she urged them to ally themselves with the French for a crusade. But an English regent cannot allow the possibility of a saintly girl opposing England's plans. Bedford called her — and believed her — a witch. Yet she acted the part of a wise Frenchwoman.

Understanding that all the ills of the kingdom had arisen from unappeased ill feeling, she required full forgiveness of Frenchmen for Frenchmen: 'If it pleases you to wage war', she wrote to the Duke of Burgundy, 'go against the Saracens.' Then, to Charles, who continued hesitant and fearful: 'Our Dauphin, no longer take so many and such lengthy counsels: follow me, and come assume at Rheims your worthy crown... Why do you doubt?' But La Trémoïlle, a professional soldier who was hostile to Joan of Arc, sought to turn Charles against her and thwarted all her plans. Nevertheless, the Maid went about repeating that she 'would last only for one year' and that they must hurry. Her march on Rheims began with the taking of Troyes and was a mere military exercise. During the consecration (July 17th), she stood beside the King, with her standard in her hand. Within five months, she had fulfilled her mission. But in that day of triumph, Joan was deathly sad: 'I should wish', said she, 'that it might please God, my Creator, that I might now lay aside arms and go to serve my father and my mother by watching their sheep, together with my sister and my brothers, who would be indeed joyful at seeing me...'

In the eyes of the English and the Burgundians, Joan was a witch and a heretic. How, had she not had the devil in her body, could she have conquered so quickly, without military strength? Now she wished to bring the King back into his capital. In the assault of September 1429, however, she was wounded in the thigh. Then La Trémoïlle's counsels of delay stopped Charles VII, who was by nature hesitant and wary. Joan rejoined the armies and was captured below Compiègne, because the gate had been closed behind her, perhaps through treason. Taken by the Burgundians (May 23rd, 1430), she was sold to the English who handed her over to an ecclesiastical court. Although the Maid was condemned beforehand, the trial lasted five solid months. Pierre Cauchon, Bishop of Beauvais, who was in charge of the questionings, had called upon the assistance of a vice-inquisitor, of prelates and priests from Rouen, plus a dozen lawyers in church courts. Seventy-five judges were gathered

together to confound this young girl in chains. Priests and laymen, English and French, all agreed to send Joan to the stake. It was only too clear that, since reasons of state required a verdict of guilty, the verdict was sure even before the trial began. Unbiased judges would have been convinced of Joan of Arc's good faith and patriotism by her admirable replies — which make this interrogation a wonderful document. A girl without education, almost a child, found answers so noble and so pure that even this dour tribunal was at times troubled by them, but she was none the less condemned to the flames and burned alive at Rouen, in the old market place, on May 30th, 1431. She was nineteen years old. Charles VII had done nothing to save her. And he waited fifteen years before starting the process of her rehabilitation.

After Joan's death, Charles VII, the Well-Served, found, for the deliverance of France, other good soldiers: Richemont, La Hire, Xaintrailles and Dunois, Bastard of Orleans. But never would they have come on the stage if Joan had not set them in motion. She had created France's moral unity. In 1435, Philip the Good, Duke of Burgundy, made his submission. The civil war was over. In 1436, Paris yielded to the King, who made his solemn entry into the capital, but did not remain there. He had no love for that city, 'which called to his mind unpleasant memories'. Province by province the kingdom was regained: Normandy in 1450; Guienne in 1453; there were no more Englishmen in Gascony. They had been 'put out of France'; only Calais remained to them.

For Frenchmen Joan of Arc has remained the purest symbol of patriotism. Everything combines to give her this character: her youth, her courage, her faith, the desperate state of the country at the time she set out to save it, the miracle of her success, the victory of a shepherdess over a triumphant enemy, and above all the stake and martyrdom. By this unmerited torment, she became associated in the popular consciousness with the saints of Christendom. Anatole France, an anti-clerical freethinker, who saw in Joan of Arc a neurotic person subject to hallucinations, a simple-minded girl cleverly managed by the clergy, nevertheless wrote these words: 'The thought came to her to restore the Dauphin to his heritage. For this thought she gave her life. Thus it was that she survived her cause and that her devotion remains an everlasting example. Here was martyrdom, without which men have established nothing great or useful in the world. Cities, empires, republics rest upon

PHILIP III THE GOOD, DUKE OF BURGUNDY The Grand Duke of the West, whose life-long regret was that of not having fought at Agincourt, wears the Order of the Golden Fleece which he instituted in 1431.
(Musée de Dijon.) Photo Bulloz.

sacrifice. Thus it was not unreasonable or unjust that Joan should have become the symbol of the fatherland in arms . . .'

The Hundred Years War had bankrupted the country, weakened the King, and raised the hopes of the great landed vassals, who constituted States within the State. For the purposes of rebuilding France, Charles VII lacked character but not intelligence. He was well served, which at least proves that he knew how to choose his servants. Above all, it was necessary to reorganize the army and the treasury.

The feudal cavalry remained only a reserve. For the infantry, each parish in the kingdom, following the English example, had to supply one archer for every fifty hearths. This man was exempt (or *free*) of the poll tax, but was required periodically to report for military training. These 'free archers' constituted a second reserve. The artillery, belonging wholly to the King, gave him great power against the strongholds of the larger vassals. In order to support

this standing army, Charles VII obtained from the States General of 1439 a perpetual poll tax of twelve hundred thousand *livres*: France, always in danger and fresh from the sight of the threat of destruction, yielded to her sovereigns the control of an army and permanent taxes. How could she refuse? Her first need was to be defended. Although Charles VII had his faults — he lived openly with a beautiful mistress, Agnes Sorel, by whom he had several daughters, and he had proved ungrateful to some of his best advisers — he left France happy and strong.

Nothing is more surprising than the speed with which the hesitant Dauphin became not only King of France, but one of Europe's most powerful sovereigns. A few years later, in Germany, in Savoy, in Italy, Charles VII appeared as the arbiter of Europe. Thanks to a merchant of Bourges, Jacques Cœur, who, starting with nothing, had enriched himself by trading in precious metals, and then had set up

FUNERAL OF CHARLES VI THE WELL-LOVED *Chroniques de Charles VII, by Jean Chartier;* ms. fr. 2691, f⁰ 11. *Photo B. N.*

The king, totally abandoned, had died in Paris at the age of fifty-three, October 21st, 1422. Before burying him at Saint-Denis it was necessary to await the return of John, Duke of Bedford, from Rouen. The funeral took place on November 11th, all Paris being in mourning. Jean Le Clerc, Chancellor of France, and the presidents of the Paris parliament are here seen in red: by this colour they show that they are not in mourning, that the monarchy continues. The effigy of the king, on his hearse, complete with all the marks of sovereignty, also reflects the idea that 'in France the King does not die'. Charles VII had already been proclaimed king on October 24th.

counting-houses throughout the Levant, there was no longer to be seen 'in the eastern [Mediterranean] sea any mast which did not bear the fleur-de-lys'. Jacques Cœur, capitalist and speculator, became the financier, the ambassador of the reign, until the moment when slanderous accusations and his too brilliant fortune brought upon him his inevitable downfall. By means of foreign alliances, Charles strengthened himself for the struggle, now become necessary, against the 'sires of the fleur-de-lys', meaning the great vassals of royal blood. This second feudality (Burgundy, Anjou, Bourbon Brittany, Albret, etc.) did not respect the royal authority. The dukes of Burgundy, 'Grand Dukes of the West', lacked only the title of king, for they had the kingdom. Besides Burgundy, they possessed Flanders through marriage and governed all the Low Countries as far as the Somme. In their capital, Dijon, they held a court at which French culture was then better represented than in Paris; Burgundian art, particularly its sculpture, was admirable. In 1429 the Duke of Burgundy had founded the Order of the Golden Fleece, a knightly brotherhood whose prestige became European. The King of France freed him of having to pay homage, because it was prudent to do so. Here was a dangerous neighbour. In 1440 the great vassals organized a rebellion against the King, to which the Dauphin, the future Louis XI, adhered. In rebellion against both parental and royal authority, the Dauphin Louis sought asylum with Philip of Burgundy. 'My cousin of Burgundy knows not what he does', Charles VII said bitterly. 'He is suckling the fox who will eat his hens'. The father knew his son all too well; he even thought him capable of parricide, but he left him his inheritance intact. The king within him controlled his rancour as a man.

Louis XI, as little knightly and feudal as it is possible to conceive, neither kept his own word, nor believed in the oaths of others. Having been a bad son, he distrusted his own children. He believed that 'every man has his price', and, were it necessary, he paid that price. Knowing the English to be 'inclined towards war against this kingdom', and fearing the possibility of a new Anglo-Burgundian alliance, he promised what amounted to a tribute to the court of England. It was Louis XI who, through these bargainings, truly ended the Hundred Years War — still smouldering under the ashes — by the Treaty of Picquigny in 1475. Ever ready to humble himself whenever he felt that he was the weaker, he exacted harsh vengeance when he had regained strength. As a captive, he promised sub-

FRANCESCO DE LAURANA: LOUIS XI The first king of France whose portrait was struck on a medallion. The inscription reads 'Div(us) Lodovicus rex Francorum'.

mission; once set free, he forced obedience. Being fearful of the great, he surrounded himself with bourgeois and lesser folk. In the end he made himself an object of detestation both to the feudal lords with whom he fought and to the masses of the people whom he taxed 'with great and awful poll taxes', but at least he laid nothing aside in the treasury, using the money instead to build 'vast edifices for the fortification and defence of the towns and places in his realm'. He has been compared to a spider; there he was, at the centre of his web, ready to scurry out along one of its strands in order to seize an unwary fly, then climbing back, execution having been done, to the centre of his gossamer.

From the moment of his accession to the throne, in 1461, the great men of the kingdom set themselves up against him in a league which they called the League of the Public Weal. United, the dukes of Burgundy, of Brittany and of Berry could have endangered the kingdom, had the English mixed in the affair. But the English were involved in civil war at home and Louis XI had inherited from his father the advantage of a permanent army. Louis, however, having saved Paris merely by a hair's breadth, decided to do some appeasing. He made promises to his enemies and then divided those enemies so that he could break his promises. The most dangerous of the great vassals was, as always, the Duke of Burgundy, Charles the Bold. Louis XI agreed to meet him at Péronne, but here the fox was caught in the trap and the King, prisoner of the Duke, promised everything the latter desired. The moment he was free, he denied what he had done, threatened, bullied. 'He who has success likewise has honour', he used to remark.

He had success, by guile and above all by good fortune. Charles the Bold went to Switzerland to meet defeat at Granson and, the following year, was killed in battle before Nancy. His daughter, Marie of Burgundy, inherited the lands which were part of the Empire, but the French provinces, which had formerly been given as an appanage, reverted to the crown for lack of a male heir. Thus, in 1477, by this stroke of luck, Louis regained Burgundy and Picardy.

There remained, though, one problem: Flanders. By marrying Maximilian of Austria and bringing these lands as a dowry to him, Marie began a long rivalry between France and the Empire. This northern French frontier was to remain until our own days one of the nerve points where European crises come into being. Along this frontier, France is dangerously vulnerable; the Germanies covet its lands because the Rhine flows down towards them; England jealously watches them because Antwerp is so close to her own shores, and this meeting of conflicting interests sets up dangerous eddies. In 1482 Marie of Burgundy died from a fall while riding. She left a son (Philip the Fair) and a little two-year-old daughter, Margaret of Austria; Louis XI succeeded in having this girl betrothed to his son, the Dauphin Charles (later Charles VIII), and it was agreed that she should receive as her dowry the Franche-Comté and Artois. Here was a great triumph. Another bloodless victory: in 1480, upon the death of King René and of his nephew Charles of Anjou, Maine and Anjou had reverted to France. Louis XI was burying his rivals; that was the surest way to dispose of them for ever.

He died in 1483 powerful and terrified. The novelists have taken delight in showing him in his castle at Plessis-les-Tours, clad in coarse, heavy cloth, surrounded by crossbow men and archers, wearing a fur-lined cap from which hung leaden medallions, while from the branches of trees the corpses of those he had caused to be hanged swung to and fro. 'King Louis's orchard'. Why so many suspicions? Did he suffer from remorse? He had squeezed his people, but only the better to defend them. He had been harsh on the feudal lords, but he had rearranged the pattern of France. A business king, with all the faults of the bourgeois, but also with their good qualities, who, in short, carried on the business of the country. He died virtuously, says Commynes, 'and better than any other whom I have ever seen die'.

The new king, Charles VIII, was thirteen years old. He was weak in body and ugly, with an oversized head, which was stuffed with chivalric romances. He had been brought up at Amboise, far from his father, whose favourite child was his daughter Anne, who had married Pierre de Beaujeu. It was to the Beaujeu couple that Louis XI left the regency. This created an outcry and even more so when Anne, under pressure of opinion, sought to 'purge' the advisers of the late king. The League of the Public Weal was reconstituted, but more than ever were the people tired of the feudal lords and favourable to the crown. Anne de Beaujeu won two victories over the rebels, one military and the other political. She called together the States General in 1484 to show that the people were on her side. The States General supported her, but demanded the freedoms of Charles VII's day, since every period looks upon the past as a golden age. The States General received stipulations of grievances and before them a wise and revolutionary speech was made by the deputy Philip Pot, Lord of La Roche in Burgundy: 'The State is the thing of the people ... the sovereign people created kings by its suffrage ... they are such, not in order to draw a profit from the people and to enrich themselves at its expense, but, forgetting their own interests, to enrich it and make it happy. If sometimes they do the opposite, they are tyrants ...' The States General asked to be convoked every two years; the next day they found the tapestries stripped from the walls and the furniture carried away. The sovereign people bowed.

Upon the death of Francis II, Duke of Brittany, an urgent problem arose. His daughter Anne was the heir. Whoever married her would own Brittany. Anne de Beaujeu acted promptly and proposed her brother to the Duchess, causing the offer of marriage to be presented by an army of forty thousand men. This form of courtship is irresistible. Anne objected that the King of France was already affianced to Margaret of Austria; the Beaujeu replied that this childish betrothal had been broken off. The Duchess resigned herself, and, despite her husband's ugliness, soon loved him. Without beauty, she herself was thin and lame, but a sharp Bretonne, highly educated and a patroness of the arts. After this marriage, the task of the Beaujeu was completed and Anne withdrew. She left her brother master of a fine kingdom wherein he no longer had anyone to fear.

II

The Transition from the Middle Ages to the Renaissance

France in the XVth century

NOTHING would be more false than to depict Western society as leaping from one social condition called the *Middle Ages* to another called the *Renaissance*. Real history is made up of individuals and of acts, not of periods. What is true is that during the fourteenth and fifteenth centuries a rationalist and richer civilization began gradually to invade Christendom and that in France the feudal lords little by little lost their mastery. We have seen Charles VII and Louis XI building up permanent armies; we have noted that the augmented part played by infantry and artillery was sure to weaken the political power of the feudal cavalry. Institutions follow inventions only after a considerable lag, but they always end by coming into step. From war to war, the King of France increased his internal power. He had become the defender of the country but also its master. The bowmen stopped the knights short, cannon made breaches in keeps. Firmly established upon personal, national and religious bases, the King — son of France, anointed of the Lord, miracle-worker and commander-in-chief — was supreme over all other powers. This supremacy had assumed various forms: St. Louis' spiritual authority, the enlightened despotism of Charles V and of Charles VII, the wily manœuvring of Louis XI. Thenceforth, however, it was almost beyond question. Neither the feudality nor the States General had been able to oppose its rise. Surely, slowly, the French monarchy moved towards absolutism. And if the King imposed rules upon himself and recognized limits to his power, those limits were the customs of the country.

The three estates of the kingdom remained distinct. The nobility kept its privileges: freedom from taxation, judgment by its peers, a matchless social position. But during the course of the Hundred Years War, it had shown itself unsuited to its military and political role. Steeped in the ideas of chivalry, it was not realistic; on the contrary, it thought realism dishonourable. With its childish vanity, its puerile concern for tournaments, banquets and passages at arms,

obsessed by personal allegiances, it had shown very little national feeling. Its passions were violent; the vengeances at the court of Burgundy testified to this. Religious sentiment restrained it hardly at all. Courtly love had become a rite. The knight, in a tourney, paraded his lady, wore her colours, her veil, and sometimes even her bodice, which he returned to her covered with blood. Bayard himself loved to break many a lance in tournament. But the time was coming when realistic soldiers would say: 'Do not break lances; keep your arms in good repair and kill your enemy.'

During the Middle Ages the clergy had acquired feudal habits. The splendour of worship had corresponded to the splendour of the tourney. The Great Schism, during which two popes had quarrelled over Christendom, had weakened the Church's prestige. The people of France nevertheless remained believers, but found fault with the sale of ecclesiastical offices and of indulgences and the absence of Christian virtues among certain members of the clergy. The priests' concubines ('priestesses') were hated. Many thought that it had become necessary to reform the Church. In 1458, the French clergy and King Charles VII had persuaded the Pope to approve the Pragmatic Sanction of Bourges, an action which shattered Roman fiscal policy and transferred to the King and to the Church of France a portion of the revenues which until then had gone to the Papacy. On the spiritual level, a new mysticism filled the needs of truly Christian souls. The *Imitation of Christ*, written about 1430, foreshadowed a devotion founded on love and on charity. Without this renewal, the Catholic Church would not have been able, during the following century, to combat the Reformation.

The active third estate was made up in the main of the middle class. This was a group distinct from the general masses, having its own privileges. You could gain admission to it, but only by fulfilling certain conditions and at the cost of an initiation fee. Paris had almost three hundred thousand inhabitants; Rheims was the second city of the

THE BATTLE OF FORMIGNY *Chroniques de Charles VII*, Jean Chartier; ms. fr. 2691, fo 197. *Photo B. N.*

This was the most glorious episode in the 'recoverie of Normandy', which was undertaken with the 200,000 crowns lent by Jacques Cœur. At Formigny, near Bayeux, on April 15th, 1450, the English under Thomas Kyriel (on the right) were cut to pieces by the French under John of Bourbon, Count of Clermont (on the left, background), and Arthur of Brittany, Count of Richemont (foreground), Constable of France. The French counted twelve dead as against the English losses of 3,774 dead and 1,400 taken prisoner.

kingdom. Many bourgeois had bought seignorial domains and, like the nobles, had farmers with a system of *métayage*. Hard-working and economical, the French peasant was prosperous as long as war and taxes spared him. But soldiers and mercenaries pillaged him, and the poll tax was heavy.

French art, during these last days of the Middle Ages, was going through a transformation. During the Hundred Years War, destruction and destitution had been such that it was scarcely any longer possible to erect great buildings. The majority of artists had then taken refuge in areas which remained on the edge of the struggle: Burgundy, Italy, a part of Flanders. Religious themes still inspired them for the most part. The story of Joan of Arc allows us to grasp the intensity of faith during the fifteenth century. But the new religious art was less didactic and more emotional than that of the twelfth and thirteenth centuries. Already the artist was leaving the City of God and fixing his eyes upon the kingdoms of this world. In the sculpture adorning its portals, the Middle Ages had expressed its idealism by means of the dematerialized bodies of their angels; during the fifteenth century, the scenes of the Passion (especially under Flemish influence) became realistic. The miniaturist took delight in depicting martyrs with the sadism of a man who has himself suffered. The idea of death haunted Villon as it did the sculptors of the *danse macabre*, and in Burgundy a fine school specialized in the carving of tombs. Meanwhile, French illuminators and miniaturists retained their own special genius (Jean Fouquet). The miniature, as they handled it, became a picture; their backgrounds were fine landscapes; their hunting scenes and their processions of state were worthy of Carpaccio or of Benozzo Gozzoli.

As for lay or profane art, in the thirteenth century it had been patronized only by wealthy communities, which ordered the construction of bell towers or city halls. In the fourteenth and fifteenth centuries, a powerful and rich man had artists working directly for him. Charles V was a great builder of town houses and castles; it was during his reign that the Louvre of Philip Augustus, enlarged by the architect Raymond du Temple, officially became the royal residence. The sons of John the Good were patrons (Angers tapestries ordered by Louis, Duke of Anjou; *Grandes Heures* executed for John, Duke of Berry). Rich merchants like Jacques Cœur had built for themselves palaces adorned with sculpture. This epoch had a taste for portraits, hunting scenes, processions. Objects of art were consigned no longer to cathedral treasuries, but to the collections of individuals. The collector encouraged an art of luxury and of rich sensory impression. Woman's body was unveiled. The profane was mixed with the sacred, and, in a 'Virgin and Child', Agnes Sorel, the King's mistress, was painted as a madonna laying bare a beautiful naked breast. Rooms were better lighted and better heated. Abbeville merchants took pleasure in having their staircases and windows adorned with wood carvings both grotesque and whimsical. The artists of the cathedrals had accepted anonymity and had found their reward in the Faith; from the fifteenth century on (above all in the sixteenth) the artist became famous, respectable, spoiled.

Literature showed the same characteristics. It likewise ceased to be anonymous and became personal. The *chanson de geste*, ceaselessly reworked and given new endings, had been composed by teams of poets. But Charles of Orleans and Villon were individuals whose lives are known to us and are reflected in their work. This is also true of historians like Froissart and Commynes. The feelings expressed by François Villon are the same as those we have seen represented in the works of art of his time: a deep sadness, a sad faith, an obsession with death. The terrors of war, the disorder of civil strife had made people weary and sceptical. Villon still knew how to pray — and pray touchingly — to the 'Lady of Heaven, Regent of Earth', in the name of his mother, 'a humble Christian', but he asserted that society was ill made, that shame and cruelty were universal, and that death, the only release, would soon carry away both the thief and the executioner, the 'Queen white as a lily' and 'Joan the good girl from Lorraine whom the English burned at Rouen'.

One characteristic which seemingly belongs to all periods bereft of hope is that their poets seek refuge in difficult forms. 'Frivolity is a violent state.' What could be more frivolous than the complication of rhythms? The ballad, the rondeau, *rimes redoublées* have the double advantage of concealing life's horrors and of giving birth to masterpieces.

It was by the Church's agency that the drama, from the tenth century on, began to revive. The custom arose, at the Easter Mass, of staging conversations among the Holy Women at the sepulchre. Then true liturgical dramas were composed in Latin. Finally 'miracles' or 'mysteries' in the vulgar tongue, representing the lives of the saints or the Passion, as well as 'plays', were performed on certain feast days by the confraternities, either in the church porch or on trestles. Folk dramas like those of Oberammergau give us some idea of these entertainments, which sometimes lasted through several days, a whole town being gathered together to witness the Mystery of the Passion. The actors, very numerous, were amateurs. Two other theatrical forms, the morality and the farce, produced a few masterpieces; the *Farce of Master Pathelin* has the speedy dialogue and the quasi-mechanical comedy of Molière, but not his poetry. As for the satirical farce, played by 'idiots' or fools, it was a parody of society which, allowing for the necessary differences, corresponds to what we know as the revue.

It is usual to attribute to the fifteenth century the 'invention' of printing. But from the bricks of Egypt to Gutenberg, the process was continuous. A number of circumstances lent it, in the fifteenth century, a new importance: the discovery of numerous ancient manuscripts, the development of the universities, travel narratives. What is called the 'invention' of printing was merely the combination of two novelties: separate characters, assembled by a compositor, and then broken up for further use, and the employment of metal characters which could be cast in great number. Laurens Coster of Haarlem and Johann Gutenberg of Mainz are reputed first to have had these ideas. However this may be, handsome books had been set up as early as 1455, and the invention reached Paris in 1470. Printing slowly transformed political life by making easier the moulding and informing of a public opinion.

The fifteenth century was basically a period of transition. Many of the nobles, while keeping their fortified castles in the country, had built in some town, be it Périgueux, Bordeaux, Rouen or Dijon, a city house adorned with sculpture. This double domicile might be interpreted as a symbol of the day. The Middle Ages continued (the keep); a new social life was beginning (the town house). For the successive layers of a civilization exist together. Even today the survivals of the Middle Ages are numerous. More than one feudal fortress still dominates the French landscape, sometimes inhabited by the same family which long ago caused it to be erected (La Rochefoucauld, Luynes, Uzès, etc.). The peasant's cottage, in many a province, has changed little. The church remains the centre of every French village. As of old, the bishop comes on his pastoral visitations. Pilgrims go to Lourdes as formerly they went to Saint James of Compostella. Country families retain something of that respect for the sacrament, of that asceticism, of that

contempt for happiness which even today makes divorces in France rarer than in the Anglo-Saxon countries.

For that rich stretch of land which is embraced as though by two open arms, the Alps and the Pyrenees, three political and territorial solutions were possible during the course of Europe's formative years. It could belong to and form part of a larger unit; it could be split up into several independent communities; or it could achieve its own unity. France, in the early days of her history, passed several times through these three successive phases. She had constituted a part of the Roman Empire; she had been shattered into Barbarian kingdoms; she had herself created a new empire, that of Charlemagne; at the time of the dismemberment of this empire, she had split up into numerous fiefs; then, bit by bit, one of the feudal lords, the King, had pieced these bits together into one domain. In the fifteenth century, France's national unity had been consolidated round a monarch.

Now the national solution triumphed not only in France, but in England and in Spain. In all three countries, a king unified the nation. For some time one might have wondered whether the Holy Roman Empire or the Church would not come to dominate Europe. United, the Pope and the Emperor could have made Christendom into a political reality. But the rivalry between the Empire and the Church had weakened both together, and they had lost all opportunity to create a homogeneous Europe. The Hundred Years War had given to the French as well as to the English an awareness of their differences. In feudal times, institutions had been approximately alike in both countries. Then the English and the French monarchies had followed divergent roads. In the fifteenth century, the English monarchy, solidly upheld by an aristocracy of squires and wealthy merchants, governed by means of benevolent justices of the peace, and annually summoned Parliaments in order to obtain funds. The French monarchy, on the other hand, sought to resurrect the Roman tradition of a central bureaucracy; it governed by means of office holders, but it had popular support because it had protected the people against the foreigner and against the feudal lords.

France owed to Rome her instinct for centralization. With her, patriotism was perennial and was bound up with national heroes, such as Charlemagne, Saint Louis, Joan of Arc; she remained Christian and Catholic; religion had infused her daily life. It had been by means of her religious art and her religious philosophy that in the Middle Ages she

THE LIMBURG BROTHERS: THE MONTH OF MAY About 1416, this shows the cavalcade which traditionally took place on May 1st; in ▶ the background lies Riom, the capital of the duchy of Auvergne which then appertained to the Duke of Berry. *Très Riches Heures du duc de Berry (Musée Condé, Chantilly.) Photo Giraudon.*

GUILLAUME REVEL: MOULINS Towards 1450 Revel depicted the towns and castles in the duchies of Bourbon
and Auvergne, together with the coats of arms of the appropriate barons. *Armorial d'Auvergne*; ms. fr. 22297,
fº 369. *Photo B. N.*

had shone throughout all Europe. Cluny and Cîteaux had spread French culture far and wide. In England, the knight evolved and became the gentleman; in Italy, he was to give place to the politician; the ancestral instinct of the French would continue to push them towards chivalric 'gestures'. Courtesy had taken root. The vocabulary of the court of love in France resembled that of feudal loyalty. It was Joan of Arc who accomplished 'what no created man could have done'; it was Blanche of Castile who moulded Saint Louis and protected him during his minority; it was Anne de Beaujeu who saved the kingdom for her brother.

The barriers between classes were higher in France than in England or in Italy. In Florence, a merchant could become a prince; in London, the middle class participated, with the knights, in the House of Commons; marriages between nobles and commoners were frequent; bourgeoisie and nobility were equal on the score of taxes. In France, trade remained debasing; the third estate sat in a section separate from the others.

It is true that ennoblement remained possible, but the ennobled plebeian, in acquiring the privileges of his new class, broke with the old. In England, the strength

JEAN FOUQUET: LOUIS XI ATTENDING THE FIRST CHAPTER OF THE ORDER OF ST MICHAEL *Statuts de l'ordre de Saint-Michel;* ms. fr. 19819, fº 1. *Photo B. N.*

By a decree issued from Amboise, August 1st, 1469, the king founded the Order and Militia of St Michael, appointing himself Head and Grand Master. Here are seen the first fourteen knights; there should originally have been thirty-six. Many of them have been identified, as also have the four officers of the Order (background). The Order was conferred up till 1830 when it was supplanted by that of the Holy Spirit.

of the aristocracy arose above all from its constituting a political and administrative governing class; in France, the aristocracy sought to remain the warrior class above all, and in a period of harquebuses and artillery, this was an anachronism. Faithful to the laws of chivalry, lacking in the practical spirit, this French nobility would have regarded as dishonourable the electoral manipulations whereby the English nobility preserved its influence. It attributed an inordinate importance to bearing, to etiquette, to a hierarchy. Such, likewise, was the case of the Spanish nobility, but in Spain there was scarcely any middle class, and class conflict was not of like importance.

In the fifteenth century, Europe was already formed, at least along its major lines. Three kingdoms — France, England and Spain — had almost reached their full development. France still needed to settle her frontiers in the north and north-east; that was to be the task of the following centuries. The danger that threatened her did not then come from Germany, which was divided into tiny States and therefore powerless, but from Austria, which, through the circumstances of feudal inheritance, gave every sign of uniting itself to Spain and the Low Countries, thereby encircling France. Truly, the feudal concept, by virtue of which a given tract of land is linked to a given person, was not suitable to modern times. National feeling is too strong for whole provinces to be able and willing to change their allegiance in accordance with the chance family alliances of their lords.

The era of personal bonds was coming to an end and the era of nationalities was beginning.

Although the kingdom was unified and national feeling was vigorous, many recently annexed provinces retained their original traits. The King respected their customs. Especially were the north and the south of France very different, both in their habits and in their style of government. Romanized earlier than the north, the south retained a feeling for Roman law, a taste for eloquence, and a more Latin culture. In Provence and in Aquitaine, the Arab occupation had

introduced elements of poetry and of history. Contact with the East had been less completely severed than in the remainder of the country. It was in the south that the Albigenses and the Cathari sought to purify the Church, and it was in the south that the Huguenots were later to find a fertile soil. Throughout the course of French history and even until our own times, without the national unity ever being threatened thereby, deep political divergencies have been visible between north and south.

Two further characteristics, which have played basic parts in the country's life, were evident even in the Middle Ages. The first is France's astonishing power of recuperation. During the course of the Hundred Years War she suffered utter disasters which might easily have discouraged her. Yet barely a few years after the end of these trials, she had once again become Europe's most powerful nation. This ability to recover arises in part from the fertility of her soil and the labours of her peasants; in part it springs from an instinctive faith in her destiny and from a deep-rooted certainty that a Frenchman can only be a Frenchman. The second characteristic is belief in France's universal mission. The French, perhaps because they belong to a border civilization — bounded on the south by the Mediterranean races and on the north by the Teutonic — are inclined to believe that it is possible to convince all men of the truth of a system of ideas. In the Middle Ages the University of Paris felt that Europe and the Church of Rome acknowledged its pre-eminence. During the seventeenth and eighteenth centuries, we shall have the opportunity to observe the same phenomenon manifest under different forms.

If the notion of a universal society should some day prove victorious, the French ought to be among the first to exercise a spiritual influence therein. They had elaborated, as early as the twelfth century, the concept of a homogeneous Christendom. The idea of a Europe united, not by the power of legions but by truths unanimously accepted, was born on the hill of Saint Geneviève.

CHARLEMAGNE, EMPEROR OF THE ROMANS Equestrian statuette of c. 802. Along with St Louis and Godefroy de Bouillon, the Emperor was one of the greatest figures of the Middle Ages.
(*Musée du Louvre.*) *Photo Bulloz.*

◀ THE DANCE OF THE SHEPHERDS A scene of pastoral life in France around 1470. *Heures de Charles d'Orléans, comte d'Angoulême;* ms. lat. 1173, f° 20 v°. *Photo B. N.*

III

Renaissance and Reformation

Charles VIII to Henry II, 1483-1559

NEVER did the writers of the sixteenth century speak of a renaissance. Culture required no rebirth because it had never ceased to be alive. Far more than with a renaissance, we are here dealing with a revolution. The discoveries of the navigators and of the astronomers had shown that the world was vaster than the Jews or the Greeks had believed. It was no longer in texts but on the earth and in the stars that truth had to be sought. No one cast doubt (at least openly) upon Christian teachings, but reformers criticized the clergy and satirists made mock of the monks. As was the case later, in the eighteenth century, men thought they dwelt in an age of 'light' which delivered them from outworn superstitions.

Why was the first flame of this new light lit in Italy? Because in its ruins, in its marbles, in its inscriptions, Italy preserved the tradition of the ancient world. Beginning with the time of Dante and of Petrarch, it had given birth to a new classical language. In its wealthy cities — Milan, Venice, Florence, Naples — rich traders gave encouragement to scholars and artists. The Renaissance was wrought in the palaces of princes and of bankers far more than in the universities. Humanist popes gave Rome a splendour beyond compare. The ideal Frenchman of the Middle Ages had been Saint Louis, a valiant and devout soldier; the Italian ideal of the Renaissance knew how to handle a brush and compass as well as he did a dagger or a sword. He was an engineer, a diplomat, a scholar.

The individual of the Renaissance did not cease to profess the Christian faith, but he no longer practised it. Not content to prepare for his salvation in another world, he wanted pleasure on this earth. In fifteenth-century Italy, Christian morality suffered an eclipse. Sexual life there was free and even licentious; murder was easily forgiven, especially if the murderer was an artist. Sixtus IV, a great patron of the arts and creator of the Sistine Chapel, showed himself more the Roman Maecenas than Saint Peter's vicar, and the Borgia Alexander VI made vice at home in the Vatican. Nevertheless, if they are sometimes forbidding, the men of the Italian Renaissance have their own special greatness. It was in their image that Elizabeth of England and Francis I of France formed themselves. There was in the men of that epoch a passion and an enthusiasm, a need for varied and bold action, a love of beauty, a respect for the arts, a *joie de vivre* which are intoxicating; yet they possessed a cynicism and a nihilism to which Europe was to owe many of its ills.

Those were the days of an insatiable desire to learn. The 'humanist' of the Italian Renaissance not only read the ancient authors, and studied all the aspects of classical life, but he knew new manuscripts, and thus broke down Christian prejudices. A new programme of study — history, poetry, literature — shaped the 'humanist'. Theology's share had been reduced. The poets of antiquity had become the 'classic texts'. As it spread over Europe, this culture was first of all to be hurtful to the simplicity of the various national literatures. But this inoculation of ancient culture, starting with the seventeenth century, was to be absorbed by the current of French intellectual energy. It was to produce Pascal, Bossuet, Racine, and would inspire Frenchmen with respect for form, the only assurance of lasting quality. The mingling of humanism and Christianity was to be the basis of Western civilization.

In the sixteenth century, however, one essential element was still lacking: the scientific spirit. Nevertheless, great artists like Leonardo da Vinci and Michelangelo would be led, through the necessities of their work, to study mechanics, descriptive geometry and anatomy; and at the beginning of the century, Copernicus showed where Ptolemy had been wrong and placed the sun at the centre of our system.

A basic characteristic of the Renaissance was that its culture belonged to the *élite*. The civilization of the Middle Ages had been popular. The troubadour and the jongleur perform-

HIGH SOCIETY AROUND 1510 This tapestry, known as 'of the Loire riverside', shows the new Italian fashion (left) and the old French fashion (right); the scene here is of the promenade in the series 'la vie seigneuriale'. (*Musée de Cluny.*) *Photo Bulloz.*

ed on the public square; mysteries were played for the benefit of the populace on the porch of the cathedral; and the cathedral itself had been built by an anonymous architect with the help of an entire community. The art of the Renaissance, on the contrary, was **aristocratic.** If Villon had written ballades understandable by every man, the sonnets of Ronsard were beyond the reach of simple folk. Humanism dug even deeper the moat between classes. Private architecture took the place of public architecture. It was intended to display magnificence and to afford pleasure. In sculpture and in painting art remained nominally Christian: the painter still clung to religious subjects, but he humanized them. Titian shows us upon the same canvas, 'Sacred and Profane Love', two blonde beauties, one clothed, proper and timorous, the other shameless, proud and naked. For the tra-

dition of the medieval artist, who had given naive expression to his faith, the Renaissance artist was to substitute the 'search for effect'.

When Louis XI died, two questions of foreign policy could claim the attention of a King of France: that of Flanders, an area coveted at once by France, England and the Empire, because each of these three Powers feared to see it occupied by one of the others; that of Italy, because the old dream of empire still obsessed Europe's sovereigns and because each of the Italian cities, at odds among themselves, would summon to its assistance any available foreign army. In the mind of a clear-thinking Frenchman, with an eye to the future, the problem of the north-east should have seemed the more important. There lay the real danger to France's frontiers. But Charles VIII, in order to free himself

JEAN BOURDICHON (?): LOUIS XII LEAVING ALESSANDRIA ON HIS WAY
TO RECONQUER GENOA, APRIL 24th, 1507 *Le livre du voyage de Gênes*, Jean Marot;
ms. fr. 5091, fº 15 vº. *Photo B. N.*

Louis XII, like certain other kings of France, was overlord of Genoa. When the city
revolted he had to proceed to its recapture; he made his entry on April 28th, with only 15,000
men. The king is here seen in a plumed helmet, followed by Charles III, Duke of Bourbon,
the future Constable (1515), who is identifiable by the device 'Espérance' on his horse's
caparison. Charles, Count of Vendôme, grandfather of Henry IV, can be identified (right)
in the cortège by his helmet bearing the fleur de lis. Jean, father of Clément, Marot was
official poet of Queen Anne of Brittany. He presented her with his manuscript about 1510.

of his first Austrian betrothal, had given up the Franche-Comté and Artois. In all decency he could no longer attack these provinces, and what was more, his own desires drew him towards Italy. All men talked of the beauty of the Italian cities, of their artists, of their poets.

France was full of *émigré* Italians, exiled and burning with hate against the factions which had driven them out. Countless were the Italians who held positions at court or in the army, and all these refugees sought to put France at the service of their own passions. Nor was it difficult to find an excuse for intervention. Under the law, the five major Italian principalities — Rome, Venice, Naples, Milan and Florence — were united by the Lodi agreement; in reality, they conspired against one another, and within each of them there were at least two political parties. The kingdom of Naples, especially, had for two centuries been a subject of dispute between the French House of Anjou and the Spanish House of Aragon. In the days of Charles VIII, the King of Naples was Ferdinand of Aragon, hated by the Pope and by Ludovico the Moor, Regent of Milan. Were France to lay claim to Naples, she thought she would surely have powerful allies. Charles VIII, surrounded 'by men of small estate experienced in nothing', allowed himself to be seduced 'by the phantoms and glories of Italy'. His Italian schemes were popular. France felt herself strong. With her astonishing power of recuperation, she had already repaired all the disasters of the Hundred Years War. Thanks to Charles VII and Louis XI, she possessed Europe's most powerful army, and it was of urgent necessity to employ these companies abroad, because they included more foreigners than Frenchmen and threatened to despoil the countryside. So the King mobilized his forces at Lyons, gloriously embraced his little Queen, and departed for the Alps with more than thirty thousand men in August 1494. At the outset there took place the splendid cavalcade of which he had dreamed. For the entrance into Florence, the residents of that town stationed themselves at their windows, bedecked with tapestries, and watched the procession of kettle-drummers, fife players, cross-bow men, archers, halberdiers, Swiss, all superbly clad in the King's colours, red and yellow. At last appeared the King's household, his standards,

and Charles himself, grasping his lance, riding a black horse, and encased in golden armour and a king's long blue mantle, which covered his horse's crupper. The sight was worthy of the romances of chivalry, but the Florentines remained hostile and distrustful. In Rome, Pope Alexander VI, who indeed had fostered Charles VIII's expedition, now appalled at what he had unleashed, barricaded himself in the Castel Sant'Angelo and appealed for help to the Sultan! Only the Neapolitans kept to their promise and, when the French appeared, revolted, in accordance with the plans which had been formulated against the House of Aragon. In February 1495, Charles VIII entered Naples, having attained his objective. For some time he enjoyed this earthly paradise, admired Italian gardens and the rich ceilings and floors of the palaces, engaged workmen capable of adorning his new château at Amboise with similar beauties. But it would be

[45]

a great exaggeration to attribute to him the introduction into France of the spirit of the Italian Renaissance. While he was abandoning himself to the delights of Naples, his army drew upon itself the hearty hatred of the Neapolitans, in whose eyes these liberators became conquerors. Now all Italy forgot its internal differences in its hatred of the occupying forces. The Pope, Venice, Ludovico Sforza and Ferdinand the Catholic formed a league against Charles VIII. He was betrayed by the very people who had summoned him.

The new Italian league armed itself. Charles realized he must return to France with the utmost speed lest his road back be cut off by the enemy. He hastily organized an imperial entry into Naples (in a scarlet mantle with a globe in his hand) and then began to retreat. In order to cross the Apennines, he had to give battle at Fornovo and won the day. The expedition had been fruitless, but the soldiers brought back with them rich booty, and popular feeling remained favourable to the Italian campaign. But the King did not long survive it. In 1498, when only twenty-eight years old, he knocked his forehead against the stone lintel of a low door in a state of disrepair at Amboise, and died within a few hours. Since the children he had had by Anne had been sickly and puny, and had not lived long after birth, his cousin Louis of Orleans succeeded to the throne. The son of the poet Charles of Orleans was a young man of thirty-six, a good horseman, charming and weak, lovable and well loved. Immediately upon his accession he announced that he would leave everything as it was, not even removing his personal enemies. He had long been silently in love with Anne of Brittany. Now that she was a widow, he hoped to marry her, but unhappily he was already married to a daughter of Louis XI, 'slight, dark, and round shouldered', Jeanne of France. Cesare Borgia, son of Pope Alexander VI, undertook, in return for a generous fee in money and in lands, to arrange an annulment. This was possible because the marriage had been forced by Louis XI. Thus Brittany remained French and the 'gentle Breton woman' remained queen.

The Italian mirage attracted Louis XII just as it had seduced Charles VIII. Were feudal pretexts needed to justify a conquest, Louis XII, who had a Visconti grandmother, could proclaim himself heir of the Duchy of Milan whence the Visconti had earlier been driven by the Sforzas. Thus began again the adventure of Charles VIII. All Louis XII's campaigns were easy at the beginning; later on Italian reversals of feeling took place and those who had been enemies before were reconciled for the purpose of opposing France; thus victories were followed by defeats. Milan, conquered at first, was then lost.

Pope Julius II, an artist and warrior, aroused against Venice by Machiavelli, swore to have all the princes of Christendom take arms against that republic. A league was formed, with France to serve as its soldier. But scarcely did Venice seem in danger, when the Pope changed his tune. Having 'cast into the Tiber the Keys of Saint Peter and taken into his hand the Sword of Saint Paul', he formed a new Holy League, this time directed against France, in conjunction with Henry VIII of England, the Spaniards, the Venetians and the Swiss. Defeated at Novara (1513), forced to return to France in order to defend his country against the English, the Swiss and the forces of the Emperor, Louis XII finally made peace and renounced his claims to Milan. The Italian mirage was fading away.

The French had fought long and to no purpose. They did not hold it against Louis XII, whom they called the Father of the People and whom the States General acclaimed whenever he appeared, thin, pale and leaning upon his small queen. Why? In part because they were prosperous. Ever since the days of Charles VII they had busied themselves in clearing away ruins and rebuilding. Louis XII took pains to protect the peasants against the landed nobility, to revise the rights of compulsory feudal service and forced labour, and to lower the poll tax.

CHENONCEAUX (INDRE-ET-LOIRE) The castle was built on the river Cher by Thomas Bohier (1513-1521), given by Henry II to Diane de Poitiers (1547) and completed by Catherine de' Medici; it passed to Queen Louise of Lorraine, widow of Henry III. *Photo Molinard.*

THE BATTLE OF MARIGNANO 'A Battle of Giants' where Francis I defeated the Milanese and the Swiss, September 13th and 14th, 1515, near Milan. *Etienne Le Blanc, Les oraisons de Cicero en françois;* ms. fr. 1738, f° 3 v°. Photo B. N.

The sickly and delicate Louis XII was succeeded by his robust son-in-law, Francis I. Francis of Angoulême had been brought up at Cognac by his mother, Louise of Savoy, a taciturn and masterful widow, but of solid intelligence and a noble woman. Francis was a splendid, strapping youth, intense, with as sturdy a stance as his crony, Henry VIII of England. He liked lovemaking, hunting, war, life. Dominated and sheltered by his mother, Francis had been spoiled and worshipped by his sister Marguerite. She liked poets and artists; she had made her brother into an amateur humanist, too much of a good fellow for serious studies, though he tried his hand 'at Florentine games and at verses, which he turned out with middling facility'. Just as later on there would be people called the 'new rich' Francis I was a 'new king' who possessed the prestige of youth, wealth and beauty and the rash optimism produced by success obtained without effort.

In search of adventure, made dizzy by his new power, he must at once seek to revive the quarrel over the Duchy of Milan. Why? For fun. He enlisted twenty-six thousand mercenaries, and 'a kind of artillery which fired fifty bullets at a time and was most serviceable'. With this well-equipped expeditionary force, he crossed the Alps, met the Swiss who were occupying the Milanese territories, and defeated them at Marignano (1515). On the very field of battle, Bayard conferred knighthood on his sovereign. It was a great day for the young king, and a fine beginning to his reign, which brought him Milan, a reconciliation with the Pope and perpetual peace with the Swiss cantons, to which he promised an annual subsidy in return for the right to recruit soldiers there. The Swiss Guard was to become a permanent feature of the French court.

The Italian wars took place outside the country, and France rejoiced in a delightful and novel prosperity. In the Loire valley, châteaux multiplied, and in the Île de France many cathedrals were built. The King completely remodelled his castle at Blois. Anne of Brittany had brought there from Amboise her tapestries, her bed 'accoutred in cloth of gold', her 'gilt and diapered chairs brought from Italy'. There she wound wool on her distaff in the midst of her women, while a poet read his verses to her or a jester amused her with his quips. France loved her Queen Anne just as she loved her King Louis XII. But Anne died in 1514, leaving only two daughters; the elder was promptly married to the heir to the kingdom, the young Count of Angoulême, her first cousin. The King took a new wife, Mary, sister of the King of England, but died on January 1st, 1515.

Under Louis XII, France had been fighting the Vatican openly ever since the betrayal of Pope Julius II. Leo X had an interview of vital importance with Francis I after Marignano. What the Pope wanted was to persuade the young king to do away with the Pragmatic Sanction of Bourges, the charter of the liberties of the Gallic Church. This conversation succeeded and a new concordat was signed in 1516, but one as much to the King's benefit as to the benefit of the Vatican; the Pope and the King each acquired vast revenues at the expense of the French Church. This concordat, which remained in force until the Revolution, partly explains why Luther's and Calvin's Reformation failed in France. Less than any matter of doctrine, it was a matter of finance. England's Henry VIII broke with Rome in order to despoil the monasteries; Francis I

GEOFFROY TORY (?): FRANCIS I LISTENING TO A READING OF DIODORUS OF SICILY (Musée Condé, Chantilly) From an edition of the first three books of Diodorus of Sicily, translated by Antoine Macault; ms. 721. *Office de documentation Pierre de la Forest.*

Towards 1532 Antoine Macault presented the king with his translation of the known fragments of Diodorus' *Historical Library*. The king is surrounded by his three sons: Francis, Dauphin of Viennois, Duke of Brittany, Henry, Duke of Orleans (the future Henry II), and Charles, Duke of Angoulême. At the king's left stands Cardinal Duprat, Chancellor of France, recognizable by his girth.

had despoiled them by previous agreement with Rome.

Young, rich, victorious, Francis I on his return from Marignano indulged in the most ambitious of plans. And what could be the supreme ambition of a king were it not the Empire? The imperial throne was elective, Maximilian was already old, and the electors were venal. Francis felt that he had some chance of gaining this impressive crown. Francis I had a dangerous rival, the grandson of the Emperor Maximilian, Charles of Austria. By the absurd interplay of territorial inheritances, this young prince, son of Philip the Fair and of Joan the Mad, herself daughter of Ferdinand, King of Aragon, and of Isabella, Queen of Castile, had title to Spain, the Low Countries, the Archduchy of Austria, and the kingdom of Naples! Already he held France in a vice; were he in addition to become Emperor of Germany, he would encircle the kingdom. The inverse proposition was likewise true; were Francis to obtain the Empire, Charles's estates would be cut off from each other. Never were two opponents more unlike. Francis I seemed the very image of strength; Charles' face was pale and he had a weak chin. But the brilliance of his eyes belied the weakness of his features. He was a man of great intelligence and determination. As against Francis I's gold, he gained the support of the powerful bankers of Augsburg, who were anxious to retain the connection between the Empire and Antwerp. Maximilian bought five votes for his grandson — a majority — and German-Flemish capitalism won the day. Charles V was elected. From that day began, between France and the Germanic peoples, a struggle in which the most recent wars are still episodes.

Henry VIII of England found himself wooed by both camps. In France he possessed a permanent bridgehead at Calais; it was near this city that Francis I came to meet him. Quite similar in their tastes, the two monarchs outdid each other in magnificence. The meeting was called 'The Field of the Cloth of Gold', because the tents of the King of France were woven of gold thread. The kings 'came to greet each other on horseback and treated each other with great kindness', but confidence was none too hearty. The King? The Emperor? Henry VIII, having weighed matters carefully, chose the Emperor for his ally, because the latter was the master of Flanders and the English merchants demanded that he do so. Now sometimes commercial counsel is bad diplomatic counsel. In sacrificing France, England destroyed the balance of power to the advantage of Charles V. She was one day to regret it.

Francis I decided to attack. Charles V was having trouble in Spain and in Germany. The moment might be propitious. This aggressive move delighted Charles V, who knew himself to be the stronger. All Europe turned against Francis I: Henry VIII, the Pope, the Venetians. Even the Constable of the Kingdom of France, Charles de Bourbon, went over to the enemy, galled because the crown had contested one of his legacies. Under such conditions, it had become folly to cross the Alps. Francis I did it, with his rash courage, and suffered a total disaster at Pavia. The army was destroyed, the King was made prisoner.

The King taken prisoner . . . A dreadful peril, had France been divided. But then was it seen how greatly she had become aware of her unity since the days of John II. The Regent, Louise of Savoy, worthy of respect, received the respect she deserved. There were no conspiracies, no turbulent States General. France displayed dignity in her misfortune. And this saved her. Unsuccessful in provoking strife within France, Charles V began to find his prisoner a burden. Francis grew ill with listlessness, hoped to die; Charles V took alarm. If the King died, someone else would succeed him. What purpose would it serve to possess a corpse? Marguerite, a devoted sister, rushed to her brother's bedside and restored hope to him. Already fortune's wheel was turning. Henry VIII, who began to find Spain too powerful, accepted two million from Louise in return for abandoning his ally. Nevertheless, Francis I, seeing that escape was impossible, decided to yield on the subject of Burgundy, fully resolved not to keep his word.

He agreed, however, to hand over his two sons as hostages in order to guarantee the fulfilment of the treaty. When he reached home and the agreement was made public, indignation against Charles V was general. The Pope declared null and void a treaty which made the King of Spain master of Christendom. In France, the Estates of Burgundy emphatically stated that the King had no right to alienate without their consent a province of the kingdom. Personal feudalism had come to an end.

The break between France and the Empire marked the end of any policy of Catholic and Christian unity. In order to destroy the House of Austria, Francis I could no longer quibble over the opponents he might incite against the Empire. On the very evening of the battle of Pavia, Francis I had sent a secret messenger to Suleiman the Magnificent. Politics was carrying the day over ideology, and even over the Faith, but could France allow herself to be overwhelmed?

CHAMBORD FLOODLIT (LOIR-ET-CHER) This castle was built by Francis I, and its owners have included King Stanislas of Poland, ▶ the Marshal of Saxony, Berthier, the Duke of Bordeaux, the princes of Parma, and now, the State. *Photo Frédérique Duran.*

In 1529, Louise of Savoy, an excellent trader, succeeded in arranging with the Archduchess Marguerite, the Emperor's aunt and the governor of the Low Countries, the Peace of Cambrai, called 'the Ladies' Peace'. The King's sons were returned to their father after payment of a ransom.

Never was France's foreign policy more confused. On the one hand there was the duel between France and Austria. In order to win against the Emperor, France needed the Turks and the Protestant princes of Germany. But through this alliance with heretics, the Most Christian King laid himself open to the discontent of his people. In France, public sentiment, especially in Paris, was inimical to the reformers. Hence internal policy pushed Francis I towards Catholic Spain whereas foreign policy made him oppose the House of Austria. From this arose a series of realistic compromises. The marriage of the Dauphin, Henry of France (later Henry II), to a relative of the Pope's, the daughter of Florentine bankers, Catherine de' Medici, showed that Francis I was anxious to maintain ties with Catholic Italy. In this he did not succeed; France's Italian venture had ended only by splitting Christendom. When Francis I died in 1547, every clear-seeing mind realized that the genuine French problem was not Italian but German.

The new king, Henry II, had the wit to be aware of this. Cold, clear-headed, silent, he had a secret hatred of Spain based upon recollections of his captivity in Madrid. He detested Charles V, but he fought him adroitly. Henry's policy was: to give up the dream of Italian conquest; to concentrate his efforts in the north-east and there to fortify the country's frontiers; and to sign a lasting peace. In order to fulfil this plan, he took his friends wherever he might find them. In England he sought support from the Catholics, who still had influence, and married his eldest son, Francis, heir to the throne, to Mary Stuart, the child Queen of Scotland. This he did to prevent a reunion of England and Scotland. In Germany, he relied upon the Protestant princes. He clearly saw that France's essential interests lay along the Rhine.

Charles V's authoritarianism annoyed the German princes. They offered the King of France 'the three bishoprics': Metz, Toul and Verdun (provisionally) if he were willing to support them. Here was security guaranteed for the French frontier. Henry II agreed, but when he sought to move forward as far as the Rhine, the Germans who had summoned him turned against him. Francis de Guise, besieged at Metz, saved that town and there founded his reputation as a hero. Charles V, held in check, ill, worn away by the gout, abdicated in 1555. He had his brother Ferdinand elected emperor, and transferred the remainder of his estates to his son Philip. Francis de Guise, strengthened by his prestige as a national hero, was determined once again to undertake the conquest of Italy. The King was weak enough to agree to this, and the expedition proved disastrous. The army sent to Italy was crushed, and France was invaded from all directions — in the north by the Spaniards and the English and in the east by Savoy. But Henry II proved himself firm in misfortune. Francis de Guise, who had sinned through rashness, redeemed himself by being bold. Hastily returning from Italy, he took command of a small army at Compiègne and, attacked at every hand, he himself attacked. Temporarily leaving the capital unprotected, he marched on Calais and took that city by surprise. It seemed a miracle. When Henry II and the Duke of Guise came back together from Calais, Paris gave them a vociferous welcome. Then the bargaining began.

This was one of those moments when, after weary campaigns, the adversaries desired peace at any price. In England, Elizabeth had just succeeded Mary Tudor, the wife of Philip II. Hence England cut herself off from Spain, and Spain ceased supporting Elizabeth in the Calais business. Henry II asked only to keep the three bishoprics, Metz, Toul and Verdun, cities securing the French border. The Emperor Ferdinand yielded. Philip II was willing to give up Saint-Quentin, which he had captured, provided that France would forswear all claims on Italy and Savoy. Such was the Treaty of Cateau-Cambrésis (1559).

This treaty was one of those which created modern France. At last France was resolutely turning her back on Italy, where she had no business and where she would always be regarded as an invader; and she was holding fast to Metz, Toul and Verdun, which were so often to save her very existence. What was more, she was recapturing Calais, which, in English hands, had been a lasting threat. Great festivities took place in Paris to celebrate the peace. But Henry II, who was an athlete, wished to take part in a tournament and was mortally wounded by the spear of Montgomery, son of the Captain of the Guards. He died in the flower of his years and his mind, at the age of forty-one. Here was a heavy loss for France, because the King, having made peace abroad, would have been able to turn his attention towards internal affairs which were becoming troublesome. And he left behind him only youthful sons and a foreign widow, Catherine de' Medici.

HOLBEIN (?): THE FIELD OF THE CLOTH OF GOLD (Musée de Versailles) A copy by Bouterwek made in 1843. *Presses universitaires de France.*

From Guines, Henry VIII of England left for Ardres where Francis I was staying (June 7th, 1520). Francis, aged twenty-five, received the twenty-nine-year-old King of England in a city composed of tents woven with gold thread and designed by Jean Bourdichon. The festivities, during which the kings competed in splendour, lasted three weeks.

THE ENTRY OF CARDINAL DUPRAT INTO SENS Bas-relief on the tomb of the Cardinal, who was Francis I's chancellor. Sens, his archdiocese, included Paris until 1622. (*Palais épiscopal de Sens.*) *Photo Hachette.*

[53]

IV

France During the Reigns of Francis I and Henry II

(1515 - 1559)

THE men of the Renaissance seemed to be saying: 'Our kingdom is of this world.' They liked luxury, the beauty of jewels, of fabrics, of dress, of palaces, of gardens and of women. Their world seemed to them huge and marvellous, and life was 'spacious'. These were the days of the great voyages of discovery, and the Normans of Dieppe together with the Bretons of Saint Malo showed themselves as bold in this as the mariners of Cadiz or of Lisbon. The French explorers had reached Newfoundland and Guinea; Jacques Cartier had discovered Canada. Spain, swollen with precious metals, imported French goods for gold. This new wealth, these opportunities ready at hand, these virgin continents, awakened prodigious energy and curiosity. The French in those days were impatient of all rule, were sure of themselves, proud of their young king, who seemed the very embodiment of the Renaissance. Vigorous, sensual, generous, cultivated, Francis I lent the 'most illustrious' crown of France a brilliance it had not possessed since Charlemagne and Saint Louis.

In those days the King's court was France's well-spring of ideas, fashions and arts. It followed the King wherever he went. It consisted of a train of twelve thousand horses, of tents, of baggage, of tapestries, of gold and silver plate. The capital was wherever the King might be. Better than his city of Paris, Francis loved his castles along the Loire. Everywhere he wanted to have near him not only his counsellors, but 'his Household', his 'company', his mistresses, and his sister Marguerite, his faithful confidante. 'A court without ladies is a springtime without roses', he said. We must picture in our mind's eye, at Chambord or at Fontainebleau, those unending revels, the beauty of the costumes, men clad in cloth-of-gold doublets, silken tights, feathered caps; the King in silver cloth; music, games, schemes of love. The court was hospitable to poets and artists. Francis I had an unbounded curiosity and was a 'lover of good

literature and learned men' to whom he took pleasure in supplying subjects on which to sharpen their wits. 'Whoever chanced to come was received, but he must needs not be a fool or stumbler', for the King's table was a true school, at which all subjects were discussed, from warfare to painting, and the King was as much skilled in one as in the other. He showered the kingdom's reserves of gold and silver upon artists exactly as he saw fit.

When it came to religion, the age was so full of inconsistency that Marguerite, a virtuous and believing princess, could write licentious stories in the *Heptameron*, and the King, as he left his mistress's arms, could proceed to a chapel to pray. The men and women of the Renaissance had so much animal violence that the scruples of their minds never put a check on the motions of their bodies. The marriage of Henry II to Catherine de' Medici was to introduce into France the intrigues of the Italian courts, unpunished murders, mysterious duels, poisoned gloves; and the consequent mixture of the *condottiere* and the knight was to produce strange fruit.

Catherine de' Medici — ten years sterile, thereafter for ever pregnant — long played a background part at a court which dismissed her father as a 'Florentine pill vendor'. Her husband the Dauphin (later Henry II) had since 1536 passionately loved a widow, the *Grande Sénéchale*, Diane de Poitiers, eighteen years older than he. Cold and ambitious, she had taken Diana's crescent moon as her emblem and had had herself painted as the lunar goddess trampling Eros underfoot, with the device: *Omnium victorem vici* (I have conquered the conqueror of all). In Rouen Cathedral she had erected a splendid monument to her husband the *Grand Sénéchal*. A widow beyond reproach, she always publicly appeared clad in black and white. This did not prevent her from having herself carved in the likeness of Diana with her stag by Jean Goujon, who knew how to make the most of her long legs, her high breasts, and her small head, nor did it

stand in the way of her accepting from the King
castles and even crown jewels. Henry II took her
everywhere with him on his travels and wrote her
ardent letters. Catherine suffered over this passion,
but with skilful obstinacy insisted that 'as for Madame de Valentinois everything was as it should
be'. Henry's romantic attachment to Diane (whom
he had created Duchess of Valentinois) lasted for
twenty-three years, in fact until death. In 1558
Henry II had passed his fortieth birthday. Diane,
a grandmother, was fifty-nine, but she remained in
his mind the triumphant victory of Jean Goujon,
glory of the Château of Écouen. Scarcely had Montgomery dealt the mortal blow to his sovereign when
Catherine, from Henry's very bedside, sent Diane
packing.

Catherine de' Medici was as ugly as Diane was
beautiful, but she had the Medici taste and in her
protection of artists continued the tradition of Francis I. The court and the Italian artists it summoned
to its service evidently clashed with the French
master masons and artisans, who naturally preferred
what they knew best how to do. The French, however, simplified Italian ornament, imposing upon it
their own sense of measure, but they added to their
traditional façades now an exterior stairway, now
an open hallway in the Italian manner. Even more
than the Italians, they studied the ancients and read
Vitruvius' treatises on architecture. Thus this artistic revolution 'was above all a restoration'. Jean Goujon's nymphs
hark back, beyond the mystical and unreal forms of the
Middle Ages, to the rational beauty of ancient statues. And
we should likewise note that the areas of France affected by
the new style were of small extent. Paris was so affected, as
well as the valley of the Loire, because it was the region
of the royal residences. Lyons, likewise, because the court
was frequently there, and Rouen because Cardinal Georges
introduced the new fashion in architecture; but at Tours
the studios of Fouquet and Colombe continued the pure
French tradition, and the portrait artists of the Valois court
have left us pencil drawings of a purity and simplicity all
their own.

In literature, at the beginning of the century, charming
Clément Marot remained closely allied to Villon. His quick,
light style, his ease, his skill at turning an epigram and at
sharpening its final thrust begin a whole lineage of French
writers, among them La Fontaine and de Musset. After
Marot, a return to the forms and the vocabulary of antiquity as well as imitation of Petrarch won over the French
poets. But it is wonderful to see the advantage they drew
from these foreign contributions for the 'defence and illustration of the French language'. The treatise bearing this
title, which appeared in 1549, was written by Joachim du
Bellay, but under the inspiration of Ronsard and his friends
in the Pléiade. An imitative art might have been dangerous
without the prodigious vitality of the period, but the

MARGUERITE, QUEEN OF NAVARRE The sister of Francis I, the 'Marguerite des Marguerites' was one of the shining lights of the French Renaissance. She leant towards the 'Reformed Church'. *Photo Hachette.*

PIERRE DE RONSARD He was leader of the 'Pléiade' poets, and was in his lifetime considered the equal of Homer and Virgil. He died in 1585. (*Musée de Blois.*) *Photo Bulloz.*

French tongue then possessed a freshness, a wealth of invention, a freedom in the use of words which it would never recapture. It assimilated much more than it imitated.

In prose Rabelais was the author who dominated the age (Montaigne came later). This was the case because he wholly represented it. Excessively fond of words, he composed lists of epithets several pages long for the sheer joy of arranging them in sequence. A Christian? Surely, but ready to laugh at monks and without the slightest taste for martyrdom. Immoral? No, but indecent, after the wanton, crude and in no sense lascivious fashion of medical students. Moreover, he knew his age completely, and, as was the case later with Balzac, was curious about everything. Nothing is more admirable than a writer who is a skilled technician of all the techniques. He was able to poke spirited fun at judges, sophists and soldiers because he had studied law, scholasticism and war. 'Pantagruelism' is at once moral hygiene, a desire for justice, a contempt for the things about which we busy ourselves, a brotherly sympathy for human affairs and an awareness of their vanity.

Like all reformers, Rabelais had ideas on education. He was horrified by pedants and 'hangmen of youth', by those 'colleges of filth' which he thought should be consigned to the flames. Ramus agreed with Rabelais on the idleness of an instruction which teaches only how to argue according to the rules of Aristotle's logic, in which the sole purpose of the student is to prove that he is right even when he knows he is wrong. The humanists were not by any means revolutionaries in philosophy or theology; they were learned men who urged sound methods in the teaching of grammar and literature. But sound methods sometimes lead minds further than one would have thought, and certain of the humanists would be drawn, through their studies, closer to the reformed Churches. Hence, to complete the picture, we must examine the part played by the Reformation in France.

The Reformation did not begin in France with an open struggle between the Catholic and Protestant faiths. Heresies had more than once divided the Roman Catholic Church; reformers had often called upon her to cleanse herself, but those very reformers held in respect the principle which the Church represented. A pope like Alexander VI (Borgia), however, was not respected because he was unworthy of respect. The sale of indulgences and the base superstitions inculcated by the monks offended religious souls. The humanists, who knew Greek and Hebrew, were no longer satisfied with the Vulgate, read the Scriptures in the most authentic available texts, and scorned the authority of ignorant clergymen. From their reading of the Bible there was to emerge a religion rather different from what the rest of Catholicism had become.

On October 31st, 1517, the German monk, Martin Luther, nailed his ninety-five theses on the door of the castle church in Wittenberg. In them he asserted that faith alone saves, that pilgrimages, the recitation of

FLEMISH SCHOOL, XVIth CENTURY: A PARISIAN GATHERING ON THE BANKS OF THE SEINE, EPOCH OF FRANCIS I (Musée Carnavalet) *Photo Bulloz, plate made by Hachette.*

The locality is the quai Saint-Bernard. Notre-Dame is visible, and the Ile Saint-Louis, which was not to be built up till the reign of Louis XIII.

the rosary, the lighting of candles and the worship of relics turned men away from true faith. Gradually he became more and more violent, for he was by nature intemperate, and he proclaimed that Rome was Babylon and the Pope Antichrist; here was no longer a reform but a break, and in 1521 he was excommunicated. Meanwhile, Marguerite, Duchess of Alençon, sister of Francis I, had taken as her adviser and spiritual director a liberal prelate, Briçonnet, Bishop of Meaux. Neither Briçonnet nor Marguerite had any thought of opposing a new religion to Catholicism; they sought, rather, within the bosom of this faith, the best means to enter into mystical intercourse with God by means of prayer. It had been Briçonnet's wish to assemble around him in Meaux the boldest minds of the Church; he chose the unorthodox professor Lefèvre of Étaples as his vicar general in spiritual matters and made his bishopric one of the French centres of the new reforming doctrine. Through affection for his sister, Francis I shielded Lefèvre, whom he called his 'bonhomme Fabri'. The whole French court, attentive only to fashion, to the pleasure of understanding the Scriptures or of singing the Psalms in French, came very close to being Lutheran without knowing it. But Luther's condemnation came like a thunderclap. The Sorbonne in its turn became greatly zealous, condemned Lefèvre of Étaples; the stage was set for a shift from erudition to inquisition, from the pulpit to the stake.

From 1525 on, the King's bondage at Pavia made his patronage less effective. The Regent, Louise of Savoy, felt weak and did not dare withstand the Pope and the Sorbonne on matters of dogma. The debate grew more and more bitter. In her efforts to maintain order despite the affliction of a kingless kingdom, the Regent needed the Church's support and so she countenanced a policy of harshness. The *Parlement* began sending heretics to the stake.

The return of Francis I was to determine the direction in which France would go in religion. Torn between his sister, a Catholic but of evangelical tendency who appealed to the King's natural kindliness, and the *Parlement* which invoked reasons of State, for several years Francis vacillated between indulgence and harshness. But partisan asperity disheartened the King. He withdrew his protection from the reformers when they began a direct attack on the Mass, and everywhere fires began to lick at their victims. Human cruelty is cunning: martyrs were roasted over slow fires to make them suffer the longer; the King himself agreed to take part in a procession around the stakes. From 1538 on, utterly discouraged by the fanaticism of his subjects, the King resolutely espoused the Catholic party.

Francis I and the 'flower of the Marguerites' had, to the extent of their power, put a check on intolerance. Henry II, of a more sombre temperament, was frightened by the spread of the Lutheran movement. Anxious, in 1549 he established a 'Burning Court' within the *Parlement* of Paris which was instructed to make inquiry against heresy, now become a 'common plague'. The decree was far-reaching: every heretic was subject to the death penalty, and the bench itself was to be purged — that matchless weapon in the arsenal of tyranny. For the very judges had been tainted with the new ideas. The criminal chamber of the *Parlement* was no longer bringing convictions. Princes of the blood — Navarre, Bourbon, Condé — members of the Coligny, Châtillon, Andelot families had been won over. In 1559, during a solemn session of the *Parlement*, brave judges declared that no one could deny the existence of grave abuses in the Church. Henry II, enraged at discovering judges 'gone astray from the Faith', stated that he would 'go watch them burning with his own two eyes'. But into those eyes was to plunge Montgomery's lance, depriving him of this comforting spectacle.

Prior to this the heretics had merely been Catholic reformers; for an open rebellion, a doctrine and an organization were needed; Calvin supplied the former and, even more, the latter. Before allowing themselves to be won over by a new theology, the French would have insisted that it possess clarity, and Calvin urged upon them a doctrine as French as Luther's had been German. His father was an attorney in Noyon. In 1536 the son published his *Christian Institutes* and in that same year reached Geneva, a liberal imperial city which had adopted the Reformation. In Geneva, Lutheranism had won over the majority and had at once begun persecuting the Catholics: beliefs change, but the passions dwell eternal. So Geneva became the asylum for reforming Frenchmen, Calvin among them. In time he graduated from being a refugee to being a minister of the Gospel, and then became the power behind the throne of a theocratic government. Seemingly this theocratic government was democratic, since pastors and elders were elected, but in fact the election was not free. A Consistory, which amounted to a private inquisition, spied on every citizen; it concerned itself with the reform of men's customs and even with censuring households. The Bible was the law, and Geneva's judges applied the Mosaic code. From that city Huguenot propaganda spread throughout France and Europe.

Calvin's tenets were harsh. Every man is predestined either to salvation or to damnation, and he cannot redeem himself through works; on the contrary, good works are the proof that he already possesses grace. The worldly effect of this dogma is paradoxical: a Calvinist constantly tends to fall back on a life of action, for indeed why should he meditate on his own soul since he can do nothing to change God's judgment? This strangely practical aspect of Calvinism pleased a portion of the French middle class; and to Calvinism likewise were attracted men of cultivation: professors, doctors and lawyers; the lower clergy and the friars; and a section of the nobility which, stripped of its benefices by the 1516 concordat and full of resentment against Rome, constituted the 'assault troops' of the Huguenot movement. The new faith grew especially strong in Lyons, where there existed a traditional bond with Geneva, in Normandy, Languedoc and the valley of the Rhône. Paris to a large extent remained Catholic. Since a military organization matched the religious, the Huguenot party soon became a State within the State, and we can understand why the kings of France were worried. For centuries these sovereigns had struggled to prevent the Catholic Church from assuming too much authority within their kingdom. They could not allow an aristocratic party, alleging religious reform, now to attempt dividing it politically. For there soon sprang up a whole school of Huguenot publicists who denied the King's absolute power. Had it found popular support, this propaganda would have been dangerous indeed for the monarchy. But unlike his fellows in Germany, the French peasant remained loyal to his traditional Catholicism. In France, Protestantism was the religion of a liberal, semi-aristocratic *élite*.

In a world upset by wars of religion, God seemed greater than ever, but further away. Man had been given over into his own hands. In his *Essays*, Montaigne showed that the individual can emerge with honour from this struggle to reshape a philosophy for himself, and France was not to forget Montaigne. Those who were to oppose him, like Pascal, were to combat him within themselves, for he was to be thenceforth an essential part of every French mind. Montaigne did not deny God — far from it — but he mounted Him upon a 'magnificently isolated' throne and lived as though God did not exist. Montaigne was the fullness of nature without Grace. Already he foreshadowed Spinoza and his abstract God. For a man like Montaigne, neither Saint Augustine nor Saint Thomas were the masters of his thinking; his references are all pre-Christian, Latin and Greek. By name and baptism he was a Christian; he went to Mass as a matter of convention, but Christianity played no part in his inner life; if it had left any traces in him, they were mere habits of conduct and speech. Montaigne was no more Christian than Voltaire; he was far less Christian than André Gide.

MICHEL EYQUEM, SEIGNEUR DE MONTAIGNE He was the greatest social commentator in XVIth century France. Right up till his death (1592) he tried to reconcile the Catholics and the Reformers. The arms here represented are not his. (*Musée Condé, Chantilly.*) *Photo Bulloz.*

V

The Wars of Religion

Francis II to Henry IV, 1559-1610

HERESY, a deficit, and a king not yet old enough to reign make up a dangerous mixture. The situation which Henry II left behing him was indeed explosive. The country needed peace and a strong hand, yet who had the power to rule? The new king, Francis II, was a child of fifteen, ailing, pimply, adenoidal. The Queen Mother, Catherine de' Medici, a large, mannish woman, conciliatory and intelligent, had brains, but the brains of a politician, not a statesman. She meant to put up the best fight she could for her sons, yet her double disadvantage of being a commoner and a foreigner compelled her to be prudent. Three parties were struggling for control: first, the Bourbons, princes of the blood who would succeed to the throne were the Valois to die out, whose leaders were Antoine de Bourbon (King of Navarre through his marriage to Jeanne d'Albret) and his brother, the Prince of Condé; next, the Guises, princes of Lorraine whose star had been rising ever since they had given a queen to Scotland (Marie de Guise), a queen to France (Mary Stuart), and a hero to the armies (Francis de Guise); lastly the Montmorency family, loyal to the crown but rivals of the Guises. Anne de Montmorency, High Constable of the Kingdom, was a Catholic but had three Huguenot nephews, among them the sober and admirable Admiral de Coligny. The Guises represented fanatical and intransigeant Catholicism. Antoine de Bourbon welcomed Huguenots at his court in Nérac because, ever since the dismissal of the Constable Bourbon, that family had withdrawn into opposition, and also because he had inherited the tolerance of his mother-in-law, Marguerite of Navarre, the 'flower of the Marguerites'.

Since the young king had married their niece, Mary Stuart, the Guises seized the reins of power; they did so by admitting the majority of young Francis II, a convenient fiction which permitted him to summon whatever councillors he might choose. The French people embraced the Guises who at once became 'providential men', called by God for the defence of the Catholic religion. Francis, the soldier, was the most popular; the Cardinal of Lorraine, the real leader, was at once 'dictator, pope and king'. The Guises and their extremist friends wanted to purge the realm of heresy; thanks to their violence, they forced the adherents of reform into rebellion.

Thus it was that the 'Huguenots by policy' joined forces with the Huguenots by religion. Every variety of malcontent, suffering persecution, decided to get rid of the Guises. It was agreed that armed bands would converge towards Blois and Amboise and would capture the court; the Guises, however, were warned, the scheme was uncovered and the schemers were apprehended. Frightful repressive measures followed; all the pinnacles of the castle of Amboise bore the heads of those put to death. The result was savage hatred, passed on from generation to generation. Even Condé himself became worried when a sudden and fateful situation arose: Francis II, who was sickly and prey to a chronic inflammation of the ear, was stricken with a high fever. What a blow to the Guises! The Cardinal outdid himself with processions imploring Heaven to heal the King; the General threatened the doctors with hanging were the King to die. But death respects neither powers nor persons. Francis II breathed his last. The Guises had lost the first round.

The new king, Charles IX, was ten years old. He was a Valois through and through, weak, likeable, an aesthete and lazy. This time there must be a regency, and Catherine de' Medici secured it for herself by threatening the Guises with the Bourbons and the Bourbons with the Guises, at the same time calling upon all the parties to make peace. Feeling herself without authority, she smiled on both enemy camps. Because she failed, she is considered a knave; had she succeeded, history would have bestowed upon her the honour it accords Henry IV. In 1560, for the first time since 1484, the States General of the realm assembled at

FLEMISH SCHOOL, XVIth CENTURY: NAUTICAL GAMES DURING FESTIVI-TIES AT THE COURT OF HENRY III (Uffizi Gallery, Florence). *Tapestry woven at Brussels c. 1580, after a cartoon by Antoine Caron (or François Quesnel). Photo Alinari.*

Henry III and his wife Louise are seen in the foreground, right. In keeping with the Age of Discovery, the island is peopled with savages wearing head-dresses. The 'Europeans' wear either the costume of the era or Roman garb.

Orleans. The Chancellor, Michel de l'Hôpital, in the noblest of terms urged them
to reconciliation. The notion that a matter
of faith might be settled by a public debate
seems bizarre, but l'Hôpital hoped for it
in all sincerity, and Catherine opened a
'colloquy' at Poissy in 1561. The Chancellor opened with a speech in which he
pointed out that a civil war would weaken
the country, that consciences cannot be
forced and that the reformation of the
Church would make possible the reunion
of all Christians. Théodore de Bèze defended Calvin's teachings in moderate terms;
to this the Cardinal of Lorraine replied.
After several days, it was decided to ap-
point a committee to find a compromise.
None was found and the whole business
went no further.

But Catherine did not forsake the idea
of a possible reconciliation between the
two forms of the Christian faith. With
courageous persistence she retained Théodore de Bèze and Coligny at court and did
everything she could to assure the Huguenots relative toleration without at the same
time over-exciting the Catholics. Her 1562
edict allowed Reformed persons to hold

SEAL OF CATHERINE DE' MEDICI On the left half of the shield, the lily of France; the right half is quartered, 1 and 4, the Medici *palle*, 2 and 3, the Tower and Auvergne, with Boulogne. *Arch. Nationales.*

their meetings on the outskirts of towns and prohibited
both parties from carrying arms. But the Catholic and
Protestant masses regarded all tolerance as sinful; in Paris,
the Catholic crowds set fire to the dwellings of Protestants;
in the south, the fury of the Huguenots was wreaked on
Catholic churches. The Catholic nobility, incensed, sought
ways and means to get rid of Catherine; she, taking
fright, turned towards Coligny and asked him what forces
the Huguenots had at their disposal for the defence of
the monarchy. It amounted to an appeal for civil war.
Everyone was polishing up his weapons. In March 1562 the
Duke of Guise, who happened to be passing with his men-at-
arms through the town of Vassy, came upon a Huguenot
prayer meeting. In the battle which soon was raging, twenty-
three of the faithful were slain and a hundred and thirty
wounded. This episode was the spark that started the fire:
Condé summoned the Huguenots to battle and Guise marched
upon Paris. The policy of appeasement had come to naught.

So there remained civil war. It began with strong foreign
support for both sides: Philip II of Spain spurred on and
helped the Catholics, Elizabeth of England encouraged the
Huguenots. Well-born prisoners were decently treated:
Francis de Guise shared his bed with Condé. But this kindliness was strictly limited to the leaders; the forces on the
fighting front, small though they were in number, since they
never consisted of more than eight to ten thousand men,
plundered, slaughtered and raped with all the cheerful fury
of partisans. Perhaps at the outset men fought for their
faith; very soon indeed they were fighting for the fun of it.
In 1563, universal fatigue led to a sort of timping peace
in the permanence of which no one believed.

There followed a period of confusion and ferocity. In
Paris the Huguenots were outlawed; in Normandy, the
Catholics; in the south, cathedrals and monasteries were
sacked. Everywhere families split up. Fanaticism made
assassination legitimate; banditry found its sanctons in faith,

MICHEL DE L'HÔPITAL He wrote latin verse, and was Chancellor of France from 1560 till his death.

a policy. Above all she dreaded the influence which the Admiral, thanks to his quiet seriousness, was beginning to exercise over the young King. Charles IX was even planning campaigns with Coligny without informing his mother. Catherine lost control of herself: this Admiral was stealing her son from her and preparing to hurl France into a hopeless war. With the assistance of the Guises, she made the necessary preparations to get rid of Coligny, and on Friday, August 22nd, a harquebus was discharged at the Admiral from the shelter of a window, but he was merely wounded in the arm. The indignant King promised an investigation of the matter, which would surely have led to the Guises and, eventually, to the Queen Mother. Catherine made a desperate decision. On August 23rd, she confessed to her son the part she had played and told him that she was lost — and he as well — if they did not now drive matters to an extreme, by which she meant a slaughter of the Huguenots. Charles IX hesitated, and then suddenly resolved to join with the Queen his mother. On the twenty-fourth, at one-thirty in the morning, the alarm bells of Saint-Germain-l'Auxerrois gave the signal for the massacre. Lists had been drawn up so that no one might escape. Guise himself went to the Admiral's dwelling, and Coligny died heroically. In Paris three or four thousand Huguenots perished amid scenes of horror; in the provinces there were thousands more, particularly at Lyons and Orleans. Only the princes of the blood — Henry of Navarre and Condé — escaped death, but they were held prisoner in the Louvre and 'invited to change their religion'. Abroad, Elizabeth went into mourning; Philip II sent congratulations.

A massacre is no solution, especially when the decapitated body has spare heads to take the place of the old. 'The Religion' could lose five or six thousand of its leaders and still possess resolute fighters; and in Henry of Navarre they had a protector. After his pretended abjuration, he had remained at court, amusing himself with dalliance; finally, on a 'very dark and frosty night', he fled, forswore his recantation and, in his own Béarn, rejoined that new Huguenot republic, cut off from the rest of the State, which Catherine had found confronting her immediately after the massacre.

Since Saint Bartholomew's Day, Charles IX had seemed overwhelmed with melancholy. He spat blood, and the doctors called him 'pulmonary'. In May 1574 he became so weak that he had to take to his bed. On the thirty-first he died, aged twenty-four, in the arms of Catherine de' Medici. Henry III, his brother and successor, was in Poland, of which country Catherine had had him elected king; she recalled him in all haste.

This third son of Henry II had a strange and disturbing charm. Tall, thin, fastidious, gracious, a wag, he showed

for all men insisted that they owed obedience only to their consciences, which meant their fancies. Catherine turned alternately to Spain and to England; she sought to please all men, which led to her being accused of betraying all men. Henry of Navarre, grandson of Marguerite, had become the dynastic leader of the Huguenots, whose political chieftain was Coligny. The Peace of Saint-Germain (1570) was due to the influence of a new party, the Politiques, or Catholic moderates, 'who prefer', as the true fanatics scornfully put it, 'the salvation of the kingdom to that of their souls'. The Cardinal of Lorraine and the Guises left the court; Admiral de Coligny came back. In order to cement the peace, Catherine considered bestowing her daughter Marguerite on Henry of Navarre and her son, the Duke of Anjou, on Elizabeth of England. Two Protestant marriages!

But slaughter lurked behind the wedding feast. When, in 1572, the marriage of Marguerite to Henry of Navarre had been arranged — to the great wrath and horror of the Catholics — Coligny was imprudently triumphant; he now wanted a reversal of alliances: war against Spain, friendship with England. But Catherine feared the Spanish armies and felt that France, with a Catholic majority, would resent such

FRANÇOIS CLOUET: KING CHARLES IX Catherine de' Medici had him undertake a tour of
France, 1564-1566. He wrote a treatise on
hunting and was an amateur goldsmith.
(Musée du Louvre.) Photo Bulloz.

intelligence and innate liberalism, but inspired no respect; his effeminate manners, his bracelets and necklaces, his liking for perfumes upset people, as did even more his suspect 'little darlings', gentlemen who were altogether too bedecked and beruffled. Compared to him, the virile Henry de Guise, called 'the Scarred', seemed to the Catholics a desirable leader. This all the more because they were greatly annoyed at finding Henry III, after Henry of Navarre's flight, once again pursuing a policy of appeasement towards the Huguenots. Through the Peace of Monsieur (1576), members of 'the Religion' gained places of refuge, freedom of worship, the right to any employment. And Saint Bartholomew's Day had only been four years before! It passed understanding. The truth was that the Treasury had almost no funds. Since royalty lay in default, there sprang up the idea of a league which would re-establish the authority of the Church and be under the leadership of Henry de Guise.

In 1584 the Duke of Anjou, the King's last remaining brother and the great hope of the Catholics, died suddenly of an infection of the lungs. Since Henry III had no children and there was no likelihood that he would have any, the heir by primogeniture would thenceforth be Henry of Navarre, a heretic. An odd situation — a King of France who could not even be consecrated. Henry III, solid partisan of legitimacy, accepted his cousin of Navarre as heir presumptive while asking him to become converted to Catholicism, but Navarre replied that this was a matter of conscience. The Guises were already on the look-out for a king; why not one of themselves? Henry of Navarre (descended from a son of Saint Louis) was related to Henry de Valois only in the twenty-second degree. The court tacked back and forth, while Catherine begged her son-in-law, Navarre, once again to be a Catholic. He wisely put her off without an answer, for had he acquiesced, he would have lost his partisans and placed himself at the mercy of his enemies. Henry III, scorned and detested, had to yield to the League and the Guises; in 1585 he granted them everything. Ten years earlier he had tolerated Protestantism, now he outlawed it; he had granted places of asylum, now he withdrew them. And all this he did against his inclination, for he knew that these measures would bring war.

This war was called that 'of the three Henrys' (Henry III, Henry of Navarre, Henry de Guise), but in fact King Henry and his mother continued to play the thankless part of mediators, which won them the contempt of the members of the League. Paris, aroused by the preaching monks and by the

Duchess of Montpensier, sister of the Guises and a League amazon, was ready to declare against the King. In May 1588, Henry III forbade Henry de Guise entrance to the capital. The Scarred One came alone, with a retinue of only eight or nine men. He was greeted with such joy that he was almost smothered. Furious, Henry III had troops brought into Paris and wanted to resist; the town was bristling with barricades; the students were marching on the Louvre. Guise was master of the situation.

King Henry succeeded in finding safe refuge at Blois, but he had lost Paris, where Guise reigned, and when he convoked the States General, he asserted that all France supported his enemies. He yielded, humbled himself, but astute observers felt that the 'day of daggers' was drawing nigh: the Duke of Guise, a rebellious subject who threatened the throne and the life of his master, must be killed. Many of his friends told Guise of his danger, but he relied on the King's weakness. 'He would not dare', he said. The King dared, without even consulting his mother. Henry de Guise was assassinated in the Château of Blois, whither he had been summoned for a council; the Cardinal of Guise was arrested and killed next day by halberd blows. Catherine de' Medici was appalled: 'What have you done?' she exclaimed. 'Now I am the only King', was her son's reply. The Cardinal of Bourbon roundly scolded the old Queen: 'Ah, Madame, here are some more of your tricks! You'll be the death of us all!' Catherine, at the end of her tether, fell ill and died three weeks later.

Saint Bartholomew did not wipe out 'the Cause'; the Blois murders did not at once wreck the League. Quite the opposite; Paris rose against the 'tyrant' whom the preachers thereafter referred to only as 'Henry III, late King of France'. The League refused to deal with 'M. Henry de Valois'. The fury of the League's priest members rose to delirium. Yet however alarming these antics may have been, they were those of a monster mortally wounded. Without the Guises and their popularity, the League could only fade away and 'burden the kingdom with the weight of its impotent death-throes'. Henry III settled down at Tours and, abandoned by the Catholics, resolutely summoned to himself his cousin of Navarre. A truce was arranged between the brothers-in-law and they jointly besieged Paris. Henry of Navarre knew how to wage war. Soon the kings were at Saint-Cloud, and the League realized it was lost; in desperation it also betook itself to crime: preachers publicly asked if no man would avenge the murders of Blois. The Dominican Jacques

JEAN-BAPTISTE VAN LOO: HENRY III RECEIVES THE DUKE OF NEVERS DURING THE FIRST CHAPTER OF THE ORDER OF THE HOLY SPIRIT (Musée de la Légion d'honneur).

Henry III, King of France and Poland, founded by a decree of December 1578 the Order and Militia of the Holy Spirit, appointing himself its Head and Grand Master, as were to be all his successors. The first chapter was held in the Augustinian church in Paris, on December 31st; the king administered the oath and received the new knights. The first was Ludovic of Gonzaga, seen here kneeling before the Grand Master, surrounded by four officers of the 'royal orders', i. e. those of St Michael and of the Holy Spirit, this latter order now taking precedence.

THE RECEPTION OF HENRY III AT THE LIDO OF VENICE On his return from his kingdom of Poland, he passed through Venice. Landing from the *Bucentoro*, he is received under a canopy by the Doge Mocenigo (July 18th, 1574). *An engraving. Photo B. N.*

Clément wormed his way to the King (August 1st, 1589) and stabbed him with a *poignard*. Henry III died better than he had lived, as a king who thought only of the fate of his realm, when he said to Henry of Navarre: 'I die happy at seeing you by my side. The crown is yours . . . I order all officers to recognize you as their king after me . . .' Then he urged him to change his religion: 'You will suffer many a rebuff if you do not make up your mind to accept another faith. I exhort you to do it . . .' He breathed his last at three in the morning. The directing committee of the League announced through its propaganda agency that this murder was legitimate and that the excommunicated King of Navarre could not succeed to the throne.

Protestant King of a Catholic country, Henry IV had to play a difficult hand; however, he held many trumps, of which the first was his own person, so well shaped to please the French. They were grateful to him for saying: 'We are born not only for ourselves, but above all to serve the country.' He wanted to be king of a whole nation, and

not of a part of one: 'Those who honestly follow their conscience are of my religion, and as for me, I belong to the faith of all those who are gallant and good.' He believed that kindness and mercy are a prince's primary virtues. Yet the role of the sovereign is not to provoke partisan feeling: 'All men want me to string the bow of my business with the cord of their passions'. Endlessly Henry called the French to union: 'We are all Frenchmen and fellow-citizens of the same fatherland; therefore we must be brought to agreement by reason and kindness and not by strictness and cruelty which serve only to arouse men'. He pleased also because he was brave and a good soldier: 'I have leaped upon cities' ramparts; surely I shall gladly leap upon barricades.' Just as briskly did he write, with a mixture of country warmth and Gascon poetry. Always in love, he sent his mistresses beautiful and passionate letters. Nevertheless, Henry the king held Henry the lover in check: 'Regarding whatever may be the actions of a soldier, I seek no advice from women.' His sparkling

[65]

eyes, his arched nose, his square beard, his Gascon accent, his delightful character and even his love-affairs soon became popular.

On the morrow of Henry III's death, Henry IV was king, but who recognized him? Many a Catholic said, 'So be it if he is converted', and he knew that he would have to come to that, that Paris was utterly Catholic, that 'if France is a man, Paris is his heart', and that, as he was later to say, 'Surely Paris is worth a Mass'.

Moreover, his religion, which was one of feeling rather than of dogma, could adjust itself to a conversion. What mattered for him was to remain a good Christian and to preserve his dignity; he would not reach a conclusion except in his own time: 'I have often been called upon to change faith. But in what circumstances? With a dagger at my throat. Had I had no respect for my conscience, respect for my honour would have prevented me ... What would those most devoted to the Catholic religion have said about me if, having lived to the age of thirty in one condition, they saw me suddenly change my belief under the expectation of thereby winning a kingdom? ...' He promised to look into the matter, to seek light. Those who were unwilling to wait, he said, had the right to forsake him. 'Among the Catholics, I shall have with me those who love France and honour.' And indeed he had them, plus a small Protestant army.

The League organized itself against him; the Duke of Mayenne (brother of the Duke of Guise) proclaimed the aged Cardinal of Bourbon king under the style of Charles X, and made himself Lieutenant-General of the realm. In Paris, the sectarian demagogy of the Sixteen (district representatives) annoyed the Catholic aristocracy, which refused to follow; Henry IV believed that it was possible for him to conquer his kingdom, and with a thousand men he undertook this great task.

He could have withdrawn into Languedoc, but that would have been to forsake Paris, so he marched on Normandy where he knew he would find friendly cities. Thither Mayenne followed him; at Arques, near Dieppe, by his own qualities of leadership Henry IV won a first victory which guaranteed him Frenchmen of all parties, who turned by instinct to the nation's king. On the League's side there were the King of Spain and the Duke of Savoy, all France's enemies; such ill-made alliances upset decent people. The Paris middle class, which had embraced a Catholic party, was astounded and weary to see this party turn revolutionary. Even Mayen-

ne wrote: 'The merchants think of their business, will have nothing to do with war, and advise peace.' The members of the *Parlement*, persecuted by the Sixteen, were secretly partisans of Navarre; the *Satire Ménippée* describes the anger of the well-to-do: 'In olden times, each man had wheat in his attic and wine in his cellar', the authors kept repeating; 'each had his silver plate, his arras, and his furniture ... Now who can boast of having enough to live on for three weeks, apart from the thieves? ...' Everyone wanted order, everyone awaited an energetic and forgiving ruler; what was more, this ruler existed and he was the King. All that was told of him was delightful: 'If you are losing your standard-bearers, rally to my white plume; you will find it on the road to victory and honour.' Then, on the eve of a battle: 'Quarter for Frenchmen, death to foreigners.' When at last he came to lay siege to Paris, he had not the heart to maintain too harsh a blockade and allowed the entry of foodstuffs: 'I do not want to rule over a cemetery', he said.

In 1593, the States General of the realm had been summoned to Paris. The deputies were few in number, but the people seemed to expect a decision from them. Mayenne made a speech from the throne and said that France wanted a Catholic king: his candidate was Mayenne. Philip of Spain wanted to seat on the throne of France his daughter, Isabella-Clara, grand-daughter of Henry II, and make France a more or less autonomous Spanish province.

Meanwhile, Henry IV bargained at Suresnes. He felt that the time had come for his conversion. Were the States General to choose a king other than he, his legitimacy would thenceforth be contested; if, on the other hand, the legitimate king were to become a Catholic, Paris and France, weary of these long wars, would yield to him. 'Instruct me', he said to the bishops. 'I am not stubborn ... You will win God a fine advantage, a handsome conquest of conscience.' Was he acting in good faith? During his life he had been twice Protestant and twice Catholic ... Experienced in abjuration, he had created for himself a kind of faith which was at once very broad and at the same time very sincere. It cost him nothing to surrender to the popular will and, as he put it in his own Gascon, 'to jump the ditch'. But he wanted to be given the necessary time. He led the bishops a rare dance by his questions and his remarks, going as far as to refer to the cult of the saints as a form of leg-pulling. Finally on July 25th, 1593, at Saint-Denis, Henry IV, clad in white, was 'received

into the bosom of the Church'. The League had no further reason for existence. In March 1594, after he had promised a full amnesty, the King entered Paris, his great city, and went to Notre Dame to hear Mass. His amnesty was honestly fulfilled. When France saw that the King wished no reprisals, it followed Paris's example.

Nothing could be more admirable than the patience with which Henry IV completed the pacification of France. It was no easy task; bad feeling ran high. Many were furious at his leniency: 'If there are those who have forgotten themselves', he said, 'I am satisfied if they come to their senses and people stop talking to me about it.' He even bought many a submission, saying that this cost him ten times less than the use of force. He paid the debts of his worst enemy, Mayenne, limiting his vengeance to making the big rheumatic fellow keep up with his quick strides for a time. He made peace with the Spaniards. There remained the necessity of reconciliation with the Holy See; in this negotiation, Henry was very firm, and the cardinals advised the Pope to yield because France's Gallican clergy supported the King and there was risk of a schism. Agreement was reached on the basis of the concordat of 1516; the liberties of the Gallican Church were retained; the King was to select the bishops and have the benefices in his gift. The Church, however, kept its possessions: a quarter of France's area, a hundred millions in revenue plus tithes, in return for which it pledged itself to maintain the places of worship and the schools. This left open the question of the Prince of Condé who, a Protestant, remained heir presumptive to the throne as long as the King had no legitimate male child. It was agreed that this young prince should be reared in the Catholic religion, and the Pope thereupon lifted the excommunication. Thus the monarchy kept the benefice lists and its authority over the French Church. The matter of the Jesuits alone remained unresolved; this order, founded in 1540, a real spiritual militia in the service of the Papacy and removed from the authority of the national hierarchy, had played a major part in the wars of religion. In 1594, the Jesuits had been banished from France as enemies of the King and the State; in 1603, Henry IV called them back, despite the remonstrances of the *Parlement*.

As for the Protestants, true tolerance for them did not yet dwell in men's hearts. A few worthy men such as Bodin had as early as 1577 conceived the idea of separating the Church from the State. But the majority of Catholics and Protestants still wished for the annihilation of their adversaries. Henry IV had hoped that his conversion would lead to that of the mass of Protestants, but nothing of the sort happened; they held his abjuration against him and continued to call the Catholic Church the 'beast of Rome'. All the King was able to obtain from the Huguenots was the acceptance of a kind of armistice — the Edict of Nantes. This act contained wise provisions: the right of Protestants to all State employment; religious worship to take place in fixed places and under set conditions; the right to make wills; the organization of the Protestant clergy into a synod, colleges and consistories; the creation in the Paris *Parlement* of a Chamber of the Edict and of a bipartite chamber in the *Parlement* of Toulouse. Certain secret articles were dangerous: the Protestants retained one hundred and fifty strong places and castles and hence did not abandon the erection of a State within the State. Their past sufferings and experiences were such that we cannot blame them for having insisted on these safeguards, but the continuance in the kingdom of a party with separatist tendencies was a danger to France.

Religious pacification was not the only problem — far from it. 'You know to your cost, as do I to mine', said Henry IV to the notables of Rouen, 'that when God called me to this crown, I found France not only half ruined, but almost entirely lost to the French... Through my care and toil I have saved the heritage; I shall now save it from ruin.' There was much to be done. 'Destruction everywhere', wrote the Venetian ambassador. 'A great part of the cattle has disappeared, so that ploughing is no longer possible... The people are not what they used to be, courteous and honest: war and the sight of blood have made them sly, coarse, and barbarous.' Peasants were to be seen who, for lack of beasts of burden, themselves drew the plough 'and served as animals, with ropes over their shoulders'. In the towns, the population had decreased, at times by two-thirds. Looms had stopped. The financial situation was deplorable. 'All my shirts are torn', wrote the King himself, 'my doublet is worn through at the elbow, I often can entertain no one, and for the last two days I have taken my meals now with one, now with another.' But Henry IV knew that this land and this people had hidden resources; he bravely undertook to rebuild France, to restore to the French confidence in themselves, and to set things to rights. For this purpose he relied above all on his friend and companion, Maximilian de Béthune, Baron of Rosny (whom, in 1606, he made Duke of Sully).

FRENCH SCHOOL, XVIth CENTURY: A PROCESSION OF THE LEAGUE IN PARIS
(Musée Carnavalet).

Henry IV laid siege to Paris but his assault of May 12th, 1590 failed. The defenders took heart, and the Sixteen, dictators of Paris, organised a great procession to celebrate the success, May 14th. Monks and laymen, armed, pass under the arch of St John at the town hall; they sport the Cross of Lorraine on their hats, for this is the emblem of the Guises and of all the League.

Sully had more than genius; he had good sense, integrity and a vast capacity for work. 'Here I am', he wrote, 'locked up in my office, where I examine minutely and with the greatest attention all the abuses which remain to be rooted out.' He arose at four, worked until six-thirty, breakfasted, worked until noon, dined, worked and went to bed at ten. He was crusty and obstinate; even after the conversion of the King, he kept portraits of Calvin and Luther hanging on his walls. His very frankness made him dear to Henry IV: 'That hour when you no longer contradict me, I shall believe that you no longer love me', the King told him. Industrious and diligent, economical and even mean, Sully carried on the business of the realm like a French peasant. 'It must not be known', he would say, 'that the King has a few pennies.' He felt that States were built upon 'prudence, order and gold'. Towards those tax collectors and paymasters who stole on a large scale, he was pitiless. He went over their accounts with a fine tooth-comb and made them disgorge — sometimes unjustly, which led to the saying that he was more a soldier than a master of finance. He was indeed a soldier, and was put in charge of the artillery at the same time as the King entrusted the finances to him. He liked to stroll, between the Louvre and the Arsenal, in great market places full of cannon. 'Never will the artillery have its day in the sun unless it is managed by a superintendent of finances', he used to remark. When he came into office, he found a debt of three hundred million *livres*, and twenty-three millions in annual income which, after the deduction of local charges, only supplied seven millions as the King's net revenue, all of which went straight into warfare, pensions and gifts. With the co-operation of the chief men of the kingdom, much harshness, much pushing and pulling, debt conversion and repudiations, Sully succeeded not only in restoring equilibrium, but in laying away a reserve of thirteen millions in the Bastille and in enlarging his beloved artillery.

'Tilling the soil and keeping flocks — these are France's paps, the real mines and treasures of Peru.' The words are Sully's, who believed that the land was the only form of wealth and that those who worked it were the only nursery for the army. He performed wonders to repair the damages of war, rebuilding France's roads, lining them with elms, repairing bridges (he built Paris's Pont-Neuf in 1604), laying out a network of canals, re-establishing peace in the countryside by disarming the partisans, making illegal the seizure of the peasants' cattle and tools, requiring that every

three months the feudal lords should destroy 'the wolves, foxes, wildcats and other noisome beasts', creating breeding studs, reorganizing the administration of the forests, draining marshes. Trade and colonies, however, did not interest him. Fruitlessly did men talk to him about Quebec (founded in 1604). 'Things which remain separated from our body by foreign lands or seas will be ours only at great expense and to little purpose.' Like him, Henry IV loved the peasants and hoped to see 'a chicken in their pots every Sunday', but he wanted also to reorganize industry. Sully had no faith in this. He opposed the King's efforts to encourage the raising of silk-worms, he opposed Champlain's voyages, he opposed luxury trades, he opposed revenue-contractors, he opposed the marriage of nobles to the rich daughters of commoners, he opposed lazy, idle and pleasure-loving ways of life. Had the King allowed him to do it, Sully would have set up in each bailiwick an inspectorate of morals. Here was Calvin turned artilleryman and financier. Henry IV, more progressive, had hoped that the kingdom would produce at least the manufactured articles it needed. At the beginning of the sixteenth century, this had not been an idle hope; France was then developing her industry much more rapidly than England.

But in 1600, everything had changed. The Italian wars followed by the wars of religion had ruined individuals, and therefore no private capital was available. Reconstruction had to be carried out by the State; it could concern itself only with luxury trades because the great masses of the people, impoverished by the poll tax, had no purchasing power. The King stimulated the establishment of factories for the making of cloth of gold and cloth of silver, rugs and crystal ware. The results were less astonishing than legend would have them, but at least Henry IV and Sully gave France ten years' truce, and the country remembered it as a golden age.

In the French monarchy the problem of the Dauphin was always serious. Now Marguerite of Valois, long separated from Henry IV, had never given him any children. Most certainly it was not because of his impotence, since he produced a flourishing crop of bastards. His amorous escapades were beyond number: history has dug up the names of more than fifty-six of his mistresses, and Clio knows not everything. His best-beloved was the beautiful Gabrielle d'Estrées, by whom he had three children and whom he hoped to marry. Yet if 'Queen Margot', who had never loved her spouse, was ready to agree to an annulment, she was unwilling that it be used to encourage a misalliance, to be followed by the coronation of a hated rival. Gabrielle, however, died suddenly. In order to wipe out his debt to the Grand Duke of Tuscany, in 1600 Henry married Marie de' Medici, the niece of this creditor. At twenty-eight the Florentine was heavy and fleshy; the whole court nicknamed her 'the fat banker'. Marguerite kept in the background, but lived in Paris, and was even friendly to the royal pair. Beginning in 1601, Marie de' Medici presented the King with a son who was to be Louis XIII and then asserted herself by an annual pregnancy. The King, however, never became attached to this rather foolish and very jealous consort. Henriette de Balzac d'Entragues (daughter of Marie Touchet, who had been Charles IX's mistress) inspired in him a violent passion. For one hundred thousand *écus* and a promise of marriage written in his own hand — a promise Henry IV had not kept and which he would later redeem at great cost — this young girl had sold herself to him. The three children whom Henriette bore the King were, like those by Gabrielle d'Estrées, ennobled and acknowledged, and their mother was created Marquise de Verneuil. The pranks of the ageing King displeased his people as much as his wife; that which had been charming in a young hero was offensive in a greybeard. Towards the end of his reign, open complaints were to be heard. Dissoluteness ages badly, and Henry was no longer the wise and lighthearted boy of his younger years.

In foreign policy he continued to the end his opposition to the House of Austria, not as a Protestant, but because he viewed that house as dangerous to France. In his book, *Économies Royales,* Sully attributed to his master a 'Great Design' which would have made Europe into a Christian Society of Nations governed by a council of sixty elected members. Whatever the merits of the idea, it was fathered by Sully and not by the King, who had little use for great designs and who, at the time of his death in 1610, was thinking, rather, of going to war with the Habsburgs. On May 14th, 1610, a man jumped upon the running-board of Henry's coach and with a stroke of his knife severed the King's aorta. Henry had been occupied in reading a letter; he died instantly. His assassin, Ravaillac, seemed to be insane and without accomplices, but it has been proved that in 1610 several plots were in hand. Henry IV had been attacked by all the parties because he would not allow himself to be a partisan. A victim's death always restores some greatness of heart to those who have not defended him during his lifetime: Catholics and Protestants praised to the skies him whom they had so bitterly attacked. Ten generations have confirmed this judgment, and Henry IV remains, together with Charlemagne, Joan of

CLAUDIUS POPELIN: HENRY IV An enamel representing the king in court dress; the horse's caparison is black and patterned with the fleur de lis. (*Musée Condé, Chantilly.*) *Photo Hachette.*

Arc and Saint Louis, one of France's heroes. He typifies not France's mystical aspect, but its aspects of courage, good sense and gaiety.

Six months before his death, in conversation with the Marshal de Lesdiguières, Henry IV had said that 'he well knew that the foundation of all France is the prince's authority. That is why he wanted his son, the Dauphin, to be, as it were, the centre towards which led all the lines of public power ... that it was his intention to establish him as absolute king and to give him all the true, essential marks of royalty, to the end that there might be no one in the realm who would not have to obey him ...' *Absolute king*; he himself was that. After so much division, horror of civil war had united the French behind him. His charm had established the power of the crown on love as much as, and more than, on force. For a century France would be 'mad about the Bourbons'. From 1610 on, the country and the King were one, not through constraint but by instinct. The suffering occasioned by disorder and the skill of the peacemaker had together begotten a willing submission. The people accepted and even desired the substitution of a central power radiating throughout the land, for the multiplicity of local authorities.

All the same, monarchical absolutism was limited by privileges (or liberties) and by custom. We must recall the fashion in which the realm had been built up, by marriages, inheritances, acquisitions, annexations of provinces and towns which gave themselves over to the King. One of the last of these annexations, that of Brittany, had been freely elected by the States General of the duchy because 'the hope of peace which we may entertain through union is preferable to everything that can be said against it'. In return for their adherence, provinces, manors and towns had been granted by the King guarantees which were called privileges or liberties. The privilege, an intermediate stage between such divided authority as had existed in the Middle Ages and that which was to be the equalitarian total power of the great democratic States, had been the means for winning acceptance of centralization from those whom it despoiled. From the King's point of view, it was a legitimate survival. The crown respected its commitments and did not try to apply a uniform law to all France. Each province was judged according to its custom; some had their provincial States General.

The jurists had long maintained that the States General, the nation's assembly or committee, was the most aged and the most worthy of the respect of the nation's institutions. In the sixteenth century, it was possible that the States General, thanks to French internal discord, might assume an authority similar to that of the English Parliament. But the States, composed of the three orders — the people (third estate), the nobility and the clergy — had always been weakened by the absurd traditional rule of voting by orders. That is, each order voted as a unit, so that the privileged orders were assured a two to one majority. Furthermore, the moment the States General began to talk too much out of turn, the King ordered the tapestries to be taken down from the walls and had the halls locked up, leaving the deputies with nothing to do except go home, which they did without too much outcry.

Who, then, watched over the observance of the custom of the realm? In theory, the *Parlements*. At the beginning of the seventeenth century, there were *Parlements* at Paris, Toulouse, Bordeaux, Rouen, Aix, Grenoble, Dijon and Rennes — powerful and respected companies. The First President of Paris, one of the greatest personages in the kingdom, gave precedence only to the princes of the blood and the chancellor. The councillors judged all matters as a court of last resort. They registered the royal edicts and,

if they considered them contrary to the fundamental laws of the realm, they had the right to make remonstrances. Under a strong king, indeed, remonstrances were ineffective, in the first place because no one knew clearly what the fundamental laws of the realm were, and secondly because the King had the right to hold a 'bed of justice' at which he himself presided over the *Parlement*, and that body had to submit to his wishes. Henry IV treated it cavalierly: 'You have told me the burden this edict places upon our finances; but you supply me with no remedy to escape it and even less to keep my armies alive. Were each of you to offer me two or three thousand *écus*, or to hint that I might take your salaries or those of the paymasters of France, this would be a means for not making edicts; but you want to be well paid and think that you have done a great deal when you have made me remonstrances full of fine sayings and handsome phrases, whereupon you go to warm your hands at your own hearths and do everything to your own convenience.'

JEAN III LECLERC, after JEROME BOLLERY: THE SPANISH ARMY LEAVING PARIS The governor of Paris, Charles II de Cossé, later the Duke of Brissac, surrendered the city, and Henry IV watches the foreign troops leave by the Porte Saint-Denis, March 22nd, 1594. (*B. N. Prints.*) *Photo Giraudon.*

FRENCH SCHOOL, XVIth CENTURY: HENRY IV AT THE SIEGE OF AMIENS
(Musée de Versailles.) *Office de documentation Pierre de la Forest.*

When the Spaniards took the town, on March 11th, 1597, France was greatly shaken, and the king lost his principal artillery depôt. The town did not surrender until September 25th, after the Spanish leader had been killed. This was the last action of the war which ended with the Peace of Vervins, May 2nd, 1598.

In the administration of the kingdom, the King in part made use of his judges. Until the time, later on, of the *intendants*, bailiffs and seneschals were as much administrators as magistrates. In case of need, the first president of a provincial *Parlement* took the place of the governor. Directives were given by the King in his council, in which sat the chancellor, the superintendent of finances, and the secretaries of State, whose duties, in Henry IV's day, were still rather ill defined. (The chancellor was the fountainhead of justice, irremovable, the keeper of the royal seals.) As for defence, ever since Charles VII, the King had possessed an army and was himself its commander-in-chief. It consisted of the nobility (younger sons, above all); the French troops, cavalry and infantry; and mercenaries, Swiss, Scottish and German.

Finances had been the great weakness of the French monarchy. Sully, loathed as must be a good finance minister, re-established a temporary equilibrium. In 1610 receipts amounted to about thirty million *livres*, which corresponded roughly to the expenditure, and a war chest had been set up. Moreover, the tax system had been slightly improved. By contrast, indirect taxes had been made heavier. The most famous impost, which was to play a major part in France's consequent history, was the *paulette*. It was an annual levy equal to 1 per cent of the purchase value of government posts, which judges and other officials were henceforward to pay, and in return for which they would have the right to bequeath their offices to their sons. The *paulette* made government jobs hereditary and created a genuine 'nobility of the robe'. The day on which this tax was inaugurated, the monarchy 'sold its power to the middle class', but it took two centuries for the monarchy to become aware of it. And finally, the clergy (ever since 1560) had annually to give the king a portion of the Church's revenues. This sum was known as the 'free gift'; there was nothing free about it except its name.

At the beginning of the seventeenth century, a cross-section of the pyramid of French society would have presented approximately the following picture. At the apex was the King, surrounded by a ceremonial which, under the last Valois, had become wholly Oriental, but to which Henry IV had restored some humanity. We may well wonder whether the King's mistresses, so damned by the historians, did not play an essential role by supplying next to an all-too-flattered sovereign women who dared speak to him as a human being. The privacy of the bedroom has a healthy levelling effect upon rank and dignity, and Agnes Sorel, Diane de Poitiers, Marie Touchet and Gabrielle d'Estrées were intelligent and well-informed women. After the king came the Great Ones. The highest aristocracy was made up of the princes of the blood, without peer, too highly placed and corrupted with power. Dangerous likewise were the foreign princes, like those of the House of Lorraine, who were dependent on France but retained sovereign rights. Belonging also to the caste of the great were the provincial governors, in principle nominated for three-year terms, but in fact often irremovable, powerful in their domains and bargaining with the King for their support of his cause. It should be noted that this high aristocracy had power only by the King's will; it was he who created governors; they were no more than his officers. The medieval hierarchy had been broken and a rebellious prince of the blood no longer possessed a whole chain of vassals with which to build himself an army. The Fronde would demonstrate that a rebellion was still something to be feared, but from 1660 on, the Great Ones would be altogether domesticated.

The next lower level was that of the middling and small nobility, representing about seventy thousand holdings. The greater part of these nobles, half peasant, half warrior, still dwelt in castles with drawbridges and turrets. But they were beginning to discover that they had been ruined by the depreciation of the currency and that the sole means of rebuilding their family fortunes would be to live under the King's shadow, he being the dispenser of posts and benefices. The King encouraged the concentration of the nobility at court because it placed at his mercy a turbulent class which had afforded his ancestors much trouble. In short, everything took place as though he had said to his nobles: 'Give up the relics of a feudal past which no one can bring back to life; give up dispensing justice, collecting taxes; above all give up private wars and civil war. *In return for this, your wages will be many a scrap of every sort — chicken bones, pigeon bones, without mentioning many a warm caress.*' — to quote La Fontaine. At court the King gave them a friendly reception; all were his companions at arms. But life at court was costly; the stakes were high and one's clothes had to be splendid. Soon, farms and tenant lands, meadows and mills were eaten up; one must fall back on the King's bounty. Under Henry IV the crown spent a third of the budget on pensions. Such was the price for keeping the nobles loyal.

The clergy was dependent on the crown as much as on the Holy See. Bishops were appointed by the King. When a diocese was vacant, its revenues went to the King. He also kept the roll of benefices. In return for the support of the Gallican Church, the crown granted the clergy a preponderant status in the country; bishops and archbishops were entitled to great honours, and numerous seats were set aside for them in the various councils. Like the nobility, the clergy was exempt from the polltax, the salt excise and a number of other imposts. The Assembly of the Clergy met from time to time to vote the free gift, and it took advantage of the occasion energetically to defend the privileges of the Gallican Church. Intimate union between the Church and the monarchy remained in France one of the elements of stability.

It has often been asserted that the nobility in France was a closed caste; nothing could be less accurate. Every wealthy burgher could make his son into a noble by having him educated and by purchasing for him a public office. A judge's or counsellor's robe conferred nobility, and the *paulette* allowed this nobility to be made hereditary. In order to satisfy the ambitions of the bourgeoisie, the King multiplied government posts. No country in Europe had been, as much as France was, turned into a pasture for lawyers and financial agents. The upper middle class, comfortably wrapped in furs, 'spread its red or black robes on every seat bedecked with fleur-de-lys'. In earlier days the nobility had chosen war for its speciality; the French middle class had taken advantage of this to capture administration and justice. For these tasks it had great aptitudes — a liking for order and economy, often great intelligence, sometimes courage, as was the case with Harlay, First President, who defied the League. But it had its faults — vanity, stinginess, jealousy.

When reference is made to the third estate of that day, it would be mistaken to believe that the true people were represented therein. Posing as the third estate was a clever dodge of the upper middle class (actually, at the base of the pyramid lay the unprivileged, those who paid the poll tax). In France's towns there then lived a whole people of small merchants — prudent, hardworking, timorous. There was very little of that financial boldness common enough in Italy and England. The French merchant was satisfied with little, laid something aside, dreamed of becoming an alderman and retiring. If he could, he would push his son towards the King's service; if not, he would leave him his business. The habits of this class changed very little between the seventeenth and the nineteenth centuries. The artisans worked in small groups — a few apprentices and a master. They were joined together in corporations for their trade, in confraternities for their fun. Moreover, the workers in a given craft constituted a sort of freemasonry; they had special jargons and means of identification. The mass of little people did not like corporations; they had had their usefulness in the Middle Ages, but were now simply burdensome, authoritarian organizations which secured the masters the fattest of unjust privileges. Hence in the seventeenth century the tendency of the majority of the people was to ask the King's intervention in order to lessen the power of the corporations.

It is difficult to give an account of peasant life with any accuracy. The legend built up about this period, perhaps by contrast with the horrors of the civil wars, is that of a Golden Age, of a chicken in every pot. In fact, the French peasant was destitute, while the land was more and more split up and the population grew. The French peasant is a steady worker; he is never discouraged; but he counted on the King to free him from feudal survivals. A lack of firmness towards the nobility on the part of the sovereigns of the seventeenth and eighteenth centuries was to be one of the causes of the Revolution.

Had the Renaissance and Reformation produced lasting effects in France, or were they not merely an interlude, without effect on the main course of the drama?

Sixteenth-century man imagined that nothing essential had changed because he saw the King upon his throne, the lord in his castle and the parish priest in his church. Yet he failed to observe that from then on the King would be dependent on the banker or the gold mine, allowing him to maintain an army and do without the feudal nobility; he failed to see that soon wars would be declared, no longer to ensure the triumph of the true faith, but to defend the independence first of the middle class, then of the masses; he failed to note that humanism leads to scientific agnosticism. While the Renaissance thought itself no more than a search for a compromise between the ideas of ancient philosophy and those of the scholastics, it bore within it the seeds of nationalism, the French Revolution, modern science and world wars.

On the political level, national had taken the place of feudal conflicts. Patriotism had been born in France long before, and it had been sturdy ever since the Hundred Years War; since Henry IV, no other feeling would be strong enough to vie with it in French hearts. When the nobility,

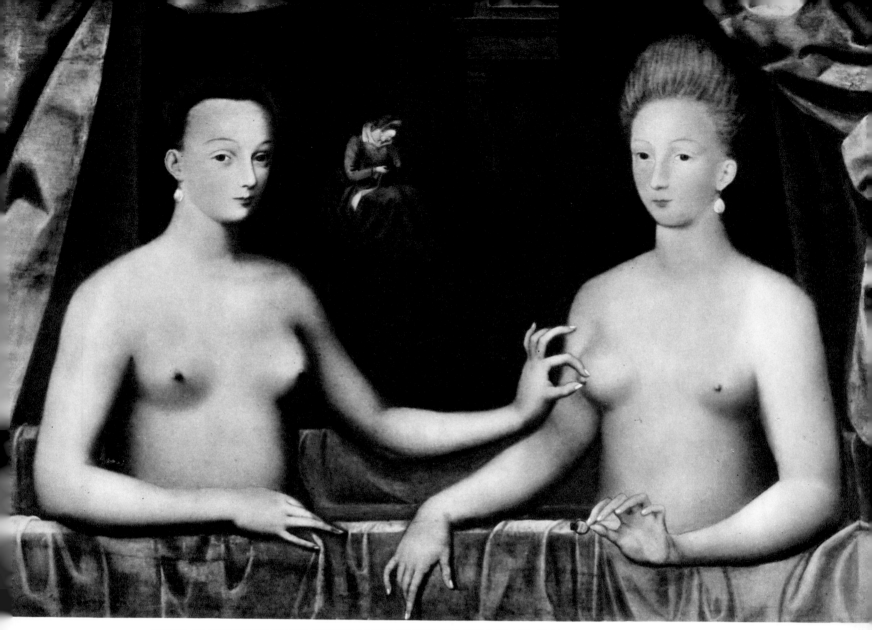

SCHOOL OF FONTAINEBLEAU: THE DUCHESS OF VILLARS WITH HER SISTER-IN-LAW, THE DUCHESS OF BEAUFORT
On the right is Gabrielle d'Estrées, Duchess of Beaufort, who almost became queen, and who gave Henry IV
three children; c. 1595. (*Musée du Louvre.*) *Office doc. ed.*

during the days of the Fronde, toyed with foreign alliances, there was instant popular revolt. The general admiration for good King Henry represented the triumph of patriotism over faction. Absolute monarchy won the day in the XVIIth century because the King embodied the nation's unity.

The birth of a great literature and the maintenance and enriching of the French language were essential factors in this unity. The best French minds had absorbed the works of the humanists, and thereafter they were to devote themselves to imitating the formal perfection of antiquity. No modern people would attach a greater importance to style, to eloquence, to the choice of words; even the preacher would become a man of letters; and by the same token Francis I, Henry IV and their successors were to be classic

writers. For a long while these shared glories, these victories of sword and spirit, would suffice to unite the French, who found so much contentment in rejoicing at the beauty and the greatness of their country that for two centuries they forgot the daring of the Renaissance. With Henry IV, the nation reached a stopping place, a landing. The republicanism of Plutarch's heroes left its mark on Corneille, just as Rabelais' heartiness is reflected in La Fontaine, but the ordinary Frenchman during the seventeenth century went to church on Sundays, cried 'Long live the King!' with all his heart, and put up with the privileges of the nobility and the clergy. He would not understand that in his father's day one of the great revolutions of the human spirit had just been accomplished.

[75]

VI

The Absolute Monarchy

Louis XIII to Louis XVI, 1610-1792

CHILD rulers are the plague of monarchies. Henry IV had bestowed the regency on Queen Marie de' Medici, the haughty Italian — a fat blonde, handsome enough when Rubens painted her, very well pleased with herself, an authoritarian without authority. The new king was only nine, a sullen, shy child who was left to the mercies of riding masters, manservants and cooks. It is possible that his mother, by neglecting his upbringing, hoped to prolong his minority. She herself was dominated by a childhood friend, Leonora Galigai, a swarthy and greedy sorceress suckled by the same wet nurse as herself, whom she had imported from Florence. Leonora had married an affected fop named Concini, and for some years this strange pair ruled over the Queen Mother and, through her, over France. Concini, made Marquis of Ancre, had himself named marshal.

The Concinis had the wisdom to retain Henry IV's old ministers, 'the bearded fellows', except for Sully whom everyone detested, and these old fellows had the wisdom to understand that the weaknesses of a regency made any war undesirable. The campaign which the late king had begun against the Habsburgs was wound up and, to make peace sure, Marie de' Medici decided to marry her son the King to Anne of Austria, daughter of Philip III, King of Spain, and great-granddaughter of Charles V. This caused an outcry among the Protestants, who felt that this was a threat to them, and it did not placate the Catholic nobility; the Great Ones of both religions formed a league and denounced the abuses of the regency. As for the country, it was against the Great Ones and for the King; so it was a reasonable step in 1614 to convene the States General. Louis XIII, who had just reached his majority, appeared before it, dressed in white, elegant and frail. He was highly applauded. The ordering of the retinues was magnificent, but these 'gentlemen of the States' showed little feeling for the national interest; each of the three estates argued in its

own behalf. The nobility of the sword went after the nobility of the robe and called for the abolition of the *paulette*, that is, of hereditary office. The clergy was most energetically represented by the young Bishop of Luçon, Richelieu, whose artful eloquence aroused admiration. With his arched nose and thin lips, his 'goatee and moustache in cavalry style', his paleness and slenderness, he cut a distinguished figure. He asked that ecclesiastics be more closely linked to power. This amounted to nominating himself, and Marie de' Medici, who had admired this pale, proud young prelate, took note of it. The States General, after bitter discussions, was adjourned by the usual means — by the removal of the tapestries — and the delegates went home without having accomplished anything. Its bequest to the country was Richelieu, whom the Queen soon summoned to the council and whom Concini made his friend. This great bishop, of a good noble family, burned with ambition; from his distant diocese he had watched the court and had drawn up for his own guidance maxims on the art of success. He urged the budding statesman to silence, dissimulation and careful answers, which are like 'those retreats that save lives and equipment'. He fascinated the queen with that glance 'no one could withstand' and, without ever laying aside his prelate's dignity, dominated her.

Yet in the very terms of the problem there was an element which the Regent, Concini and Richelieu wrongly neglected — the young king himself. He had been left to servants and a single favourite companion, Charles d'Albert de Luynes, a handsome fellow who, like Louis XIII, loved riding and hunting. No one took note that the King had become of age, and hence was master; no one knew that he was aware of his rights, hard and when necessary even cruel. Unsociable, a dreamer, he played at being bored. He loved Luynes, feared women and did not enter his own wife's bed until five years after their marriage, and only when he was led to it by his favourite. He knew, however,

PHILIPPE DE CHAMPAIGNE: ARMAND-JEAN DU PLESSIS, CARDINAL DUKE OF RICHELIEU This Bishop of Luçon was prime minister from ▶ 1624 till his death in 1643. He was among other things a playwright, founded the Académie Française (1635), and left an important *Political Testament. Musée Condé, (Chantilly.) Photo Bulloz.*

SIMON VOUET: LOUIS XIII (Musée de Versailles) *Office de documentation Pierre de la Forest.*

Vouet, chief court painter, did many portraits of the king, who was also among his pupils. The king is depicted in full martial apparel, with France and Navarre, somewhat *décolletées*, at his feet. Navarre is on the king's left, holding a shield with this country's device on it.

VAN DYCK: GASTON D'ORLÉANS
This son of Henry IV was coward-
ly and, like all the House of
Orléans, hostile to the elder
branch. He was the play-thing
of the warring factions. (*Musée
Condé, Chantilly.*) *Photo Giraudon.*

LOUIS LE PAON: THE BATTLE OF
ROCROY In this battle the Capet-
ian Louis II of Bourbon, then
Duke of Enghien, beat the Capet-
ian Don Francisco de Mello
(May 19th, 1643).
*Conservation du Musée de
Versailles.*

how to reach a decision, how to lead and how to hate. When he grew tired of seeing the Marshal of Ancre show off, he secretly gave an order to the captain of his bodyguard, and Concini was assassinated. Louis XIII was sixteen years old. At court it was as though lightning had struck. The courtiers, by profession abject, turned towards the new star. Richelieu, compromised by his connection with Concini, went back to his diocese; Marie de' Medici was exiled to Blois; on the Place de Grève, Leonora Galigai was burned as a witch. Luynes would have been the master had he possessed any mastery, but he was a weak fellow, ignorant of public affairs at a moment when the situation in Europe required the most refined intelligence. Catholics and Protestants were still fighting in Germany; Bohemia and Hungary were in revolt against the Emperor. The latter appealed for French help in the name of Catholicism, while the German Protestants asked the same country to intervene in order to put a stop to the undertakings of Austria. To have a free hand in Europe, France's ruler needed internal peace, yet the Queen Mother's party, still powerful, was a source of anxiety to the adherents of the King. Richelieu,

who had become Marie de' Medici's secretary of writs, several times tried to effect a reconciliation between mother and son, but fruitlessly. In 1621, during a campaign, Luynes died of 'the crimson fever'. The King did not weep for him; indeed he shed few tears. After this death, Richelieu, freed of an enemy, was given the Cardinal's red hat, but the red robes had no worth in his eyes were they not to become a prime minister's livery.

Up to this moment, Louis XIII had considered Richelieu a turbulent and dangerous prelate, 'ready to set fire to the four corners of the realm', and wanted to have 'no dealings with him'. But in 1624, Marie de' Medici's pressure as well as the Cardinal's abilities — at a time when ability in statecraft was rare — led Louis to yield. No sooner had he entered the council than Richelieu, 'with indescribable joy', saw his part grow greater and greater; soon the King realized that in him he would find the 'chief minister' for whom he had hoped, and forgetting his prejudices he placed the Cardinal at the head of state affairs.

Louis XIII was a harsh master who entertained the highest of notions concerning his rights and duties as king. Jealous of his authority, he even bestowed shocking humiliations on Richelieu himself. It was the King and not the Cardinal who insisted upon putting men to death. To Richelieu, who was inclined towards leniency, the King wrote: 'It is ordered that you be less easy and less moved by pity for the said lords, for they have valued too low what they owe the master of the shop.' Such was his manner of expression, commonplace and picturesque. Louis XIII stammered, but he knew what he wanted to say; his intelligence was obvious, his will inflexible. His health alone failed him, and in this he was like his minister; their ailments and their medicines drew them together.

For Richelieu likewise was a sick man, burning with fever, nervous, often on the edge of tears, variable in temper, distraught, impatient. As chief minister, he took his frugal meals alone in his room and sought silence at Chaillot or Rueil. At times his fiery temper broke out in brief yet terrible rages; whenever he said, 'Sir, your most humble servant', every prudent visitor saw fit to flee. But this irritable man had succeeded in fashioning for himself a steadfast will. His was an obstinacy of principle, not one arising from narrowness; never was there a clearer mind. He went straight to the point and at a glance penetrated to the bottom of matters. After clarity, he viewed secrecy as the greatest virtue of a statesman. The 'Most Eminent' was also the 'Most Secret'. He believed in severity, but not in rancour. Few have been more attacked and slandered; but he learned to bear this abuse calmly.

Although the greatness of the minister and the man is beyond dispute, it is false to say that he 'created' a French policy. 'My first goal', he said, 'was the majesty of the King; the second was the greatness of the realm.' He could reach these objectives only by stages. One of the obstacles was the continuance in France of Protestant fortified places and Huguenot armies. Richelieu the cardinal was tolerant; Richelieu the statesman could not suffer anything which divided the State. Hence the necessity to put a stop to the 'chronic blackmail' of La Rochelle and the other places of asylum. La Rochelle was like the Calais of old, an English bridgehead in France. The Cardinal besieged La Rochelle and vanquished it, and in 1628 Louis XIII made his entry into the town. Here Richelieu's moderation became apparent: as conqueror, he imposed a peace of reconciliation: general amnesty, freedom of worship, no confiscation of goods. A few months later the Peace of Alais, or Edict of Grace, put a stop to the religious wars. Richelieu had

EMBANKMENT AND BRIDGE OF LA TOURNELLE, PARIS In the middle distance is the Ile Saint-Louis. (*Musée Carnavalet.*) *Photo Bulloz.*

VAN DER MEULEN: THE ENTRY OF LOUIS XIV AND MARIA THERESA INTO
ARRAS (Musée de Versailles.) *Office de documentation Pierre de la Forest.*

Enlisted in 1664 by Charles Le Brun, whose niece he married, Van der Meulen, who
was a topographer, followed Louis on many of his campaigns, and painted the castles, towns
and localities as he came to them. Here, during the Flanders campaign, the king and queen
make their entry into Arras, July 30th, 1667. The king and his brother are on horseback
behind the coach occupied by the queen and her suite.

THE PARIS MARKET IN THE XVIIth CENTURY This illustration features a number of fishwives. (*Musée Carnavalet.*)
Photo Hachette.

fought the party, not the cult, and the conversion of the heretics was 'a work for which we must look to Heaven, without our applying any violence'.

The intrigues of the Great Ones were no less dangerous than those of the Huguenots, but the King and the Cardinal clipped their claws too. There was a moment when the two Queens plotted against Richelieu, and with them, Gaston of Orleans, the King's brother and heir to the throne; handsome Marie de Rohan, Duchess of Chevreuse; and the bastards of Henry IV. It was difficult to punish the Queens and the Duke, but the lesser players paid for their masters. Chalais, Montmorency, Cinq-Mars and other distinguished heads fell: Marshal de Bassompierre, a national hero, was cast into the Bastille for having played a tiny role in one of Marie de' Medici's conspiracies, and he remained there until Richelieu's death in 1643. Richelieu was of a noble family, but he regarded the nobility as dangerous in the State the moment it ceased waging war for it, since the nobles carried the warrior spirit into internal affairs. Here was the reason for the harsh edicts against duelling, which Richelieu punished with death. As for the people, the object of his government was not their happiness, but the security of the State without which there is neither happiness nor people.

It seemed to him that the first requirement for this security was a realistic foreign policy. In order to save France and 'unstring the Spanish rosary', he decided to ally himself to the Protestant princes of Germany and Scandinavia as the best expedient for the time being. From 1624 to 1635 he applied all his skill to arousing enemies against Austria without involving France in the war. First Denmark, then Sweden, urged by him, flew to the help of the German princes. Gustavus Adolphus, Sweden's Lutheran King, received from Richelieu subsidies with which to continue the war. In 1633 the Emperor's armies seemed to be disorganized by General Wallenstein's rebellion; this gentleman dreamed of establishing (to his profit) an empire in which all religions would be free. By taking advantage of this uprising, Richelieu hoped to advance without opposition to the Rhine, the kingdom's natural frontier. His troops slipped into Alsace. But within two years, Wallenstein had been assassinated, the Swedes beaten and the Protestant princes crushed at Nördlingen; Spain was sending troops to Austria, which would win the day if France did not openly declare herself. Richelieu hesitated no longer. It was now necessary to intervene on the side of the German Protestants if Austrian domination was to be staved off.

The war was not without its dangers. In 1636 France was invaded and the Spaniards penetrated as far as Corbie, their scouts reaching Pontoise; all would have been lost had not courage matched the extent of the danger. The country supplied soldiers and money. Spain was repulsed; France regained self-confidence; Richelieu's enemies were lost. After 1636 Richelieu had practically nothing but successes. His armies moved forward in Picardy and Artois; in the south they occupied Roussillon (Catalonia, Savoy, Turin). In 1642 France extended almost to the Scheldt, the Rhine, the Alps and the Pyrenees — in other words, her natural boundaries.

And there was another matter for congratulation: on September 5th, 1638, twenty-three years after her marriage, Anne of Austria had at last given France a dauphin; Gaston, Duke of Orleans, the Cardinal's enemy, lost all hope of succeeding to the throne. But in December 1642, the Cardinal, long ill, felt that he was dying. He was not to see the French peace for which he had so long laboured.

It is certain that Richelieu wanted absolute authority for the King as for himself. He had tasted the luxury of power and 'loved glory more than morality allows'. When in 1635 he founded the French Academy, he wanted even the Republic of Letters to recognize his authority — and it was a most reasonable authority — over language and the works of the mind. Someone said of him that he had been 'the schoolmaster of the French nation'.

Louis XIII did not long survive Richelieu, and the *Parlement*, which had been humbled by the Cardinal, at once sought and found an opportunity to reassert itself. In his will, Louis XIII had retained in power 'the relics of the Cardinal', by which he meant a council of men selected by Richelieu, which, during the infant king's minority, was to watch over Anne of Austria, the Regent and Gaston of Orleans, the Lieutenant-General of the Realm. Anne of Austria was a proud Spaniard, long weaned of tenderness through her husband's indifference, not ill willed but, despite her placid manner, inclined to fits of wrath which turned her voice into a shrill noisy falsetto. She brought the child King before the *Parlement* to request that the will be broken and her regency made unconditional. The *Parlement* joyfully greeted this chance to show its power and Anne won the right to form her own council. Thereupon she surprised everyone by choosing as principal minister one of Richelieu's creatures, Giulio Mazzarini, called Mazarin.

He was an Italian, born of a family 'of small estate, but not lowly'. He had served as a captain of infantry and then, through the favour of an ecclesiastical friendship, having become a canon at Rome without ever having been ordained, was made a papal legate and nuncio to France. Richelieu had espied in him a clever fellow, 'of wonderful industry and astuteness in managing men and putting them off with doubtful and misleading hopes'. Richelieu had been firm, and even hard; Mazarin was flexible and remembered neither benefits nor insults. 'Now we saw', wrote

THE PARC DE CHAMPS This magnificent château (Seine-et-Marne) was built in the XVIIIth century and became the favourite residence of the Marquise de Pompadour. *Photo Roubier.*

FRANZ HALS: RENÉ DESCARTES A native of Tours, he is the father of modern philosophy (d. 1650). (*Musée du Louvre.*)

de Retz, 'standing on the steps before the throne, whence the harsh and forbidding Cardinal Richelieu had struck with lightning rather than governed human beings, a successor soft spoken and benign, who wished for nothing, who was in despair because his dignity as a Cardinal did not allow him to humble himself before everyone as much as he would have desired...' Everyone suddenly discovered himself to be pro-Mazarin — everyone, and especially the Queen Mother. What was the nature of the bond? Did she unite herself to him in secret marriage? The letters demonstrate a more than tender feeling; the facts show that she soon could not do without him and lodged him near her both at the Palais Royal and during the court's state journeys. The sequence of events would show that her choice had been good. Mazarin had less style than Richelieu, and his methods were less direct, but he followed the same pattern with the same tenacity, and he would leave Louis XIV in 1661 a kingdom stronger than ever.

At Rocroi (1643), the young Duke of Enghien (later the Great Condé) had defeated the 'fearsome Spanish infantry'. Turenne had moved into Germany. Now the task was to harvest the fruits of victory. France was extremely lucky to have in charge of her business a master diplomat. The peace conference which was, perhaps for centuries, to settle Europe's fate began in 1644; not until 1648 were the two Treaties of Westphalia (Osnabrück and Münster) signed upon the same day by the Catholic and Protestant Powers, which had deliberated separately. These treaties constituted a triumph for France and for Richelieu's policies. They left the Empire more than weakened, gave France full sovereignty over Alsace, and made France the arbiter of Europe.

It might be thought that this diplomatic triumph would make secure the glory of the minister who won it. Not at all; no man has ever been more slandered than Mazarin. As early as 1648, Paris was in the process of rebellion. Why? Because two foreigners, a Spaniard and an Italian, were governing France; because no more cardinals were wanted as 'first ministers'; because finances were in a bad way and finally because, during those days, revolution was in the air, in Naples, for instance, and in England. The Paris *Parlement* had nothing in common with the Parliament of London but the two institutions bore the same name, and this alone was sufficient to give ideas to the Paris Parlementarians and their First President. Far more determined was the attitude of the people of Paris, which thought itself strong, feared Mazarin less than Richelieu, and had found a leader in a demagogic prelate, Paul de Gondi (later Cardinal de Retz), an ambitious cynic bitterly opposed to Mazarin.

These combined forces came very close to endangering the monarchy. Their successive uprisings, which are referred to as the 'Fronde' (the French word for a sling) because stones were shot into the windows of the Cardinal-Minister, amounted to an advance version of the French Revolution. The royal family had to leave Paris, and the people stormed into the palace, forcing the Regent to show them the small King lying in his bed. Louis XIV would not forget these scenes, which so strangely resembled those during the course of which his family was to perish. There were several clashes followed by limping settlements. But the people were not satisfied. They were insistent that Mazarin should disappear. The court fled to Rueil; it would have been in serious peril had its opponents been united. But what idea had they in common? Among the military men, Turenne campaigned against the King and bargained with the Spaniards, whose intervention alarmed those still possessed of patriotism and common sense. Turenne's army abandoned its general; the *Parlement*, justly scandalized at the Spanish alliance, which stank of treason, decided to talk things over with the court.

[84]

THÉODORE GUDIN: THE FRENCH IN LOUISIANA (Musée de la France d'Outre-Mer).

Continuing the work of Marquette and Jolliet, de la Salle sailed down the Mississippi to its mouth, April 9th, 1682. He called the country Louisiana in honour of the king. On a second voyage from France he was killed by his companions while exploring the delta country.

PIERRE-DENIS MARTIN (?): A DETAIL FROM THE BATTLE OF FLEURUS Near Charleroi, the Duke of Luxembourg
beat the Prince of Waldeck with his Dutchmen and their allies, July 1st, 1690. (*Musée de Versailles.*)
Office doc. ed.

The peace of Rueil settled nothing. Both parties remained strong; what was even more important, the Great Condé, bulwark of the court, suddenly turned against it. A man of vast pride, he thought that without him Mazarin would have been defeated. Gondi, the better to destroy Mazarin, pretended to become reconciled to him and urged him to have Condé and the princes arrested, their insolence having become unbearable. Now to place the victor of Rocroi and Lens under arrest was a rash move; it aroused the whole country. The *Parlement* took sides with Condé. Were the uniting of the two Frondes, that of the *Parlement* and that of the princes, to take place, Mazarin would be lost. In January 1651 he had to retire for a while, after having freed Condé. But Anne of Austria played her cards well; she won Gondi to the crown by offering him a cardinal's hat, and secured the support of Turenne, the only general to match Condé. Mademoiselle de Montpensier, the 'Grande Mademoiselle', a mannish girl, took command of an army, and determined to join Condé. However, Mazarin knew that there was one man on whom he could always rely against Condé, namely Condé himself — who was so intolerable and vainglorious that Paris would end by preferring even Mazarin to him! The patriotic populace was aroused at seeing Spanish flags in the army of the Fronde; the mob was beginning to turn against those who had spurred it on. Now merchants' deputations were arriving with tears in

[85]

their eyes begging the King to return to Paris. In October 1652 Louis XIV made a military entrance into Paris, and everyone who counted came to pay him court. The Fronde was finished.

Mazarin waited for several months before returning. He was retained by the King until his death. Louis recognized the worth of this tight-mouthed and discreet 'stepfather' who showed him the principles of politics, and above everything else, he would never have discharged the minister whose return betokened the King's victory over the Fronde.

Mazarin lived until 1661, and during the last years of his life did good work for France. Spain had to be dealt with, once and for all; that country persisted in poisoning all France's domestic quarrels. In order to beat Spain down, Mazarin did not hesitate to ally himself with Cromwell's regicide and Protestant England. He was merely following Richelieu's tradition. Thanks to this alliance and Turenne's genius, he won the Battle of the Dunes. Yet to ensure peace an alliance was needed, and the King had to marry the daughter of the King of Spain. The Peace of the Pyrenees completed the re-establishment of France's borders, giving her the Roussillon, the Cerdagne and Artois. Maria Theresa, eldest daughter of Philip IV, married Louis XIV. In return for a dowry of five hundred thousand gold *écus*, she gave

up her rights to her father's throne. Spain, however, was very poor; the dowry could never be paid; and all hopes remained legitimate, even that of one day seeing the two crowns united, since Philip IV had not at that moment any male heir. Mazarin had more than completed Richelieu's work; Louis XIV's personal rule had begun.

For all Europe the King of France was then 'the great King'; his century was to remain the Great Century. Everything about it had indeed been great, and first of all Louis XIV himself. Having known Mazarin's tutelage, he had resolved to be his own minister. He presided over his council, worked six hours a day, and tied himself down to signing the vouchers for the smallest State expenditure. Saint-Simon, who disliked him, said that he was born with a mind below the mediocre, but 'a mind able to shape itself, to refine itself, and to borrow from others without imitating and without embarrassment', which, coming from a foe, is the handsomest of tributes. Louis had perfect manners, not allowing himself even the kindliest and most innocent chaffing, and never passing a woman without lifting his hat; 'I add that this was true of chambermaids and those he knew to be such', Saint-Simon naively adds. He had been born kind and patient; his weaknesses lay in loving flattery, in welcoming and encouraging the most clumsy praise, which

quickly produced an unawareness of truth and a confusion of the State's interest with care for his own glory. Even though he was a pious and believing man, he was willing to have his court make of him a god; little by little he became majestically selfish, judging men solely by their devotion to his person.

The shifting of the court at this time from Paris to Versailles strengthened the monarch's despotism by withdrawing him from the controls of public opinion. It had been with Mademoiselle de la Vallière, when their love was still a secret, that Louis had gone on his first visits to Versailles, staying in a small castle built by Louis XIII. Gradually he erected there 'innumerable buildings', and finally, beginning in 1682, he made of it his principal residence. Five thousand people, the pick of the French aristocracy, then dwelt at the château, and five thousand others in its neighbourhood. By its absence, the French nobility lost its local prestige in the provinces, but on the other hand any great lord who failed to live at court cut himself off from favours, posts, pensions and benefices. Life at Versailles was ruinously expensive, and this was a deliberate part of the system. As a matter of policy, Louis forced magnificence upon all, and thus reduced the courtiers to dependence upon his bounty for their existence, whence came the amazing prestige of all

those who could get near him and beg favours: mistresses, bastards, doctors and serving men. At court he regulated with extreme care the least details of ceremonial. Saint-Simon thought that this arose from his having 'a mind by nature tending toward smallness', yet likewise admitted that, not having enough real favours to bestow, the King was clever in substituting imaginary privileges for those more substantial.

'L'état, c'est moi.' ('The State—I am the State!') Louis XIV never uttered these words, but the idea was in his mind. Louis XIV ruled France by means of councils on which, in theory, he alone made decisions. The ministers were few, and he rarely changed them. At the very outset of his reign, he brought about the arrest, trial and life imprisonment of the Superintendent of Finances, Nicholas Fouquet, a bountiful patron of the arts, but who had acquired the dangerous habit of confusing the credit of the State with his own. An overhandsome entertainment which Fouquet gave the King at his Château of Vaux-le-Vicomte (and perhaps his attentions to Louise de la Vallière) brought about his downfall, probably undeserved.

But the generation of ministers which followed was ably chosen. Colbert, Le Tellier and his son Louvois, fulfilled their tasks as 'chief clerks' as scrupulously as any men could.

In the field of finance, Colbert's job was a hard one, for he had to deal with a lavish sovereign. In Colbert's view, endowed as he was with common sense, that rarest of qualities among technical men, there was no other means of balancing the budget than to increase receipts and diminish expenses. He tried also to simplify public accounting, to lessen the number of exemptions from the poll-tax, to soften the harshness of the means of compulsion used against tax receivers. But his task remained ever incomplete because of the wars which endlessly caused new deficits. The King's solicitude for 'glory' outmatched his concern for straightening out his finances.

Colbert established state manufactures and monopolies which still exist (Gobelin tapestries, the striking of coins, tobacco, the royal printing houses). He took an interest in Canada and established, without great success, the Company for the Commerce of the Western and Eastern Indies. But he died before the harvest was gathered; his successors did not continue his effort, and France was outstripped by England.

Louvois, son of Le Tellier and Colbert's rival, worked like the latter for the King's greatness. He was opinionated, arrogant and without scruples, but he created for France the first true standing army of modern times. Before him, regiments and companies belonged to their colonels and captains, who recruited them, paid them and had a personal interest in maintaining phantom units on paper. Louvois (1670) forced upon them a uniform and severe discipline and armed them better than any other troops in Europe. Soldiers armed with the bayonet, invented by Vauban in 1687, took the place of pikemen. Cavalrymen were given carbines. For the management of supplies, Louvois inaugurated the army *intendants*, and in 1674 the Invalides was founded to serve as a home for old soldiers. But admirable organizer though he was, Louvois was a dangerous counsellor for Louis XIV; in order to make himself indispensable, he urged towards war a sovereign who was all too inclined to seek glory.

At the moment when Louis XIV took over the management of affairs, however, a long peace seemed possible. Towards 1665, France was the strongest Power on the Continent. Her aim should have been to rectify her northeastern frontier bit by bit and without armed conflict. Vauban, a great military engineer and architect, was building covering strongholds for her, the ramparts, curtain walls and demilunes of which protected and adorned the country for two centuries.

Upon the death of Philip IV in 1665, a conflict called the War of Devolution broke out. Louis XIV had laid claim to a part of the new Spanish king's territorial inheritance. Turenne marched into Flanders, this being the only means to make sure of a royal inheritance. Holland, alarmed, called the Swedes and certain German princes to its assistance. Rather than yield, it opened its dykes and put in power William of Orange, the man who symbolized resistance to France. With heroic obstinacy, she fought on from 1672 to 1678 and, by raising coalitions, succeeded in putting France on the defensive. Louis XIV had to make peace; the treaty, signed at Nijmegen in 1678, gave France a portion of Flanders and the Franche-Comté. The frontiers of modern France had been approximately settled. Strasbourg was still lacking; by a judicial decree in 1681 Louis XIV annexed it without a blow. Nothing better shows what was then France's strength than Europe's acceptance of these 'juridical' annexations.

In 1685 Catholic James II succeeded his brother Charles II, and in 1688 a Protestant Whig revolution placed on the English throne the most constant of France's foes, William of Orange and his wife, Mary. Thenceforward England and Holland, acting jointly, would seek to beat down Louis XIV. William III continued England's traditional policy: the defence of Flanders, the mastery of the sea and the shaping of a coalition against the Continent's greatest Power. Against Louis were then leagued England, the Empire, Holland, Spain and Sweden. The purpose of this league, called that of Augsburg, was to push France back into the frontiers which had been defined for her by the Treaties of Westphalia and the Pyrenees. When the French fleet was destroyed at La Hogue, Louis XIV wanted to come to terms. At the Congress of Ryswick he agreed to give up the Low Countries and to recognize the House of Orange in England.

The only matter which remained threatening was that of the Spanish succession. Charles II, Spain's slow-witted king, was soon to die without an heir (1700). Who would get his throne? A son of the Emperor? A French prince? Believing that French support for a weakened Spain was more valuable than any other, because it was geographically closer at hand, the Spanish ministers had obtained from their dying king a will which appointed as his successors the Duke of Anjou or the Duke of Berry, grandsons of Louis XIV. Thus was Louis' hand forced; he could no longer refuse the kingdom of Spain on behalf of his grandsons

LOUIS DE SILVESTRE: LOUIS XIV RECEIVING FREDERICK-AUGUSTUS OF
SAXONY (Musée de Versailles).

On September 27th, 1714, the future Elector Frederick Augustus II, Duke of Saxony,
was presented to the king at Fontainebleau, under the name of Count of Lusace, by Madame,
Duchess of Orleans. He had recently become a Catholic in order to succeed to the Polish
throne, and he had a good three hundred and fifty bastard brothers and sisters, including
Maurice, Count of Saxony, who was to be the famous French Marshal. The Duchess of
Berry, grand-daughter of Madame, is here seen in mourning, her husband having died four
months previously.

EUGENE ISABEY: THE BATTLE OF THE TEXEL The Texel is an island at the entrance to the Zuyderzee, off which, on June 19th, 1694, Jean Bart defeated a more numerous Dutch fleet. (*Musée de la Marine.*)

without himself re-establishing Charles V's empire. He accepted the perilous honour and sent the Duke of Anjou, under the name of Philip V, to Madrid (1701). The War of the Spanish Succession sadly filled the last days of the reign and lasted until 1713. The purpose of the English remained the same: to preserve the balance of power in Europe, to prevent Louis XIV from uniting the forces of Spain and France and to force him to evacuate the Rhine delta and Flanders. Marlborough crushed the French and the Bavarians at Blenheim (1704), then reconquered Flanders at Ramillies (1706). In France there was great discouragement; nevertheless the English demands were such (they asked Louis XIV himself to drive his grandson from the Spanish throne) that the King refused. Marshal de Villars encouraged him not only to resist but to attack: the Battle of Malplaquet in Flanders was far from being as fortunate for the Allies as those which preceded it; the victors lost more than a third of their forces and Villars withdrew in such good order that pursuit was impossible.

An unforeseen event confirmed the English in their desire to come to terms with France. The unexpected death of the Emperor of Austria threatened to join in the person of the Archduke the crowns of Spain and of Austria, were Philip V to abdicate; here again the balance of power would

[89]

be broken and Spain would be in Flanders — all the things England had feared for a century. Turning a somersault — one of the features of its foreign policy — England made a separate peace with France. The Dutch and the troops of the Empire still continued to fight. Louis XIV said to Villars: 'If a mishap takes place, write to me. I shall gather together in Paris whatever men I may find; I shall proceed to Péronne or to Saint-Quentin to perish with you or save the whole State.' The Battle of Denain (1712) cooked the Dutch goose. In 1713 the Treaty of Utrecht put a stop to this long conflict. France retained approximately her present frontiers, but she was debarred from Belgium, and lost Newfoundland and Acadia. England emerged mistress of the waters and at ease on the Continent. The days of British domination were beginning.

The age of Louis XIV was in France an age of masterpieces. During the seventeenth century French literature set Europe a model. Bossuet, La Fontaine and Racine, Saint-Simon and Madame de Sévigné were to inspire subsequent writers, especially in the matter of style. Molière remains our greatest writer of comedy; Corneille, Pascal, La Rochefoucauld, La Bruyère — each of these names calls to mind so much that is splendid. Now what is the essence of this French classicism? The imitation of Greek and Roman writers? Such imitation had been much more narrowly required during the preceding century. The Cartesian method? Yet Descartes thought like his contemporaries; he did not teach them to think like him. Respect for reason? Corneille's heroes are not reasonable any more than those of Retz. The abstract and impersonal approach of this artistic flowering? But we find Pascal and Madame de Sévigné wholly personal. What makes a writer classical, said Valéry, is that he seeks not 'to make the new' but to 'make enduringly'. La Rochefoucauld observes himself, but analyses within himself the everlasting man; Racine transposes dramas of his own time into ancient or biblical tragedies. From Madame de La Fayette to Proust, there was to be an established and continuous tradition of analytical novels in which France excelled.

In art even more than in literature, French classicism ordered nature. All the works of this age possess their simple, intelligible unity. This is true of the landscapes of Poussin or Claude Lorrain, of Puget's or Coysevox's sculpture, of the Louvre's colonnade as much as of the dome of the Invalides. Versailles above all lays before us the unity of the age: there the landscape is made for the castle and the castle for the King. He it was who directed the labours of his architect Mansart, his gardener Le Nôtre, his painter Le Brun, the countless artists who wrought those door handles, those balusters, those candelabra. The French garden had replaced the Italian pleasure ground. Symmetrical, intellectual, regularly bestrewn with statues and fountains, it satisfied the mind while preserving the illusion by virtue of the distant and hazy countryside which stretched beyond the Great Canal.

'Although he has been blamed for meannesses', wrote Voltaire of Louis XIV, 'for harshness in his zeal against Jansenism, too great arrogance with foreigners in the days of his success, for his weakness regarding several women, too much severity in personal matters, for wars lightly undertaken, for ravaging the Palatinate with fire, for persecuting the Protestants, nevertheless his great qualities and achievements, when ultimately weighed in the balance, are preponderant over his faults. Time, which ripens men's judgments, has put its seal upon his reputation; and despite everything which has been written against him, his name will not be uttered without respect and without associating with it the idea of a century eternally memorable.' Unfortunately greatness is not the same as stability; the regime bore within it the germs of the disease which would destroy it. The King wanted himself to be the sole source of power. 'This was to make a revolution not only desirable, but conceivable and possible.'

Suddenly, in 1712, death struck Louis' whole family a series of blows. The kindly Duchess of Burgundy was the first to go; then her husband the Duke; after them followed the little Duke of Brittany, their eldest son; and in 1714 died the Duke of Berry, Louis XIV's third grandson. The only survivor, on the death of Louis XIV in 1715, was a child of five, the Duke of Anjou, later Louis XV.

Philip of Orleans, nephew of the late King, was appointed Regent; he was agreeable, congenial, intelligent, with infinite grace of manners, a natural eloquence and a memory which made him seem well informed on government matters. It was one of his weaknesses to believe that he resembled Henry IV in every particular, and 'cultivated this resemblance no less in the vices of that great prince than in his virtues'. The regency was a reaction against many aspects of the Great Century. Louis XIV had ruled as an absolute king, with a few clerks; the Regent set up seven councils of ten members each, and highly valued the advice of the aristocracy. Louis XIV had protected the Jesuits; the

THE COUNCIL OF THE REGENCY This is a composition-portrait. The Council functioned from 1715 till 1723, during Louis XV's minority. *Conservation du Musée de Versailles.*

Regent protected their enemies. Louis XIV had exalted his illegitimate children; the Regent stripped them of their standing as princes of the blood. At Versailles Louis XIV had boarded ten thousand voracious families; the Regent eliminated most of the expenses of the court. In foreign affairs his adviser was the Abbé Dubois, a weasel-faced diplomat, the master of his own weak master, that Dubois who had 'servile and low' beginnings, but wanted the cardinal's hat and got it. As England's man he succeeded in convincing the Regent of the dangers of the Spanish alliance; might not Philip V of Spain one day revoke his agreement and covet the throne of France? Dubois carried the day, and an English-French-Dutch pact made war with Spain inevitable.

To replenish the exhausted exchequer, the Regent called in a Scots banker, John Law, a great gambler and a great schemer, but in no sense a swindler. A bold and ingenious

banker, he had one idea which is basic to the modern concept of credit: to create apparent resources by printing money. In 1716 Law set up a General Bank to discount commercial paper, and in 1718 it became the Royal Bank with the State as its sole shareholder. His error lay in using as backing for the bank's notes shares in a company of the Indies, which was the heir of Louisiana and of the concessions made to Colbert's *Grandes Compagnies.* A nation's credit cannot be established upon a fluctuating basis. At the outset came success beyond belief, values soared, and Law went up like a balloon. He sought in good faith to recruit settlers for America and to transform his Utopia into real wealth; he cannot be held culpable for all the speculators' follies. But when the crash came, as it had to come, the system was swept away with the fools. He tried to put up a fight; in order to save his own currency, he

NICOLAS DE LARGILLIÈRE (?): THE REGENT POSED AS BACCHUS Philip II, Duke of Orléans, a royal grandson, portrayed c. 1720. (*Musée du Louvre.*) ▶

JEAN-FRANÇOIS DE TROY: THE OYSTER LUNCHEON (Musée Condé, Chantilly.)

This painting, executed in 1737, shows gourmets consuming oysters in a lavish setting;
some of them are following the trajectory of a cork burst from a bottle.

GABRIEL LEMONNIER: D'ALEMBERT GIVING A READING AT MADAME GEOFFRIN'S, 1755 Marie-Thérèse Rodet
was left with a considerable fortune on the death of her husband Geoffrin, and was thus able to maintain one
of the most brilliant salons in Paris. (*Académie des Beaux Arts, Rouen.*)

outlawed the circulation of gold and silver. Still values
tumbled. Now there was 'slaughter' near the bank's doors;
on October 10th, 1720, the bank was put out of business
through the influence of the farmers-general. Law fled, and
died in Venice (1729), 'a sorry beggar, timidly making
excuses'. This failure shook the country. Here was no
matter of one financier's downfall; the State was involved
in this business; the great disentangled themselves, the poor
lost everything. Serious discontent and disaffection followed,
for a single big scandal weakens a regime more than hun-
dreds of little ones, and the weakening of a regime already
weak is perilous. In 1723, the Regent died (as he had lived,
a libertine). The Duke of Bourbon, who succeeded him,
was of even less worth. He was induced to ship the Infanta,
Louis XV's betrothed, back to Spain and to choose for the
young king a princess unburdened with any dowry—Maria
Leszczynska, daughter of the dethroned King of Poland.

Louis XV was a handsome young man, frail and gloomy,
with the pretty face of a girl, unfeeling and cold. In his
fearfulness, his lassitude, his sometimes cruel teasing, he
recalled to mind Louis XIII. None of his tutors had taught
him his duties as a sovereign. Cardinal Fleury had won
his affection, and the moment he had to rule, he turned
everything over to this prelate, who had not 'the slightest
notion of anything when he took the helm of all things'.
The fact is, though, that he governed better than most
ministers. He was well advised and, as early as 1738, the
eternal deficit had been covered. In foreign affairs the paci-
fist Fleury encouraged understanding with England, whose
prime minister, Robert Walpole, shared his horror of war;
neither could spare his country this ordeal, but they struggled
to contain its evils within limits.

The death of the King of Poland, Augustus II, in 1733
made the danger more threatening. As was natural, the

[93]

VAN BLARENBERGHE: THE BATTLE OF FONTENOY On May 11th, 1745, the Marshal Count of Saxony defeated the Anglo-Dutch forces ▶
under the Duke of Cumberland. Louis XV was present (right), as well as the Dauphin Louis who wanted to lead a charge of the
king's household troops. (*Musée de Versailles.*)

Queen of France supported her father as candidate for the Polish throne; the King helped her through pride, having been humiliated at his marriage to a 'demoiselle' no longer the daughter of a king. A small French expedition was shipped off to Danzig, fought heroically and was finally captured by the Russians. Only one road remained open: to attack Austria. Fleury did what he could to make this war short and inoffensive. By the Treaty of Vienna (1738) he agreed to acknowledge Maria Theresa's rights to the throne on condition that Stanislas Leszczynsky, king without a kingdom, would be given Lorraine, which at his death would revert to France. Here was one of the finest compromises in diplomatic history. Austria was satisfied, the father-in-law once again had a kingdom and France acquired a wholly French area.

But brief are the triumphs of wisdom. The Emperor, Charles VI, had died in 1740, and his legacy had awakened the greed of others. Frederick II, King of Prussia, a Machiavellian prince, unburdened by religious or chivalrous principles or by respect for engagements into which he had entered, laid claim to the rich province of Silesia. An irresistible current drew France, violently opposed to Austria, towards the Prussian alliance and war. Fleury, weakened by age (he was eighty-eight in 1742) refrained from interfering. On May 11th, 1745, in Louis XV's presence, Maurice de Saxe won the victory of Fontenoy over Austria's allies the English, Dutch and Hanoverians. Meanwhile Frederick II with total cynicism threw his weight on one side, then on the other, was faithless, retracted, made his own arrangements; and the Peace of Aix-la-Chapelle (1748) pleased no one save Frederick, who kept Silesia.

The King's public and private life added to the general confusion. Louis was not a fool: but generally, being born tired, he let 'the well-oiled wheels turn'. His gallantries became more degraded with the passage of time. Starting in 1732 he took on, in the order of their ages, the three Nesle sisters — Madame de Mailly, Madame de Vintimille and Madame de la Tournelle. After them a woman of the middle class, Madame Lenormand d'Etiolles, née Poisson, became official mistress. The King made her Marquise de Pompadour, and she governed him, France and all Europe for twenty years. A middle-class woman detested by the nobility and a royal mistress branded by the clergy, she needed the support of public opinion and hence of the literary men; the latter hoped that the Marquise would help them fight 'superstition', which annoyed her as much as

it did them. And support them she did. Thanks to the *Encyclopédie*, the *philosophes* enlisted the whole country in the defence of their own ideas. Diderot, who coupled a stormy genius with the solid virtues of a managing editor, was entrusted with the direction of the enterprise. He took as collaborators Montesquieu, Voltaire, d'Alembert, a whole constellation of stars of the first magnitude. We must add Rousseau, who represented a reaction against the rationalism and free ways of the century's early decades, and who did not have the same admiration as Diderot or Voltaire for the 'progress of enlightenment'; he believed not in reason, but in the feelings and emotions, and he made their outpouring into virtues. Politically he wanted a society based on a *Social Contract* by which men of goodwill would pledge themselves to live in accordance with natural morality. From 1750 to 1789 the Encyclopaedists' rationalist revolution and Rousseau's sentimental revolution progressed side by side.

Art in the eighteenth century followed the same line of development as literature. The painters were weary of the grandeur of the Great Century. Watteau was above all a decorative painter, and his enchanted world lies half-way between the theatre and life. Fragonard likewise joined dissoluteness and melancholy, and thus preserved a certain greatness while Boucher rounded out the movement of reaction. To Rousseau's sentimental reawakening there corresponded the sentimental painting of Greuze. Chardin, one of the greatest — and most French — of French painters, marks the appearance in art of the very lowest middle class. Madame de Pompadour and Madame Geoffrin encouraged artists: Nattier, La Tour and Boucher painted the former; Chardin and Hubert Robert the latter.

The difficulties arising out of the peace of 1748 led France to reverse her alliances. What advantage did she win from new Prussian victories? Bernis, the new French foreign minister, understood the Prussian danger, but unhappily the country did not support him. Indeed, Frederick of Prussia's victory at Rosbach was greeted in France almost with joy. After Rosbach, Bernis was greatly discouraged. The King and the court did not react. 'I seem', said Bernis, 'to be the minister of foreign affairs for Limbo'; in vain did he point out the danger. Then, with deliberate purpose he made way for Choiseul, friend of Madame de Pompadour and the *philosophes* and the most brilliant of French ambassadors. Choiseul had one policy — that of the Family Compact with Spain where the Bourbons reigned. This was a

CLAUDE-JOSEPH VERNET: FISHING FOR TUNNY IN THE GULF OF BANDOL
(Musée de la Marine).

In 1752, Vernet was commissioned by the Court to paint the ports of France. Fifteen of the paintings were carried out, of which thirteen are in the Musée de la Marine. This one was painted in 1754. The fishing was done by driving the tunny through a carefully laid out labyrinth of nets into an inner compound where they could be caught and killed. The battles between man and fish were so spectacular that people from the neighbourhood would come out to watch. In the background, the castle destroyed during the Revolution.

CARLE VAN LOO: A BREAK DURING THE HUNT This painting shows the less strenuous side of hunting in 1737.
(*Musée du Louvre.*)

treaty of mutual assistance which, by uniting the two fleets, was to establish some sort of balance of maritime power. Yet on the world's oceans England was too strong even for this combination; the war turned out as badly for France at sea as it did for Austria on land. In 1763 the Peace of Paris had to be signed, and it was one of the saddest in French history. It cost France her empire and created England's.

In this Seven Years War France had lost Canada, all the territory east of the Mississippi, India (apart from five trading factories), and Senegal. Frederick II retained Silesia. It must be granted, to Choiseul's credit, that immediately after the defeat he worked his hardest to rebuild a fleet, and also that it was he who annexed not only Lorraine (a legacy which came to France upon the death of Stanislas

MAURICE-QUENTIN DE LA TOUR:
VOLTAIRE (*Ferney.*)

MAURICE-QUENTIN DE LA TOUR: ROUSSEAU
(*Musée de Saint-Quentin.*) *Arch. Photo.*

Leszczynski) but also Corsica, an island to become one of the most loyal of French provinces.

In 1770 Choiseul received a *lettre de cachet* exiling him to his estate at Chanteloup; his policy of revenge on England and of building up naval armaments worried the King. Before his downfall, Choiseul had had time to arrange for the Dauphin's marriage to one of Maria Theresa's daughters, the Archduchess Marie Antoinette, which strengthened his pro-Austrian policy. The coalition which had overthrown this minister was composed of the Chancellor Maupeou, the Abbé Terray, Controller of the Finances, and Madame du Barry, the King's mistress. Maupeou succeeded in making Louis XV understand that the aggressive power of the magistracy was becoming a national danger. In 1771 he suppressed the *Parlements*, abolished the sale of offices, and established new and simpler courts — which were dubbed Maupeou *Parlements*. Meanwhile the Controller Terray, a pitiless and therefore rather capable minister of finances, reduced the arrears on government obligations, postponed the repayment of borrowed funds which had reached maturity, reformed pension abuses and established the 5 per cent tax (on capital) and real-estate taxes. These were wise measures, but the Maupeou *Parlements* were treated with contempt, and the Abbé Terray's taxes, which were indispensable, gave rise to endless protest. In 1774, Louis, who had become the Little-Loved, died and was regretted by no one. And yet during the last years of his reign Choiseul, Maupeou and Terray had done good work; a sovereign with wisdom could still rescue the regime. Louis XVI was crowned. Would he be a god, or a cypher? He was an honest blockhead.

In an absolute monarchy, the King's personality counts for everything. The worth of the regime and that of the sovereign are one: under Henry IV absolutism had seemed legitimate, under Louis XVI it seemed intolerable. Not that the King was worthless — far from it. He was constantly anxious to do well; he was devout and chaste, and he loved his people, nor was he entirely a fool. He knew some history, geography and English, but government and politics did not attract him. Heavy in mind and body, with a tendency to fatness, he was actively concerned with only two things — hunting and the work of a locksmith. Choiseul had married him off at sixteen to the Archduchess Marie

◀ MONTESQUIEU
(*Académie des sciences, Bordeaux.*)

LOUIS-MICHEL VAN LOO: DIDEROT ▶
IN 1767 (*Musée du Louvre.*)

Antoinette, in order to seal the Austrian alliance. Marie Antoinette possessed grace and dignity; her imperial mother had commanded her to please and, working through her husband, to influence French policy, and so she tried, long without success, to win over this doltish adolescent. Her husband seemed terrified by the realities of love, so she fell back on feminine friendships — the weak and charming Lamballe, later the dangerous Polignac — and on her young brother-in-law, the Count of Artois. After she had become queen, she wished to continue 'to afford herself the sweets of private life' which wounded those not admitted to her intimacy; from this sprang gossip and slander.

Louis XVI belonged to the pious and humanitarian breed of Bourbons; 'I should like to be loved', he said on his accession to the throne. Together with all his generation, he had an instinctive faith in the excellence of human nature; when he chose his first cabinet, he summoned into it several of the fashionable reformers. At its head he had placed Maurepas, an aged, frivolous and sceptical man of state who was a bad choice for such a moment; yet he chose such colleagues for him as Malesherbes, the protector of the Encyclopaedists, and Turgot, the hope of all bold spirits. Had Turgot been kept in power by a strong king, he might perhaps have accomplished the needed reforms and spared France a revolution. But he was to remain minister for only twenty-one months, and he was impeded in his work by three powerful forces: the Queen, because he supervised her expenditures and because she wanted her friend Choiseul, the ally of Austria, to be minister; the bankers and tax collectors, because he threatened their profits; and the masses, because they had been aroused by agents who led them to believe that the free trade in grains was impoverishing them. Thereupon the King, because he was worried and mawkishly sentimental, called back the members of the *Parlement*. It was sheer folly: scarcely had it been recalled when indeed the *Parlement* began to block all reforms. Finally, he was ordered to resign his office; the Turgot experiment had come to naught. It was a serious business, but Versailles and France scarcely suspected it.

There were external as well as internal reasons for this failure; in order to set the finances to rights, Turgot needed peace; but in order to be revenged on the English, Vergennes, the Foreign Minister, needed a war. Ever since 1768 Choiseul had been rubbing his hands over the warning signals of the American Revolution. Vergennes was in 1776 confronted with a *fait accompli* in America; should he support the rebel colonies? The young nobles admired them, just as they praised to the skies Voltaire and Rousseau. Every young man wanted to fight for the insurgents. At first the French troops in America were volunteers. Then, in 1777, Louis XVI recognized the independence of the United States and signed a treaty of alliance the following year. The new Finance Minister, Necker, was faced with supplying funds for a war; he was a Geneva banker and an honest man, who had managed his own affairs competently, which was not sufficient assurance that he would manage well the business of France. But he had a wife whose *salon* gathered together *philosophes* and physiocrats. In order to support Vergennes's American policy, Necker did what Turgot was unwilling to do — he borrowed, and the popularity of the American cause ensured the success of his loans. In five years, from 1776 to 1781, he increased the debt by almost six hundred million *livres*.

Nevertheless, Vergennes, by means of a skilful Continental policy, was imposing a European peace on Austria and Prussia. In 1780-81, Rochambeau's army and Admiral de Grasse's fleet made certain an American victory and the surrender at Yorktown. France seemed to the world the protectress of freedom, and never had she been greater. Above all, Vergennes, Rochambeau and Lafayette had erected the foundations of a Franco-American friendship.

At the moment of victory, Necker had already fallen from office — like Turgot, driven out by the hatred of the court. The financial problem seemed no longer open to solution; anyone seeking to cut down expenses was hated at Versailles; anyone trying to meet expenses through financial reform found the *Parlements* arrayed against him. The Queen and the 'Countess Jules' (de Polignac), after an interval, obtained the appointment of their man Calonne to the Finance Ministry. Between 1781 and 1786 he sought to expand the country's economic activity; it is true that during the same period he continued the policy of borrowing — eight hundred millions more — but what could he do? The privileged classes defended themselves with might and main; a man of finance was helpless against them; it was an author who launched the real attack.

Like Figaro, Beaumarchais was a Jack-of-all-trades; he knew intimately the great lords, their superficiality, their self-indulgence, and he painted their portraits. For a long time the King forbade any performance of the *Mariage de Figaro*, with the result that, when the *Mariage* was finally allowed on the stage, the public found a hidden allusion in every sentence.

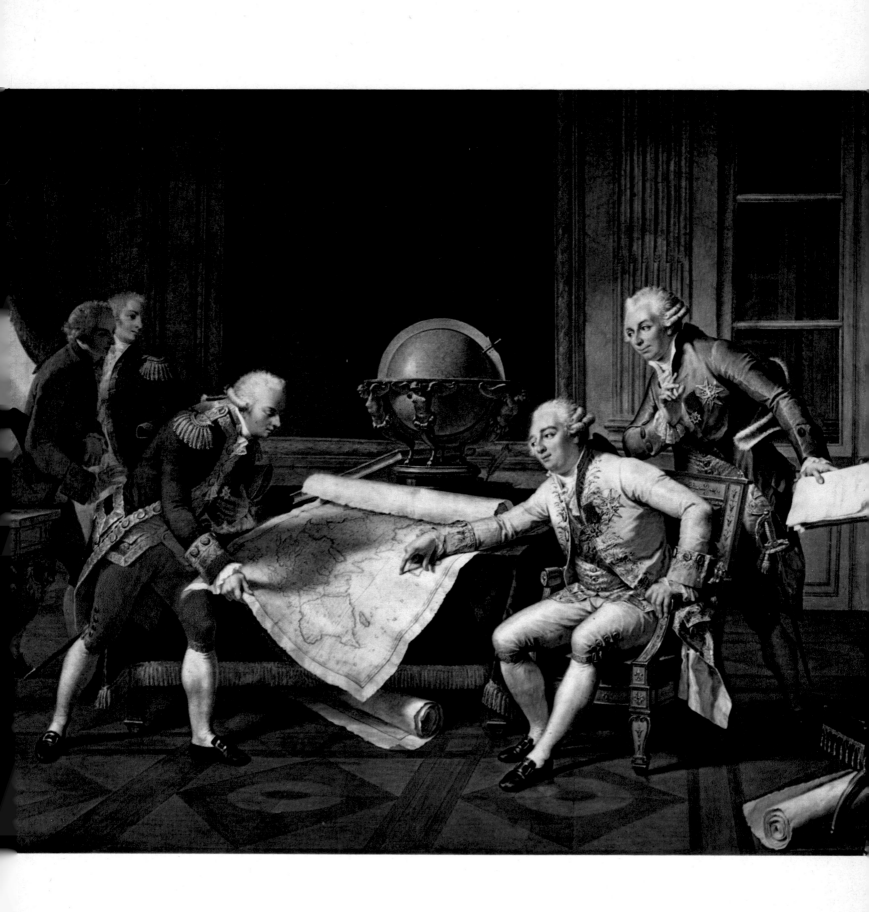

NICOLAS-ANDRÉ MONSIAU: LOUIS XVI GIVING INSTRUCTIONS TO LA PEROUSE (Musée de la France d'Outre-Mer.)

The Count of La Pérouse had distinguished himself during the American War of Independence. Louis XVI sent him at the head of an expedition to the North Pacific, giving him instructions personally, for he was well versed in geography. He left Brest on August 1st, 1785 with two frigates and vanished after a long voyage. Not till 1826 were the relics of the expedition discovered on Vanikoro Island, where the explorers must have been massacred after a shipwreck. This painting shows the scene just before the departure; the Marquis of Castries, Minister for the Navy, is also represented.

VAN BLARENBERGHE: MARIE-THÉ-
RÈSE-LOUISE DE SAVOIE-CARIGNAN,
PRINCESSE DE LAMBALLE She was
a friend of Marie-Antoinette and
superintendent of her household.
She died in the massacre at La
Force, September 3rd, 1792.
(*Musée de Versailles.*)

AUGUSTE COUDER: THE CAPTURE OF YORKTOWN, 1781
Washington is to be seen, together with the Vicomte
de Rochambeau (pointing), commander of a force of
six thousand sent by Louis XVI. On Washington's
left is La Fayette. Lord Cornwallis surrendered on
October 19th. (*Musée de Versailles.*) *Arch. Photo.*

summoned Monsieur Necker, who possessed the art of creating an illusion that he would extract more from the taxes and less from each taxpayer. The magician's return gave rise to the liveliest hopes.

Necker could not do the impossible, but his popularity was a source of strength and he began generously by turning over to the Treasury two million *livres* taken from his personal funds. This gave the notaries confidence and they brought him six million *livres*; then the financiers and creditors took heart. By virtue of expedients, Necker was able to hold on until the opening of the States General.

A revolution, which is a change in the managing class, can be brought on by a breakdown of the managers — excessive injustice, destitution and misery, military defeat. But certain revolutions are set in motion by the abdication of an *élite* which no longer believes in itself or its rights. In 1789 France was still the most powerful State in Europe, with a population of twenty-six millions. She had just won the American war; her military and naval prestige had never stood higher. Throughout Europe was to be found the influence of the French *philosophes* and artists. Thus no one could justly have said that the French monarchy in 1789 had come to grief abroad. At home, the liberals had held power for fifteen years. Malesherbes, Turgot, Calonne, Necker, Loménie de Brienne were certainly not tyrants. Yet France boiled with unrest and her Government had lost its reputation. Why?

First of all because the kingdom's ancient (unwritten) constitution no longer worked. The King could summon the States General; true enough, but since 1614 he had never done so. *Parlement* could require respect for the unwritten laws; quite so, but *Parlement* had become the bulwark of privilege. The nation was not hostile to the monarchy, far from it; but feudal survivals were no longer tolerable to public opinion. Between the bourgeois and the nobility there continued a deep social inequality which was no longer accepted. Everywhere an impulse was afoot against a nobility which continued to enjoy privileges while it was no longer expected to perform its corresponding duties.

The religious framework was shattered, no less than the political. The mass of the people remained loyal to their churches and to their pastors, but these themselves were tainted with the prevalent irreligion. The bishops and court abbés, who performed no spiritual ministry, drew upon vast revenues and lived lives often little edifying. Cardinal de Rohan, Archbishop Loménie de Brienne and others of the sort scandalized the faithful. The lower clergy was shocked at the injustices and subscribed to the *Encyclopédie*. France in 1789 wished great changes not because the coun-

In August 1785, convinced that with the systematic opposition of the *Parlements* other methods must be sought, Calonne decided to convene an assembly of notables. The assembly met in February 1787 and Calonne opened it with a revolutionary speech against abuses. But towards Easter, 1787, the privileged groups, enraged by this assault upon their ancient rights, won the dismissal of Calonne, and Loménie de Brienne, Archbishop of Toulouse, became first minister. Between Brienne and the *Parlements* a battle was joined which resembled the Fronde. In Dauphiné, where an alliance had been formed between the third estate and the nobility, a gathering of the three orders took place at Vizille. The Vizille Declaration proposed the taking of a reasonable step: no taxes or subsidies which had not been approved by the States General. As early as August 1788 Loménie de Brienne announced that the States General would be convened on May 1st, 1789; he was planning an appeal to the third estate against the privileged and the *Parlement*. But public opinion was already tired of Brienne. And the Treasury was literally empty. The King, seeing no means of escape from actual bankruptcy,

LOUISE-ELIZABETH VIGÉE-LEBRUN: MARIE-ANTOINETTE AND HER CHILDREN (Musée de Versailles.)

The birth and death of a royal baby, Sophie-Hélène-Béatrice, 1786, delayed the completion of this painting which was shown at the Salon in 1787. On the left is Marie-Thérèse-Charlotte, who was to become Duchess of Angoulême: on his mother's lap sits Louis-Charles, Duke of Normandy, the future Louis XVII; holding the crib is Louis-Joseph-Xavier-François, Dauphin of Viennois.

LOUIS-LÉOPOLD BOILLY: THE GOHIN FAMILY A family group, done in 1787, of the wealthy ship-owner of Nantes.
He traded with 'the islands', i.e. the Antilles. (*Musée des Arts décoratifs*.)

try was in misery but because it was, on the whole, fairly well off. Relative prosperity gave birth to ingratitude towards those very institutions which had brought that prosperity into being. No one troubled himself over what would be the reaction of the mobs were the barriers suddenly to be let down. Men believed that they saw in the American Revolution the pattern of all revolutions; there lay the example of a free society which with seeming ease had shaped itself by virtue of abstract principles. Lafayette and his friends had erected at the very heart of the managing classes a centre of propaganda for the new ideas; George Washington's moderation hid from them the danger of political

catastrophe. An enlightened minority believed it could keep any revolutionary movement under control. By means of books, pamphlets, intellectual groups, the new ideas had won over the bourgeoisie; already political clubs had opened in Paris.

As for the French, few among them in 1789 wished for a constitutional monarchy of the Anglo-Saxon sort. The King, they thought, should hold his privileged ones in check, and public opinion should hold the King in check. The French of Louis XVI's day had a mind to repair the house, not to tear it down. They had a dread of intolerance and social inequality, but they continued to respect their sove-

[105]

reign. They were able to tumble, therefore, without foreseeing it, into a sanguinary revolution which those who began it had never wanted.

What exactly did they want? They wanted what they had once had — a king meting out justice who could restore order. It was expected that Louis XVI would bring to heel the last of the privileged. The third estate had acquired wealth, culture and power; it hoped for equal rights and careers open to talent; it also demanded the removal of the barriers which prevented a capitalist liberalism from taking the place of a medieval economy. One *élite*, the middle class, was seeking in France to supplant another, the aristocracy, which had overlooked its duties.

The financial disorder which, by leading to the convocation of the States General, started the Revolution, was not the cause of the trouble, but one of the symptoms of the disease. Making up the deficit was out of the question only because it was impossible to tax the wealth of the aristocracy and clergy. This refusal on the part of the privileged, the attitude of the *Parlements* which sustained this rebellion against the State, and the just displeasure of public opinion at the unconcern of the public authorities were what made thorough changes necessary. Over these changes the King of France could preside, as British sovereigns several times have done in the course of history. It was his task to guarantee, without violence, the transfer of power from one class to another. Had Louis XVI chosen this position, the monarchy would have been saved. But the King could likewise make himself the champion of the threatened classes; in that case, he would perish with them.

LOUIS-PIERRE DESEINE: LOUIS XVII This bust was executed in 1790 when Louis was Dauphin. He was recognized King at the Temple by his mother, his sister, his aunt and Cléry on January 21st, 1793, and then by the princes at Hamm in Westphalia, and later by the royal and Catholic armies of the West. (*Musée de Versailles.*)

VII

The Revolution and the Empire

(1789-1815)

THE French Revolution began not in tumult but idyllically: when, on January 1st, 1789, Necker announced that the King was summoning the States General and granting the third estate double representation, the news was greeted with affectionate enthusiasm, and His Majesty's kindness caused 'torrents of tears' to be shed. But ideas were far less clear than feelings were lively. And what meaning could be attached to consulting the voters in a country without political education? For want of candidates and creeds, the electors were being asked to draw up statements of policy by means of memoranda. Pamphlets supplied them with advice; of these the most celebrated was that written by the Abbé Sieyès, a soured clergyman with a cold, moderate outlook, '*What is the third estate?* Everything. *What has it been until now?* Nothing. *What does it seek to be?* Something.'

The court refrained from campaigning, but individuals, particularly the Duke of Orleans, had fewer scruples. In Provence, Count Mirabeau, a speaker of genius and a profound political thinker, was pushed aside by the nobility because he had led a scandalous life and because his violence aroused fears. Spurned by his own estate, which was dismayed at his past and which he annoyed by his talk of 'necessary sacrifices', Mirabeau offered himself to the voters of the third; he was elected by Aix and by Marseilles, and he was to be the greatest orator of the States General. Each parish compiled memoranda which were brought to the assembly of the bailiwick, and this body worked out a collective memorandum. The peasants complained of the poll-tax, the salt tax, the tithe; the bourgeois asked for a constitution, a representative assembly. All wished for the suppression of feudal rights and privileges; the right to vote taxes and to control their expenditure. With these things accomplished, the French monarchy's golden age would begin.

The deputies chosen were of high moral and intellectual quality. About 50 per cent were lawyers, the rest being great nobles, businessmen, priests. Ill assorted by the very nature of the three orders, this assembly seemed homogeneous in culture; throughout France, education had been clerical and Latin; Robespierre and Mirabeau were both of them readers of Seneca and Plutarch; Rousseau had more disciples among the deputies than Montesquieu. Where now was the States General to meet? The King chose Versailles. His advisers should have told him that the nearness of Paris would inflame the assembly and the capital, that court life there would be at once a humiliation and a scandal to the third estate. An uneasiness made itself felt straightway; beginning with the royal opening session (May 5th), the third estate, which was obliged to wear black, found itself penned up in a special enclosure, while prelates' robes and nobles' many-coloured clothing blazed around the King. The speech from the throne disappointed and chilled. Necker was as spiritless as the King. The third invited the members of the two privileged chambers to unite with it in verifying credentials. A dozen democratic priests responded to this invitation; together with these, the deputies of the third estate proclaimed themselves the National Assembly.

This illegal assembly expected to be dissolved from the very beginning; it was not. The deputies, made bold, demanded that France should have a charter. This constituted a seizure of power, and it aroused intense excitement among the nobility and the clergy. Each of these two orders numbered in its ranks liberals and irreconcilable conservatives; among the clergy the liberals won the day: six prelates and one hundred and forty-three priests joined forces with the Assembly, which welcomed them with deep feeling. The opposition prelates and the nobility entreated the King to put a stop to this usurpation; a royal session was announced for June 23rd and, during the intervening time, the hall where the Assembly had been meeting was closed. The deputies rushed to the 'Jeu de Paume', a large indoor tennis court. Standing upon a table the astronomer Bailly presided;

the Assembly swore 'never to separate and to meet in any place where circumstances might require until such time as the Constitution should be established on solid foundations'. On June 23rd the royal session took place; Louis XVI announced that the States General would deliberate by orders and that it could discuss taxes but not privileges. Nobility and clergy marched out behind the King. The third estate remained, in dejected silence; when summoned to withdraw, they boldly refused. 'They want to stay?' said Louis XVI. 'Well, damn it! Let them': an expression, perhaps, of his natural pliancy, but also of his military weakness.

The court had yielded; the nobility capitulated. The King himself 'commanded' the three orders to meet; already optimists were saying that the revolution was over and that it had not cost a drop of blood. Unfortunately on July 11th the court party of resistance won him over; and a little later Necker was dismissed. The people of Paris feared a *coup d'état* and the city bristled with rumours. Bread was scarce; brochures and pamphlets abounded. The Palais Royal gardens had become an open-air club. There a youthful attorney without briefs, Camille Desmoulins, on this July 12th, clambered upon a chair and cried out: 'To arms!' Out of a horse-chestnut leaf he had fashioned himself a green cockade; the dictatorship of the mob was beginning. Crowds stripped the gunsmiths' shops, carried away from the Invalides twenty-eight thousand muskets and five cannon; then, all turned their steps towards the Bastille.

The taking of the Bastille is one of those events about which it is not easy or even fair to write objectively. If we are to understand the part played by this event in French history, we must consider less what the Bastille really was

EDOUARD DETAILLE: THE DEPARTURE OF THE VOLUNTEERS (Musée de l'Armée.)

On July 11th, 1792, the Legislative Assembly declared the country in danger and called for 450,000 volunteers. On the 22nd, a march-past took place to mark the publication of the decree. Here is seen the tribune at the Pont-Neuf where the officials enrolled the recruits. The flags still sport the fleurs de lis as the monarchy was not to be overthrown till later in the summer. A war was now to start which would not end for twenty-three years.

JACQUES BERTEAUX: THE CAPTURE OF THE TUILERIES This painting, exhibited at the Salon in 1793, shows the red-coated Swiss troops defending the side of the palace facing the Carrousel. A contingent of revolutionaries still carries the fleurs de lis, August 10th, 1792.
Conservation du Musée de Versailles.

than what it was symbolically. Its crenellated towers in the very centre of Paris seemed like a dark shadow of feudalism; the *lettres de cachet*, its mysterious imprisonments, added to its sinister repute. The effect of the fall of the Bastille was stupendous: suddenly the people knew its own strength. July 14th, 1789, had been the first of those great revolutionary 'days', brief dramas which would each time change the face of France.

The King, on July 14th, had been hunting all day; on the morning of the fifteenth the Duke of Liancourt awakened him to tell him the news. 'Is this a rebellion?' asked Louis XVI. 'No, Sire, it is a revolution'. The King's promise to withdraw the troops meant that the monarchy was giving up its own defence. At first the Assembly was appalled; it was by majority middle class, opposed to violence. On July 17th, Louis came to Paris and went to the Hôtel de Ville,

where he received the tricolour cockade, and so accepted the Revolution. Anarchy was getting the upper hand with incredible speed; without trial, the mob hanged the minister Foulon 'from the lamp-post'. In the provinces, the fear of hunger and the fear of 'brigands' engendered the 'great dread'. Speaking before the Assembly on the night of August 4th, the Viscount de Noailles asserted that the sole means to bring this agitation to an end was the abolition of feudal rights. The third estate declared itself deeply touched by this generosity on the part of the privileged, each of whom, in the enthusiasm of the occasion wished to forfeit something. All at once there existed in France only equal citizens, endowed with inalienable rights. On August 26th, the Assembly defined these rights in its *Declaration of the Rights of Man and of the Citizen*. The nation had become sovereign, but the Government remained monarchical. When

[109]

J-B MAUZAISSE after E-J HORACE VERNET: THE CANNONADE AT VALMY On September 20th, 1792, the French under Kellerman·

the question arose of a royal veto, the Revolution's second crew began work. Marat, a fanatical, disillusioned and sickly doctor, summoned the poor to battle. This second crew would have its Day — October 5th, 1789.

What would be its purpose? To go to Versailles in order to 'hurl Antoinette out of the throne'. At once several thousand women were recruited to march on Versailles; the

court would never dare order the use of firearms against such a procession. Soon the palace was overrun; the King had to promise to live at Paris and the Assembly had to agree to follow him there. The King came back to the Tuileries castle, where he was the prisoner of the Paris Commune. He came in state to attend the session of February 4th, 1790, in order to announce his acceptance of the princi-

...shed back the Prussians under the Duke of Brunswick-Luneburg near Valmy (Marne). *Conservation du Musée de Versailles.*

ples of the Revolution. Once again on that day you might have thought that the Revolution was over.

The Constituent Assembly had had no political experience; it was unaware of the need for rules; it tolerated disorder in its meetings; it laid itself open to pressure from the galleries; it forbade the King to choose his ministers from among its members. In short the Assembly wanted parlia-

mentarianism without any of the conditions which make parliaments possible. Moreover, the real power lay outside the Assembly: a society called the Jacobins moulded public opinion. It was this group of incorruptibles which asserted what it called the unity of the nation, which was really only the unity of a party. In 1790 the Jacobins still accepted the monarchy, and the Constitution created by the Assembly

was monarchical. The King had been given the power of
veto. Suffrage was not universal; only active citizens voted,
meaning those who paid taxes. The bourgeoisie was relishing
its day in the sun. During this time, bankruptcy stood at
the door. Now the Church owned three milliard *livres* in
property; Talleyrand, a bishop and turncoat grandee, suggested placing this property at the disposal of the State;
and on April 10th, 1790, ecclesiastical properties were duly
declared the property of the nation. Louis XVI would probably have remained loyal to the new Constitution if an
insoluble problem of conscience had not arisen to face him.
The confiscation of their property by the State had made
the clergy dependents of, and therefore employees of, the
State. The State therefore demanded of priests an oath of
loyalty to the nation, that is, to the King and the Constitution. All the bishops save four refused to swear and a
great number of pastors followed their example. This inter-

vention by the Assembly in the spiritual realm had deeply
upset him and produced in him an abrupt change of attitude:
he ceased thinking that in would be possible for him to
accept the Revolution and co-operate with it. On June 21st
he fled with the Queen and the Children of France. At
Varennes, he was recognized, arrested and brought back to
Paris through mobs hurling insults at him; thereafter he was
to be the enemy of the people. The spell was broken.

The Right in the new Assembly, called the Legislative,
was made up of moderate Jacobins, the Feuillants; in the
Centre sat the 'independents'; to the Left were those later
called the Girondists. At the extreme Left were to be found
the Cordeliers, but the real leadership of this group — Robespierre, Marat and Danton — were outside the Assembly.

Danton, powerful and ugly, pitted with smallpox, had
realistically thrown himself into the Revolution, in the success of which he believed. Robespierre, the diminutive
Arras lawyer, seemed as sad as Danton was jovial. His
green, near-sighted eyes, his icy manner, his intellectual
arrogance, repelled the best of his contemporaries. But the
weak were attracted.

The Girondists wished to declare war against feudal Europe; were not the Revolution's worst enemies the Coblenz
émigrés and the Emperor of Austria? In Austria a new and
younger emperor, Francis II, asked nothing better than to
take up the Girondist challenge. On April 20th, 1792, war
was declared; the King of Prussia immediately joined forces
with the Emperor. The campaign began with a rout. The
Jacobins, feeling themselves in danger, took violent steps
which the King refused to sanction. The Jacobins felt that
they needed a 'Day' to frighten Louis XVI. A mob armed
with pikes and sabres overflowed the Tuileries. The King,
astoundingly calm and courageous, refused to reconsider his
veto despite being elbowed and ridiculed by a crowd more
chaffing than ferocious.

Meanwhile the danger of a reaction which might sweep
away the whole fabric of the Revolution temporarily drew
the Girondists and Robespierre together. On July 11th the
Assembly proclaimed '*the Fatherland in danger*'; this formula
was to permit the conscription of men and the gathering
of arms. Outside France, Louis XVI's brothers, Provence
and Artois, behaved as though they wanted to ruin him:
they had had the impudence to threaten Paris, and the people
of Paris decided to rid themselves of the King.

The Commune planned a Day for August 10th which was
to settle Louis XVI's fate. When the Tuileries had been

LOUIS-LÉOPOLD BOILLY: MAXIMILIEN-FRANÇOIS-ISIDORE DE ROBESPIERRE
(1758-1794). (Musée de Lille.) *Studio Gérondal*.

He came from a bourgeois family of Artois and was a lawyer. He was deputy of the
third estate for Arras, and he came to the fore with his speech against the death penalty
delivered before the Constituent Assembly, May 30th, 1791. By virtue of his integrity, his
declarations to the Jacobins, his propriety, he became the idol of the people, who elected
him to the Convention. He voted to send the king to his death without trial, overthrew the
Girondists, and joined the Committee of Public Safety as head of the 'Mountaineers', July
27th, 1793, where he organized the Terror. He reached the presidency of the Convention,
but on July 27th, 1794 (9 Thermidor, Year II) this body arrested him with his accomplices
and had him guillotined, amid general rejoicings, the following day.

J-B VÉRITÉ after P. BOUILLON: LOUIS XVII TAKEN AWAY FROM HIS FAMILY The Committee of Public Safety had Louis-Charles Capet separated from his parents, July 2nd, 1793; the idea was to induce him to make a deposition against his mother. This royalist print was published c. November 1794.
(*Prints. Coll. de Vinck.*) *Photo B.N.*

captured by the rioters the Assembly voted for the 'suspension' of the King until a national convention should have reached its decision. The Commune insisted that he be taken to the Tower of the Temple, where he would be under the people's guard. The party of legality was beaten; the party of violence was prevailing.

Marat next urged the slaughter of the nobles and the priests; for the country must be terrified. On September 2nd the Commune, frightened at the advance of the *émigrés* and Prussians, started the performance. The September massacres were an outbreak of collective sadism; more than twelve hundred prisoners died amid scenes of horror and depravity. The Assembly, feeling the knife at its throat, dared not intervene; the Commune approved; public opinion remained curiously indifferent and cynical. Meanwhile, half Europe was marching against France. Brunswick, having captured Longwy and Verdun, marched on the capital. But he ran into Dumouriez and Kellermann, and above all clashed at Valmy (September 20th, 1792) with the artillery of the old French army, the best in Europe. In this brief burst of cannon fire the fate of France and of Europe had been settled. The invaders began a general retreat; the French Revolution had for the first time revealed its military strength. On the very day of Valmy, the Legislative Assembly disbanded; and on September 21st the Convention met in place of the now defunct Assembly.

As a whole, the Convention was middle class, elected in opposition to the September massacres, but in Paris the Commune had triumphed. In the new legislature, the Girondists sat on the Right; once more the old advanced party had become — without changing its programme — the moderate group. Facing them, on the Left, sat the Mountain, dominated by Danton. Robespierre, icy and correct, awaited his hour; near him sat the hardest and the most intelligent of the fanatics — Saint-Just. At the Mountain's summit stood Marat. Between the Gironde and the Mountain there extended a third group, the *Plaine*, or the Swamp (*Marais*). Yet to the left of the Mountaineers sat the section of the Rabid (*Enragés*). At first it looked as though the Gironde was going to run the Assembly.

The armies of the Republic continued victorious. The occupation of Belgium was easy and the Austrians were ousted. Many of the Mountaineers adopted the thesis of the natural frontiers — the Pyrenees, the Alps and the Rhine. Here was an announcement that Holland would be invaded and therefore assurance of English enmity.

[113]

Was it necessary to try the King? The Gironde did not want to; it feared dividing France. Saint-Just and Robespierre, on the other hand, wanted the King's trial and death. The King, during his questioning, showed much calm and dignity. Death was the vote, by a small majority; on January 21st, 1793, the King's head fell. The regicides, slowly becoming aware of their awful responsibility, understood that thenceforth they must maintain the Revolution or perish. The Vendée, shocked at the fate of its 'martyr king', rose, and civil war was used to justify the establishment in every commune of revolutionary committees. When, in April 1793, a nine-member Committee of Public Safety was created, no Girondist had a seat on it, Danton was its head. Dumouriez's treason was the final blow for the Gironde. Having sought to involve his army against the Commune and having failed, the General went over to the enemy. Belgium was lost; the Vendée was in rebellion; the English fleet was at Toulon; these military reversals made inevitable the Gironde's political defeat. The greater part of the country was showing itself weary of the Revolution; from this the Mountain concluded that they must force it to revolutionary action. A

violent campaign was started against the Girondists. The Commune decided to defy the Gironde and to produce a Day. On June 2nd, eighty thousand men surrounded the Assembly. Robespierre called for the indictment of twenty-two Girondist deputies.

In Paris, after the fall of the Girondists, hard and energetic men took power. Even Danton seemed too spineless and was eliminated on July 10th through a clever stratagem of Robespierre's. The latter wholly dominated a second Committee of Public Safety. Lyons, which had revolted, was retaken; Toulon, where the insurgents had called in the English, was recaptured after a brilliant siege during which a young artillery officer, Captain Napoleon Bonaparte, rendered distinguished service. In the Vendée, the success of the royalist insurgents (*chouans*) dismayed the local republicans and caused them heartily to desire reconciliation with the Convention. This body presented them with an excuse for such a compromise in the new Constitution of 1793, one of history's greatest swindles. Never did freedom seem better safeguarded and never was there less freedom. But this conjurer's trick gave minds time to calm down. Marat's

PHILIBERT-LOUIS DEBUCOURT: PROMENADE AT THE PALAIS-ROYAL Palais-Egalité or Palais-Royal, this ancient residence of the Orleans was the great centre for pleasure-seekers at the end of the Ancien Régime and during the Revolutionary period.

PHILIBERT-LOUIS DEBUCOURT: FRASCATI'S DURING THE DIRECTORY One aspect of a society which, once the dust had settled, returned to its normal distractions. This artist was held in great renown by his contemporaries for his aquatints.

assassination afforded excuse for harsh measures; from then on the Jacobin minority could rule under the banner of patriotism, and the regime of Public Safety was far more absolute than the monarchy had ever been.

The Terror became the order of the day. The guillotine, a new device, speeded up the slaughter through the simplicity of its operation. Even though the September massacres had 'emptied the prisons', there were about two thousand eight hundred heads severed in Paris and fourteen thousand in the provinces. For fourteen months the Revolutionary Tribunal sat without recess; Fouquier-Tinville, the public prosecutor, a frightful man with pale lips and a low forehead, a failure in private life, called for heads, and they fell with bloody monotony. Thus perished Marie Antoinette, Madame Roland, the scientist Bailly, so popular three years earlier; the poet André Chénier. Danton and Camille Desmoulins had both been appalled at the trial and death of the Girondists, their opponents but not their enemies. Desmoulins, in his paper *Le vieux Cordelier*, supported the idea of a 'committee of clemency' which Danton wanted to see

formed. And thus arose the faction of the Forbearing (*Indulgents*), in opposition to that of the Rabid (*Enragés*) led by the horrible Hébert. Robespierre watched both Forbearing and Rabid factions with disgust; Robespierre admired only Robespierre. In perfect good faith he confused his personal enemies with the enemies of France; he knew himself to be so incorruptible that he denied himself no crime. But Robespierre was capable of commanding and organizing: when he took power, he found all Europe lined up against France and two-thirds of France against the Committee; in six months he had re-established order. He set about beating down the factions because they disturbed the monstrous egoism of his system; now should he begin with the decapitation of the *Indulgents* or the *Enragés*? He chose Hébert as his first victim, then it was Danton's turn.

With Hébert and Danton dead, Robespierre was the master of France. With great ceremony, he celebrated the feast of the Supreme Being on the Champ de Mars; during this weird ceremony, you might briefly have wondered whether he were the priest or the idol. The Convention, no longer able to protest, murmured. Ever since Robespierre had insisted upon the right to indict deputies without the Convention's consent, that body had trembled; from cowardice it had allowed France to be beheaded; now it was ready, from cowardice, to behead Robespierre. There was nothing to justify the Terror any longer. The armies of the Republic, especially that of Sambre-et-Meuse, were winning victory upon victory. France then had the greatest army in Europe; the troops knew it, felt it. Robespierre was all-powerful, and he was undone. For he lost all sense of proportion. In the Committee of Public Safety, Carnot and his friends, threatened by Saint-Just, were turning against Robespierre. On 9 Thermidor, Robespierre was greeted by the Convention with yells of 'Down with the tyrant!' and was refused the right to speak. At the President's orders, some policemen arrested Robespierre, Saint-Just, and others. He was guillotined together with his companions, before a vast multitude which applauded.

Tallien and Barras were hailed as the conquerors of the Terror. On 7 Thermidor it would have been difficult to find in all Paris a hundred men with the courage to condemn the excesses; on the eleventh Robespierre had not a friend left. Suddenly the accusers were accused, and the guillotiners guillotined. Fouquier-Tinville and the jurymen of the Revolutionary Tribunal suffered the fate of their own victims, and then the tumbrels ceased carting their daily contingent to death. Hastily Paris changed. The surviving Girondists came back. Gilded youth sported heavy sticks with which the 'dandies' and the 'incredibles' belaboured the Jacobins.

The peasants, enriched by supplying the black market, and the 'Jacobins with feathered nests' were agreed in demanding that the Government should not molest the positions they had won; they would give up nothing, nor would they tolerate reprisals. The royalists, for their part, wanted and expected a return to the Old Regime, the punishment of the terrorists, the restitution of confiscated properties; the young fops sought to stir up the people of Paris against the Convention. In the provinces such campaigns had some success; armed partisans brought about a White reign of terror in the Midi and in Lyons. The prisons filled with republicans. The new King, Louis XVIII (Louis XVII had died in the Temple) proclaimed from Verona that the monarchy would return as absolute, that liberties would be suppressed and the revolutionaries purged. Had it not been for royalist stupidity, a restoration might perhaps have been possible, but this stubbornness gave courage to the Frogs of the old Swamp. They had to keep themselves in command or perish.

The Thermidorians had passed the Constitution of the Year III, which served their interests since it was republican without being democratic. The executive would be a Directory of five members, assisted by two assemblies, the Five Hundred and the Ancients. The system would be one of qualified electors: in order to be a voter, one had to be a property owner. This, of course, favoured the peasants at the expense of the workers. When it was submitted for popular approval, this Constitution was approved, although there were millions of abstentions. In Paris the young swells

LOUIS-PHILIPPE CRÉPIN: THE SEA-FIGHT OF 'LA BAYONNAISE' The French corvette *La Bayonnaise* (20 cannon) overcame the British frigate *Ambuscade* (42 cannon), December 14th, 1798, but at such cost to herself that she had to have herself towed in to Rochefort by the vanquished. (*Musée de la Marine.*)

GENERAL BARON LEJEUNE: THE BATTLE OF LODI Napoleon defeated the Austrians, May 10th, 1796. *Conservation du Musée de Versailles.*

JACQUES TAUREL: THE FRENCH ENTER NAPLES General Championnet made his entry on January 21st, 1799 and founded the Parthenopean Republic. This painting was exhibited at the Salon this same year. *Conservation du Musée de Versailles.*

◀ LÉON MOREAUX: THE FRENCH ENTER TRÈVES Formerly a seat of an Elector-Archbishop of the Holy Roman Empire, Trèves was to remain in French hands from 1794 till 1814. This painting dates from 1853. *Conservation du Musée de Versailles.*

CHARLES THARDIEU: THE FRENCH ARMY STOPS AT SYÈNE The expeditionary force passed through this town in upper Egypt on February 2nd, 1799. *Conservation du Musée de Versailles.*

organized demonstrations against the Convention. This body, seeing itself in danger, entrusted its defence to Barras, who thought that against White Terrorists the best champions would be the former Red Terrorists, who knew that their lives were at stake. Barras determined to entrust the command to Jacobin officers; among others he summoned a diminutive Corsican brigadier-general, Bonaparte, whose part in quelling the Vendémiaire rising resulted in his becoming second-in-command of the Army of the Interior, and one of Barras' close friends; it was at his house that the General met Josephine de Beauharnais, a charming and daring creole from Martinique, whom he would shortly marry.

On 4 Brumaire of Year IV (October 26th, 1795) the Convention declared its sessions at an end. The Directory

took power. The 'Five Sires' elected by the Assembly were five regicides; Viscount Paul de Barras was a dissolute and sadistic rake, filled with contempt for men and convinced of the possibility of ruling them by means of their passions; the four others were reputed austere republicans. At first the 'masquerade at the Luxembourg Palace', with the five Directors in plumed hats, laces and silken breeches and stockings, had provoked laughter; it was soon to cause outcries. Only war still afforded some prestige to the Government. Weak at home, it made vast plans abroad — to strike at Austria in Italy and at England in Ireland. But who would command these expeditions? Jacobin generals were needed, good soldiers and honest men. Hoche was chosen for Ireland, Bonaparte for Italy; 'General Vendémiaire' had a right to

[120]

Vue d'Aboukir, en Egypt, avec the
Buonaparte, Grand etc &c.

GENERAL BARON LEJEUNE: THE BATTLE OF ABOUKIR (Musée de Versailles.)

On July 25th, 1799, General Bonaparte, commander-in-chief of the Army of Egypt, defeated the Turks under Seid Mustapha Pasha. This painting gives an accurate view of the battlefield: the army of the Janissaries is entrenched across the Aboukir peninsula; standing off the peninsula is the fleet which had landed the Turks, commanded by Sir Sidney Smith. General Murat distinguished himself with his cavalry and captured the pasha. The ten thousand French killed fifteen thousand Turks and took three thousand prisoners, as well as a hundred flags and thirty-two cannon.

Barras' gratitude, and the Director thought he could be sure of him since he had just installed one of his former mistresses, Josephine de Beauharnais, in the young Corsican's bed. None yet realized the measure of the slender general with a Roman profile, whose burning love for a somewhat lively creole made the Directors smile. The son of a Corsican patriot, educated at the École de Brienne, a fine officer, this 'skinny mathematician' had for ten years, in shadow and in silence, made himself ready for the highest destiny. He had a taste for detail, liked to read reports and inventories and had a contempt for men, whom he looked upon as objects, not as beings; he subordinated everything to his ambition and his person. The moment he reached the Army of Italy, he dominated those magnificent soldiers of fortune, Augereau, Lannes, Murat, Masséna. He presented the Directory, which had expected him to furnish a diversion, with a whole harvest of victories — Montenotte, Dego, Millesimo, Lodi. By a lightning campaign, Italy was conquered within a month. Though a trifle worried at his triumphs, the Directors, elated at the silver and gold he was tossing them, wrote to him, 'You are the hero of all France'. It was true. For two years, in the horror of slaughters, corruption and famine, France had forgotten the taste of glory; now she was rapturously rediscovering it. Bonaparte, succeeding where the kings of France had failed, was soon, through the victories of Arcole and Rivoli, to conquer the peninsula.

With the first free elections, those of 1797, Catholicism and peace won a majority in the councils. But the remaining Jacobins did not want peace; it would hasten the day when accounts would have to be settled. They caused addresses to be dispatched from the armies protesting against the enemies of the Republic. Bonaparte, who still supported the Directory, let it have Augereau, a masterful general who invaded and subdued the new assembly. This was the *coup d'état* of Fructidor; the war party had triumphed. Before Fructidor Napoleon had opposed the peace party; after Fructidor, he supported it and himself signed, against the orders of the Directory, the Treaty of Campo Formio. He did not care a rap now for the Directors. He said he had only one ambition — to lead an expedition into Egypt, take Malta, Alexandria, perhaps India, away from England. In 1798 he wished to disappear for a time, return laden with new glories, and, if circumstances then favoured him, take power.

The Egyptian expedition succeeded, at least to the extent that Bonaparte was able to land, despite Nelson, free Egypt of the Mamelukes, and proceed as far as the Levant; but

FRANÇOIS BOUCHOT: THE BATTLE OF ZURICH General Masséna beat the Russian commander-in-chief Suvarov, September 1799. Here he is seen giving orders to Oudinot and Reille. *Conservation du Musée de Versailles.*

then Nelson destroyed the French fleet near Aboukir, and the Army of Egypt, blockaded, no longer could obtain supplies. He soon learned that at home everything was not well with the Directory. Internally, elections were going against the Government. And in occupied countries uprisings were beginning to take place against the armies of the Republic. The Austrians and Russians were entering Milan; Jourdan had fallen back across the Rhine. Bonaparte's decision was made; he must return. At the risk of being censured, he left the Army of Egypt to Kléber and outwitted the English patrols; he arrived in France at the moment that the Abbé Sieyès, newly a member of the Directory, 'was seeking a sword' for a *coup d'état*. People were tired of the Directors, of executive weakness, of hateful laws, of unjust banishments. Neither Jacobins nor royalists — such was the feeling of the country. Since Sieyès had already made sure of the co-operation of the Ancients, there remained only the Five Hundred. Sieyès decided to call a meeting at Saint-Cloud, in order to get them away from the people of Paris; Lucien Bonaparte, Napoleon's brother, who was chairman of this body, gave his approval to the move. The manœuvre took place on two days: 18 Brumaire at Paris and 19 Brumaire at Saint-Cloud, and the second day almost turned out badly. Napoleon, in a state of nerves and easily disconcerted by a hostile audience, lost his head. Lucien Bonaparte saved the situation; as president of the Five Hundred he had the legal right to call for the support of the troops against any deputy who might disturb that body's deliberations. He made use of this right. Joachim Murat brought in the grenadiers, who cleared the assembly room. The *coup d'état* had succeeded. By means of a handful of deputies, recruited among the fugitives, Lucien had a motion passed whereby three consuls would succeed the Directory. The two Directors who had conceived the stratagem had taken as their associate the general who had made it possible — it was now Bonaparte, Sieyès and Roger Ducos; but the public heard only one name.

No one disputed the legality of the new regime. The French of that day did not look upon 18 Brumaire as an attempt to destroy their freedom. They had had so little of it for many years. France, after five years of fever, had fallen into a natural prostration; her wounds must be dressed, her finances restored, her spirits calmed.

Meanwhile, Sieyès was drawing up in solemn secrecy another constitution, that of the Year VIII. He created a First Consul, the real head of the executive power, who naturally was Bonaparte; Sieyès and Roger Ducos faded into the background, while the First Consul set out to create the unity of the French. This Constitution of the Year VIII, become dictatorial through the installation of a First Consul, was overwhelmingly approved in the plebiscite. When the new consuls entered office, on December 25th, 1799, they announced: 'Citizens, the Revolution is anchored to the principles which began it. It is completed . . .' It now remained to pacify the Vendée and above all to reorganize finances. In this Bonaparte showed his extraordinary gifts for administrative organization as well as his contempt for the most elementary liberties. In the eyes of the French, he alone was the government. This budding despotism was strengthened by total administrative centralization; prefects, underprefects, mayors — all were chosen by the Government. Paris was placed under the surveillance of a prefect of police. To last, he must please the French, and Bonaparte always believed that they preferred glory to freedom. He still paid respect to the externals of the Revolution; he made people address him as 'Citizen Consul'; he furnished the Tuileries with statues of Scipio, Brutus, Washington. 'I belong to no coterie', Bonaparte would say, 'I belong to the great coterie of all the French. No more factions; I don't want any and I won't allow any'. After so many perils, misfortunes and uncertainties, this policy was the only one which could succeed. France acknowledged Bonaparte as its leader.

But what the country expected above all from the First Consul was peace abroad; he himself wanted it because, as a *coup d'état* general, he feared similar adventures on the part of other generals. A Moreau, a Desaix, a Hoche, were he to be victorious on the field of battle, could become a dangerous rival. In the spring of 1800, Austria resumed hostilities. Bonaparte insisted upon going to the front so that no one else might gather the prestige of victory. At Marengo he fought one of those battles which seal an ambitious man's fate — and almost lost the day. Only Desaix's arrival saved him, and Desaix's death left him the glory. His return to Paris was triumphal, for he had bestowed peace on a country which had suffered severely from war.

Victory is nothing if it does not bring peace, and this Bonaparte obtained in two stages. In 1801 he signed the Peace of Lunéville with Austria, an excellent treaty for France since it obtained for her the left bank of the Rhine and a protective zone fashioned out of friendly republics. Then he signed the Peace of Amiens with England (1802).

He now felt himself powerful enough to impose religious peace on France, and on April 8th the Concordat was voted. But army murmurings over the Concordat gave him pause; he was not yet strong enough to talk about making his power hereditary. And the former members of the Convention were on the watch; Bonaparte decided not to ask for hereditary transmission, but a life consulate; in 1801 a crushing majority granted it to him. Peace entranced the country; prosperity was returning. For France is naturally rich; she requires only wise policies, unity and self-confidence to restore a good financial situation. This was the period of the Bank of France, the Great Book of the Public Debt, the establishment of chambers of commerce. He presided in person over meetings at the Council of State where jurists worked out a new civil code. Everything he constructed bore the imprint of his clear, geometrical mind. He organized education as though it were the training of an army. And he created the Order of the Legion of Honour. At the Tuileries, a court was being born; dress swords and silk stockings were replacing boots and sabres; Josephine had her ladies-in-waiting, with highly authentic pedigrees.

At first England had seemed to accept the Treaty of Amiens. Addington, the Prime Minister, called himself a lover of peace; British trade wanted peace; and the British aristocrats were happy to return to Paris, astounded at finding along the Champs-Élysées Greek goddesses, naked under their gauze dresses, instead of bloody heads. But the two countries promptly began to accuse each other of bad faith; and Napoleon prepared for the invasion of England. Not only did he gather a great army at Boulogne, but he

FRANÇOIS BOUCHOT: GENERAL BONAPARTE AT THE COUNCIL OF THE FIVE HUNDRED A dramatic moment during the coup d'Etat of 18 ▶ Brumaire (November 10th, 1799); the Five Hundred shout 'Outlaw', but a battalion is at hand to clear the chamber. *Musée de Versailles.*

AUGUSTE COUDER: THE COUNCIL OF STATE INSTALLED AT THE PETIT LUXEMBOURG PALACE The councillors take the oath before the three consuls of the Republic: Bonaparte, Cambacérès and Lebrun, December 25th, 1799. *Conservation du Musée de Versailles.*

undertook to build first a fleet and then a barge flotilla. But everywhere the English fleet firmly held the seas. 'I do not say', rumbled the First Lord of the Admiralty, 'that the French cannot come. I merely say that they cannot come by water.'

Because of his excessive historical imagination, Bonaparte wanted to be emperor, and once again he encountered the opposition of the former Jacobins and the republican people of France. The kidnapping and execution of the young Duke d'Enghien, who was innocent of participation in any plot, was Bonaparte's only political crime, but it was a premeditated crime. By it he expected to achieve two results: to frighten the royalists and to supply the regicides, those who had 'voted', with the certainty that Bonaparte, now become one of their number, would not make the empire into a counter-revolution. Having received this bloody pledge, the Senate, which was filled with ex-members of the Convention, no longer hesitated and offered the imperial throne. On December 2nd, 1804, Napoleon I became Em-

peror of the French; he was consecrated in Notre Dame by Pope Pius VII.

Napoleon had received from the Pope the crown of Charlemagne. He created dukes and princes, and made kings of his brothers. Yet he was too intelligent not to view this performance with a certain irony: 'Ah, Joseph!' said he on the day of the Consecration, 'if our father were to see us!' Basically, Napoleon believed only in force. His only weakness was too vivid an imagination. In immediate action, on the battlefield, he was admirable; the moment he began making great schemes for the future, he let himself be carried away. By 1805, matters had him in their train. England had sworn his downfall. By 1804 the Third Coalition had been formed — England, Austria, Russia, Sweden and Naples. To Napoleon's mind the situation was clear: he had to conquer England or be crushed by her. London must be taken and the knot of the coalitions severed there.

However, for lack of a strong navy, his plan came to grief. Villeneuve, commander of the Franco-Spanish fleet,

INGRES: NAPOLEON I (Musée de l'Armée.)

This painting, carried out in 1806, was badly received by the critics, who found it cold as marble. The Emperor and King sits enthroned, exactly as the kings of France are depicted on their seals ever since the XIth century. He bears the symbols of sovereignty which were given to him at Notre-Dame on his coronation, December 2nd, 1804.

had taken refuge in the port of Cadiz. The season was growing late. Austria now seemed ready, and were there too long a delay, Russia might join forces with her. Abruptly Napoleon made up his mind and dictated orders for a Continental campaign. Never was Napoleon more admired and worshipped by his soldiers than during this brief and dazzling campaign. Napoleon made pawns move on the chessboard and forced an Austrian army of one hundred thousand men to surrender without a fight at Ulm. But the day after Ulm, he received terrible news. Villeneuve, who had not fought when it was needful, had left Cadiz when there was no need, and the French and Spanish fleets had been annihilated by Nelson at Trafalgar (October 21st, 1805). Napoleon saw that he could no longer defeat England except by closing the Continent to her. For this purpose it did not suffice to have entered Vienna; there remained a Russian danger. But the Russians made the mistake of attacking at Austerlitz before the Austrians were ready, and on a terrain the Emperor knew well. It was December 2nd, the anniversary of his coronation.

After this victory, what were his demands? From Russia, to the great scandal of his generals, he asked nothing, for more than anything else he was covetous of the Czar's friendship. To Prussia, which, by attacking his communications, might have sealed his downfall, he offered Hanover, the property of the crown of England. From Austria he extracted both the German Empire and Italy. This was the end of the Holy Roman Empire. He made Germany into *the Germanies*, and he set up the Confederation of the Rhine, of which he was to be the president. In Italy he drove the Bourbons from Naples, and on this throne installed his eldest brother, Joseph. Louis Bonaparte became King of Holland.

CHARLES MEYNIER: THE FRENCH ENTER BERLIN Thirteen days after Jena and Auerstädt, Napoleon made his entry by the Brandenburg Gate, October 1806. (*Musée de Versailles.*)

LOUIS-LÉOPOLD BOILLY: THE ARRIVAL OF THE STAGE-COACH Painted in 18

f the best known works of this artist. (*Musée du Louvre.*) *Photo Giraudon.*

PIERRE-PAUL PRUD'HON: THE EMPRESS JOSEPHINE AT MALMAISON Marie Tascher de la Pagerie was born in Martinique six years before Napoleon, married General de Beauharnais, and was the mistress of Barras and of many others before becoming the wife of Napoleon. He divorced her in order to marry the daughter of the Austrian Emperor.

ANTOINE-JEAN BARON GROS: THE BATTLE OF WAGRAM (Château de Grosbois.)

After the bloody battles of Aspern and Essling (May 1809), the army had to wait two months on the island of Lobau before recrossing the Danube. Napoleon, whose prestige was already threatened in Spain, made the most careful preparations with Berthier before giving battle. The French crossed the river on the night of July 4th-5th, and on the 6th they beat the Archduke Charles who had to withdraw his army towards Moravia. Berthier won the title of Prince of Wagram; the Emperor Francis sued for peace. The wounded officer in the foreground is Marshal Bessières, Duke of Istria.

LOUIS-LÉOPOLD BOILLY: A GATHERING OF ARTISTS IN ISABEY'S STUDIO Jean-Baptiste Isabey was well seen as a court painter under the First Empire. (*Musée du Louvre.*) *Arch. photographiques.*

Jerome married the Princess Catherine of Württemberg. Elisa, the eldest of the three Bonaparte sisters, was Princess of Lucca, later Grand Duchess of Tuscany. Eugène, the Empress's son, was son-in-law to the King of Bavaria. With all his family clan on the thrones of Europe, he still needed more reliable anchors!

The Prussian patriots now sent the Emperor an ultimatum, at which he rejoiced; since he must prove his strength, he welcomed so auspicious an opportunity. The campaign was as brilliant as that of Austerlitz; at Jena and Auerstädt, Prussia was crushed, and the Emperor entered Potsdam. In Berlin, during June 1806, he issued the decrees which forbade the importation of British goods and which even excluded from European ports all neutral vessels that had touched at a British port. He wanted much more, however; he wanted the Russian alliance and a European federation against England. It was to bring about this great scheme that he delayed in eastern Prussia and Poland. In this latter country, he did not conquer, he 'liberated' — or at least the Poles hoped so. At last he was able to join battle. This was at Eylau (June 1807), a murderous engagement for that day and one which, despite the victory, saddened

the Emperor. Finally, in June 1807, after the victory of Friedland, Napoleon had his peace and his alliance. At Tilsit, he met Alexander I, the youthful and enthusiastic Emperor of Russia, who seemed won over and almost under the spell of this wonderful mind. Alexander pledged himself to close his ports to the English.

And so England found herself once more in splendid isolation. To paralyse her, what ports remained open on the Continent must be closed to her, especially in Spain and in Portugal. The Spanish question was a most delicate one. King Charles IV called himself Napoleon's ally, but his Prime Minister, Godoy, was betraying his king and negotiating with the English. Would it not be more prudent to place a Bonaparte on the Spanish throne? Suddenly in 1808, while the Emperor remained undecided, the Spanish people took the matter in hand; an uprising broke out in the town of Aranjuez; the terrified king abdicated in favour of his son. Napoleon enticed the father and the son to Bayonne, under colour of negotiating the issue, and then held them prisoner. There remained the Spanish people. How would they react to this little melodrama? The Emperor, with ill-founded optimism, was sure the Spaniards would welcome it. Hastily a royal 'transfer' was decreed among the Bonapartes; Joseph was promoted to be King of Spain while Murat became King of Naples. For a moment Napoleon could have thought that the conquest of Europe was completed; on her thrones he saw only relatives, friends or slaves.

The first crack appeared in Spain. Marshal Bessières and General Dupont de l'Estang were instructed to bring a guerrilla uprising there to a rapid conclusion. When he learned that these partisans had, at Bailén, won the surrender of General Count Dupont and seventeen thousand soldiers, he fell into one of his towering rages. The consequences were serious. Joseph had to fall back, and the English found the opening they had so long looked for. English armies landed in Spain and in Portugal, and Sir Arthur Wellesley forced Junot to capitulate at Cintra; a new Continental front had been opened, and the presence of the Emperor himself in Spain had become necessary.

But other events, fully as serious, kept him elsewhere. At Rome he had come into conflict with the Pope, who, as a temporal sovereign, was not applying the Continental blockade. Austria was watching with passionate interest the Spanish revolt and the English intervention, and had put forty thousand men under arms. At all costs Vienna must be prevented from going to war, and the only way to do this was to persuade the Czar to threaten Austria. Consequently at the Erfurt meeting (September 1808) Napoleon brought all his weapons into play: he flattered, wheedled, enticed, became annoyed, stamped on his hat, and calmed down when he saw that the Czar remained impassive: the atmosphere was no longer that of Tilsit. At this moment Austria, well stocked with British gold, attacked. Again victory must be quickly won, because Prussia, and perhaps Russia, would fly to the aid of a successful Austria. Once again he set out for Vienna; Wagram (July 1809) was a handsome victory, but Wagram did not give France the same joy as Austerlitz. Bad news came: Portugal was lost, Spain tottering. In Rome the Pope had been arrested and deported, and in all Europe the Catholics muttered. Napoleon would jettison one plan for the sake of something better; in place of crushing Austria, he was going to try to draw her into his team. Finally he obtained the daughter of the Caesars, Marie Louise, a plump, fresh princess of eighteen. Josephine was cast aside. His delusion was to believe that the father-in-law would consider himself bound to the son-in-law. Within a year the Archduchess had given him an heir to his thrones who, in remembrance of the Holy German Empire, received at birth the title of King of Rome.

But the Austrian marriage did not put the Emperor's affairs to rights; nothing could do so as long as England remained hostile and undefeated. During the summer of 1811, Russia allowed one hundred and fifty British vessels under the American flag to enter her ports. Napoleon could not tolerate this defiance of his system; he let Alexander

ANTOINE-JEAN BARON GROS: THE SURRENDER OF MADRID At six in the morning of December 4th, 1808, two Spanish generals brought the surrender to the Emperor. King Joseph-Napoleon could now regain possession of his capital. (*Musée de Versailles.*)

GENERAL BARON LEJEUNE: AN ASSAULT ON THE MONASTERY OF SANTA ENGRACIA AT SARAGOSSA After a sixty-two day siege, Marshal Lannes took the town (February 1809). *Conservation du Musée de Versailles.*

1813 Prussia declared war against him. After their victory at Leipzig, the Allies would have been satisfied to leave Napoleon France's natural frontiers, the Rhine, the Alps and the Pyrenees. But he refused. Napoleon knew he was lost and wanted to end handsomely. Never had the Emperor shown himself a greater general than in this campaign of France, but no longer would people help or serve him. The country seemed war-weary; the soldiers were children; and the marshals had ceased carrying out orders. At the end, he was personally directing the artillery fire. But 'victory', as he himself had said, 'belongs to the big battalions'. At Fontainebleau he was visited by a delegation of marshals, headed by Ney, which had come to ask for his abdication. On April 6th, 1814, he resigned himself to unconditional abdication. The Allies decided to make him master of the Island of Elba. Meanwhile the Senate, the Emperor's appointees, solemnly voted for the return of the king and outlined a proposed constitution. An armistice was signed, relegating France to her 1790 frontiers; the new map of Europe was to be drawn by a congress which would gather in Vienna.

Because the Bourbons brought with them peace, they profited from a prejudice in their favour; but, to win acceptance, they had still to set at rest the minds of the peasants, the army, the bureaucrats, the purchasers of the nation's holdings — all those whose livelihoods depended on the triumphs of the Revolution. Louis XVIII was ready to bind the monarchy by an inviolable charter, but he wanted to concede the charter, not to submit himself to it. From the very moment of his first governmental act, everyone was dissatisfied.

The opposition was unaware of the work, painful but useful — indeed admirable — done by the King and Talleyrand in foreign affairs. In order to preserve what was essential, Talleyrand was dexterous enough to trap the sovereigns in their own principles; if they maintained the legitimacy of their own thrones, he told them, they must also recognize that of the kingdom of France. When, in October 1814, the Congress gathered at Vienna, you might for a moment have thought you once again beheld the old Europe, freed of its fears, going on with the dance. The Vienna diplomats were still dancing when, on March 7th, 1815, after a great fancy-dress party, they suddenly learned by courier that Napoleon had landed in France and was marching on Paris.

From France messengers had arrived who told Napoleon that the republicans and Bonapartists were plotting against Louis XVIII, and that, if he did not hasten, someone else might well overthrow the monarchy.

On March 1st, 1815, he was at the Gulf of Juan. With him he had only about a thousand men and could not rely on force; his weapons were the memory of fifteen victor-

know that if the Berlin decrees were not obeyed, war would follow. Alexander no longer feared him; he had observed the campaigns of Wellesley (now become Lord Wellington) in Portugal and Spain: the refusal to join battle, the wearing out of the French forces. The Russian campaign began in May 1812 and it was exactly as Alexander had wanted; Napoleon harvested only victories, and all these victories were useless. He took Moscow; in no time the city was in flames. It was he, the victor, who made offers of peace. Alexander gave no reply. For a long time Napoleon waited — for too long a time, since he took to the road in the bad season, with an army inadequately equipped against the cold. This Russian retreat was a tragedy. There remained of this *Grande Armée* only sick men in rags. On December 5th the Emperor left his troops hastily to start off by sleigh for Paris, where the bad news might provoke a revolution.

His position was worse than difficult, it was desperate, for he could no longer win his game, and if he began to make some concessions, all would be demanded of him. In

JOSEPH FRANQUE: MARIE-LOUISE AND THE KING OF ROME (Musée de Versailles.)

This painting was exhibited at the Salon in 1812, the year of the artist's death. The Empress holds a medallion depicting Napoleon and has pulled up the veil of the crib in order to reveal H. M. Napoléon-François-Charles-Joseph, prince imperial, King of Rome, who was born on March 20th, 1811.

DENIS RAFFET: THE BATTLE OF WATERLOO The military epilogue of twenty-three years of war took place
in Belgium on June 18th, 1815. This lithograph of 1831 shows the final square.

ious years. Grenoble opened its gates, and then Lyons; whole regiments had attached themselves to the Emperor and constituted a small army; he had now enough men to take Paris. There remained Marshal Ney, who had sworn to meet Napoleon and bring him back in an iron cage, but Ney, won over, joined forces with him. On March 20th, the Emperor slept at the Tuileries; Louis XVIII and his ministers had fled. Far more than a military achievement, the restoration of the Empire had been a people's movement. Napoleon bowed to the fashion of the day and foreswore autocracy, but he satisfied no one with his new Constitution.

Between March and June the Emperor had gathered together five hundred thousand men; the Allies had a million. A defensive strategy was doomed to defeat — Napoleon took the offensive. Never were his plans more brilliantly laid than at Waterloo (June 18th, 1815), but his lieutenants gave him clumsy service, and he himself, on the day of the battle, seemed without strength of spirit or moral energy. By the stubbornness of his defence, Wellington broke the heroic assaults of the Old Guard; on the evening of Waterloo, the last French army ebbed back on Paris, beaten. Now all France insisted upon abdication and Napoleon gave himself up to the English. 'Royal Highness', he wrote to the Prince

Regent, 'I come, like Themistocles, to sit at the hearth of the British people. I put myself under the protection of its laws, a protection I beseech of Your Royal Highness, as being that of the most powerful, the most constant, and the most generous of my enemies.'

Such, then, was his exit. Fontainebleau, the Sancho Panza kingdom on Elba would have added up to an inglorious finale; the appeal to England's generosity, the internment at Saint Helena, death on that distant bit of rock would make the Emperor into a martyr. In June 1815 many Frenchmen hated Napoleon because they blamed him for the country's losses and defeats; very soon, thanks to distance, to dislike of the Bourbons, to resentment against the English, to great memories and to the greatness of things recounted about his captivity, hate would give place to pity and then to regret. The army would never cease to recall the small hat and the grey frock-coat behind which it had 'crossed the Alps and the Rhine', conquered all the kings of Europe and carried the tricolour as far as Moscow. The people were to link Bonaparte's memory to that of the Revolution. Thus the Bonapartists and the Jacobins, forced together, formed the kernel of a great opposition party, and finally, in 1830, the Emperor's shadow ended by sweeping out the Bourbons.

LOUIS-LÉOPOLD BOILLY: INSPEC-
TING A PRINT Painted in 1820.
(*Musée du Louvre.*)

VIII
Years of Wavering
(1815-1851)

THE Emperor's defeat made necessary a second Restoration; in Paris a provisional Government, organized by the eternal Fouché — a man so constant in his inconstancy — called in Louis XVIII. The senators and generals of the Empire and the revolutionaries in their well-feathered nests were all ready once again to cry, 'Long live the King!' provided that the monarchy would refrain from disturbing them in the enjoyment of what they had acquired. At first Louis XVIII accepted everything except the tricolour cockade. Talleyrand, upon whom England and Austria insisted, and who, after all, had served his country well at the Congress of Vienna, was entrusted with choosing the cabinet. That the King should accept the backing of 'Vice and Crime', of Talleyrand and Fouché, made Chateaubriand indignant, but Louis had tasted exile and, no matter what the price, did not want to go 'off on a fresh journey'. Apart from his age and his infirmities, he was not a bad sovereign. He believed in his rights, but he wanted a quiet reign, loved peace, classical tags, and risqué stories, and understood that he could retain his throne only by accepting the ideas of his subjects. Absolute monarchy seemed to him desirable, but out of the question; from this arose his firm intention of abiding by the Charter. With Louis XVIII by himself, France would probably have come to a reasonable understanding. But with him had returned the *émigrés*, the formerly privileged, who had 'learned nothing and forgotten nothing'. After twenty-five years of exile and of hardship, they were athirst for vengeance; at their head, the King's own brother, the Count of Artois, prided himself on being, with Lafayette, the only Frenchman who had not changed in a quarter-century. Everywhere, but especially in the south, the 'White Terror' reigned. The Ghent runaways were calling for the chastisement of the generals of the *Grande Armée*: 'We are going marshal hunting', gleefully remarked the Duke of Berry. Sighed Louis XVIII, 'They are relentless!' *They* consisted of his brother and his nephews,

of women become savage because they had been afraid, of the *émigrés*.

Talleyrand and Fouché, having complacently lent a hand in the proscription of their friends, were themselves soon banished. Talleyrand had first made it his business to exile Fouché, who departed for Dresden in disguise. But he was soon replaced as Prime Minister by the Duke of Richelieu, heart and soul an *émigré*, who had left the country in 1789 and returned in 1814; he had remained a patriot while abroad, had proved a good administrator, honest and tolerant, and was an intimate friend of the Czar, who had made this Frenchman, during his days of exile, governor of the Crimea. The Duke of Richelieu was at that moment the best possible choice, and therefore he did not last.

The 1815 voters — there were very few of them, less than a hundred thousand qualified to vote in the whole country — were aristocrats and wealthy bourgeois seeking above all to thrust aside the men of the Revolution and Empire. They sent to Paris a legislature made up of *émigrés* and squireens as vindictive as they were ignorant. Louis XVIII dubbed this assembly, which was too counter-revolutionary for his taste, the 'Nonesuch Chamber'. It included rabid royalists who wanted a total reaction. The Revolutionary Tribunal was coming back, but under other names; the sons of the victims had become the hangmen. To France's horror and the joy of a few women of the world, Marshal Ney was put to death. The King should have pardoned Ney and built 'out of royalty a duke to stay this tide of blood'. He probably wanted to, for all his utterances about the rabid were caustic. But Louis XVIII, who would have loved to carry on the tradition of Henry IV, was too old and too weary to hold in check the *tricoteuses de salon*.

Luckily he got support and advice from a handful of moderate royalists who, thanks to the strictness of their precepts and the dogmatic tone of their judgments, were christened the 'Doctrinaires'. Among the wise men who thought

LOUIS-LÉOPOLD BOILLY: THE GAME OF DRAUGHTS The café Lemblin during the Restoration era.
(Musée Condé, Chantilly.) Arch. photographiques.

that Restoration should not become Reaction were Pasquier, Sainte-Aulaire, Royer-Collard and their friend Decazes, who was prefect of police, a dogmatic and intelligent lawyer, and a great favourite of Louis XVIII; he was to be Richelieu's successor. To the Left of the Doctrinaires were the 'Independents', such as the Duke of Broglie and Lafayette, liberals loyal to eighteenth-century principles, to whom, for want of being able to express themselves more openly, adhered former Bonapartists, former Jacobins and peasants frightened by the return of the nobles and the spectre of feudal privileges. The Charbonnerie (literally, 'charcoal yard'), a secret society, hatched underground plots against the regime; it was international and aimed 'at all tyrants'.

This Restoration France was hard to govern: the officers on half-pay and the patriots regretted the Emperor; the people and, above all, the bourgeoisie wanted to preserve the social equality established by the Revolution; the country as a whole remained attached to the tricolour and dreamed with

mingled weariness and pride of twenty-five years of glory. Nevertheless, the French were ready to put up with the monarchy because they had suffered far too much, and a wise government would have taken pains not to arouse them. But if Louis XVIII and Decazes were capable of prudence and even of courage; if in September 1816 the King and his minister dared dissolve the 'Nonesuch Chamber', the royalists of the majority indeed proved themselves 'more royalist than the King'. They could not bear seeing skilful administrators, trained by the Revolution and the Empire, retained for technical reasons in jobs that they themselves coveted.

Unfortunately for France, the policy of reconciliation which the King so ardently desired became impossible when, in 1820, Louvel assassinated the Duke of Berry, nephew of the King and the great hope of the ultras, who at once hurled accusations at Decazes. Faced with his family's rage and tears, Louis XVIII could not retain Decazes in power. The Duke of Richelieu came back, this time with the ultras'

LOUIS DUCIS: LOUIS XVIII ON THE BAONYLC AT THE TUILERIES (Musée de Versailles.)

On December 2nd, 1823, the king attended the triumphal return of the army from Spain. The Tuileries gardens and the Champs-Elysées can be seen through the window. Louis-Antoine of Artois, Duke of Angoulême and commander-in-chief of the army, bows before the king. His father Charles-Philippe, Count of Artois, stands on the king's left. The little girl on the right, Louise of Artois, future Duchess of Parma, watches her brother, Henry of Artois, Duke of Bordeaux, waving his hat; he is in the arms of his mother, Caroline-Ferdinande-Louise, Princess of the Two Sicilies, Duchess of Berry.

support, which condemned him to follow their policy; a new electoral law created an aristocracy of money which was entitled to a double vote. Paris bestirred itself in protest; the cry of 'Long live the Charter' became sedition. An absolutist and clerical propaganda was launched by the leaders of the 'priest party', Jules de Polignac and Mathieu de Montmorency. When, seven months after her husband's death, the Duchess of Berry brought into the world the Duke of Bordeaux, who was called 'the Miraculous Child', the royalists' excitement became so outrageous that in honesty Richelieu had to resign.

This time power had to be given to the ultras willy-nilly. At least Louis XVIII chose one who seemed the least dangerous among them — Villèle, a man retiring to the point of dullness and an able administrator. This ministry remained in office because it had some success in foreign affairs; France, humiliated by the 1815 defeats, was joyful at having a new part to play in the congresses of the Holy Alliance. For the sovereigns, the European problem was this: how to combat the disease of liberalism. And, in particular: how to intervene in Spain to save Ferdinand VII from the Cortes in rebellion? Chateaubriand, who had been given the portfolio of foreign affairs, succeeded in having this task entrusted to the French army. The French love glory, and the Duke of Angoulême's victories strengthened the regime; thereafter the army accepted the white banner without aversion. The electors of 1823 were able to send to Paris a chamber much the same as its predecessor.

In 1824 Louis XVIII died and the Count of Artois became Charles X. The change cut deep: Louis XVIII was a moderate of the Old Regime and an eighteenth-century freethinker; Charles X was an *émigré* to the fingertips and a submissive bigot. From then on the ultras had the King of their hearts' choice, and, spurred on by his new master, Villèle went so far backwards into the past that he annoyed the most ardent royalists. When Villèle, having muzzled the press, wanted to make it impossible to publish hostile pamphlets by virtue of a law ironically called that 'of justice and of love', royalists, liberals, Bonapartists and republicans united in protest. A milliard-franc indemnity, granted to *émigrés* whose properties had been confiscated, angered the majority of the nation. In Paris the ministers were booed, and in the provinces they were beaten at the polls; in 1828 Villèle had to resign. 'You are forsaking Monsieur de Villèle,' the Dauphin told the King, 'that amounts to your taking the first step down from your throne.'

With Martignac, Charles X made a last stab at liberalism. It could not succeed because the cabinet lacked the King's

LOUIS-LÉOPOLD BOILLY: THE BALLAD-MONGER A street scene well captured by a contemporary painter. (*Musée de Nice.*) *Arch. photographiques.*

confidence; he was still the 1789 Count of Artois and had no faith in the Charter which he had sworn to respect. Thenceforth the regime was doomed to failure. The 1789 opposition, unanimous and bold, was reborn. A young journalist, Adolphe Thiers, remarked: 'We must lock the Bourbons up in the Charter; so hemmed in, they will explode'. This learned ambitious little man from the south had, with the support of Talleyrand and the banker Laffitte, established an opposition paper, the *National*, which the liberal public eagerly gobbled up. When Charles X dismissed Martignac and summoned Jules de Polignac to take over the government, the nation felt that a *coup d'état* was being prepared against what freedom still remained. Polignac was the son of Marie Antoinette's friend, a decent enough fellow, but an unintelligent visionary, an absolutist, who in 1815 had refused to swear allegiance to the Charter. Even if

HIPPOLYTE LECOMTE: THE FUTURE
DUCHESS OF BERRY IN THE FO-
REST OF FONTAINEBLEAU Caroline-
Ferdinande-Louise, Princess of
the Two Sicilies, meets her hus-
band's family at Saint Hérem's
Cross, June 15th, 1816. (*Musée
de Versailles.*)

FRANÇOIS BARON GÉRARD: THE CORONATION OF CHARLES X The king was crowned at Rheims on May 29th, 1825, by Archbishop de Latil. Louis-Antoine, Dauphin of Viennois, pays homage to his father, while the Duke of Orleans (later to be Louis-Philippe I) and the Duke of Bourbon, Prince of Condé, await their turn. (*Musée de Chartres.*)

Polignac had had all the family charm, nobility and courage, his obstinacy, his narrow-mindedness, the naivety of his monarchist faith could in all France satisfy only a handful of fanatics. 'Poor Jules,' said Chateaubriand, 'he is so limited.' Polignac swore that he would have respect for freedom. 'I am so sorry', retorted Michaud, the historian of the Crusades. 'Why?' 'Because, since your only supporters are the men who want *coups d'état*, if you don't pull them off, you will have no one left on your side.' Asked the *Journal des Débats*: 'Will they tear up this Charter which created Louis XVIII's immortality and his successor's power? Let them remember well that the Charter is now an authority against which all the efforts of despotism will shatter themselves'.

When the Chamber met on March 2nd, two hundred and twenty-one deputies voted an address, respectful but firm, expressing to the King the nation's anxiety. Charles X replied by dissolving the Chamber. This was stark folly. The success of the liberals in the elections which would follow was certain; Polignac and Charles X alone seemed to have no suspicion of it. 'These fellows do not know what a King is,' said their newspaper, 'now they do know; a breath has scattered them like straw.' Imagination is the mistress of illusions: the royal breath had scattered nothing whatever. Polignac showed himself resolute, 'but he did not know the object of his resolution'. When the elections brought the opposition up to two hundred and seventy (as against one hundred and forty-five supporters of the

LOUIS-LÉOPOLD BOILLY: FREE ADMISSION TO THE 'AMBIGU-COMIQUE' THEATRE (Musée du Louvre.)

French society under the Restoration captured by a painter who left many valuable pictures of daily life in France from the end of the Ancien Régime till the reign of Louis-Philippe. This painting is dated 1819.

FRÉDÉRIC-AUGUSTE BOUTERWEK after CHARLES LANGLOIS: THE BATTLE OF NAVARINO A naval force including British, French and Russian units defeated a Turco-Egyptian fleet three times its size, October 20th, 1827. The French commander was Admiral de Rigny.
(*Musée de Versailles.*)

T. Gudin

cabinet), the King could still have saved his throne by changing ministers. In the *National*, Thiers published the formula for constitutional royalty: 'The King reigns and does not govern.' To reign is to be willing to be the reflected image of the country. Charles X did not believe in parliamentary rules: 'Louis XVI was lost through concessions', he said. 'I have but one choice, to drive or be driven.' He did neither. The Charter authorized him to issue Ordinances; he signed four such, drawn up by Polignac, but greatly exceeding the powers assigned to the sovereign by the Charter. One suspended the freedom of the press, another dissolved the Chamber and the two last changed the balloting procedure; these Ordinances were unconstitutional, unpopular and intolerable. Since the King possessed no armed force to back him in his illegality, the monarchy was committing suicide.

The Ordinances aroused Paris just as Necker's dismissal had in 1789. On July 26th, 1830, the journalists published a protest drawn up by Thiers, that ambitious journalist whose superiority of intelligence dominated the opposition. The cry went up at the Palais Royal, 'Long live the Charter! Down with the Ministry!' The King instructed Marshal Marmont to re-establish order in Paris. It was a silly choice. On the twenty-seventh, barricades were raised; the troops attacked them; a parliamentary quarrel was turning into a popular revolution. On July 28th, a group of students, young men from the École Polytechnique, and workmen unfurled the tricolour flag and set it waving from atop the towers of Notre Dame. Paris had retained the tradition of street fighting, and soon the whole eastern end of the city was in the hands of the insurgents, while the King sat passively at Saint-Cloud and Marshal Marmont, in command of the soldiery, received neither orders nor supplies. On the twenty-ninth he was utterly outflanked, and Charles X, surrounded in his covert, had to sign the withdrawal of the Ordinances. But it was too late; the French people wanted no more of this regime. In three days, the 'Three Glorious Days', Paris had driven forth the King who had forsworn the Charter. The cloth was cut indeed; it remained to sew it together. Who could bring the country unity? Lafayette as president of a republic? He was almost 'as shy of responsibility as he was amorous of popularity'; he took far more delight in negotiating for the people and in the name of the people than in aspiring to rule it. Thiers had other schemes, which he laid before a meeting of the liberal leaders at the home of the banker, Laffitte: 'Charles X can

never come back to Paris; he has shed the blood of the people. The Republic would lay us open to dreadful division, and it would embroil us with all Europe. The Duke of Orleans is a prince devoted to the cause of the Revolution . . . The Duke of Orleans was present at Jemappes [Dumouriez's great victory]. The Duke of Orleans has borne the tricolour standard under fire; he alone can bear it still, and we want no other flag. The Duke of Orleans has spoken: he accepts the Charter as we have always wished it. It would be from the French people that he would accept the crown...' Would the Duke take the throne? No one doubted that he would; he was devoured by ambition. Would he be acceptable? Thiers and his associates worked out a formula to appease the victors of July. The Chambers — therefore the nation — would offer the Duke the title of Lieutenant-General of the Realm. Charles X tried to abdicate in favour of his grandson, the Duke of Bordeaux; he thought that the Duke of Orleans would govern as a regent and that the monarchists would unanimously rally 'around the ruins of the throne'. This might not have been an impossible solution, but the Duke of Orleans wanted to be king, and through Lafayette, who was his protector, he procured a popular manifestation in order to frighten Charles X. It was effective, and the King, together with his family, set sail for England.

There remained the task of getting the insurgents, largely republicans and Bonapartists, to welcome a new monarchy. The Duke of Orleans rode on horseback to the Hôtel de Ville with a rather unfriendly reception from the crowds, which cried as he passed by: 'Long live liberty! Down with the Bourbons!' Lafayette, however, with his instinct for spectacular gestures, placed in his hands a tricolour flag, led him out on to the balcony, and embraced him. Everyone applauded and the game was won. At the beginning of August, the Chamber decided that the Duke of Orleans and his male descendants in the order of primogeniture would be, no longer Kings of France, but *Kings of the French*. The Duke took the name of Louis-Philippe I; he had five sons, all strong and handsome — Orleans, Nemours, Joinville, Aumale and Montpensier; the dynasty's safety seemed assured. Those most surprised of all were the insurgents, who had thought they were making a republic and had brought to birth a bourgeois monarchy; the Palais Bourbon had defeated the Hôtel de Ville.

And so the Restoration had come to naught. The monarchy survived, but it was weakened, stripped of the prestige

FRANÇOIS BARON GÉRARD: MONSIEUR, COMTE D'ARTOIS (Musée de Versailles.)

Charles-Philippe is here depicted c. 1820 in the uniform of Colonel of the Carabiniers; he wears the blue ribbon of the Holy Spirit and the red ribbon of the Golden Fleece. He became Charles X, king of France and of Navarre in September 1824 and was crowned at Rheims the following May. He was to die in exile at Goritz in November 1836.

of legitimacy, beholden to the uprising which had created it, battered by those who grieved for the Revolution and those who wept for the Emperor. Was this failure inevitable? Could the 'bloody ditch' dug by the Terror never be filled and levelled over? *Never* is a word which politicians should never use, but the experience of the Restoration had shown that this ditch still held Frenchmen apart. Of course it is easy to say that if Louis XVIII had been able to force acceptance of his will to reconciliation, if the ultras had been more reasonable, if Charles X had respected the Charter, then between 1815 and 1830 the monarchy would have taken fresh root. The trouble is that the problem lay in governing, not the France that should have been, but the France that was, the France still trembling from the impact of the Revolution on the Old Regime, France in a turmoil of passions. That was not easy, and the victory of Thiers and his friends bore with it heavy responsibilities.

There was no more King of France; there was a King of the French. He had not been crowned at Rheims but at the Palais Bourbon. He had not spent his young days at court but with the armies and in garrets. Having wooed the Jacobin Club and fought bravely at Valmy, he had become an *émigré* despite himself, a man suspect to the revolutionaries because he was a Bourbon, hated by the royalists because his father had been a regicide, earning his living as best he could in Switzerland and America. His marriage to Marie Amélie of Naples and the Two Sicilies, conservative in religion and in her feeling for legitimacy, and his protest against the murder of d'Enghien, had ultimately won him a half-pardon from the royal family. Exile and harsh poverty had made him prudent, astute and free of illusions, 'except on his own account'. He wanted to be, and he thought he was, the happy-medium king, the incarnation of compromise between the Revolution and the monarchy. At the Palais Royal, which was his home, he set up no Versailles ceremonial; he called workmen 'my friends', and the National Guardsmen 'my comrades'. The bourgeois king strolled about the streets, an umbrella under his arm; when idlers gathered beneath his windows and called out his name, he would appear on a balcony, surrounded by his numerous family, would brandish the tricolour and sing the *Marseillaise*. And the Parisians were tickled by this obliging compliancy.

But if Louis-Philippe played up to the people, it was because he was resolved to govern; if he was willing to

be a citizen king, it was because he wanted to be a king. He had been raised to the throne less because of the Revolution than because of fear of the Revolution, and many of his advisers would cheerfully have forgotten the July days; the Duke of Broglie would have liked the King to take the name of Philip VII, to emphasize the continuity of the regime. 'There has been no revolution,' said Casimir Périer, 'there has merely been a change in the person of the Head of the State.' Actually, Louis-Philippe was far less democratic than his easy manners would have led you to think; he would never have tolerated in France an English parliamentary system, under which the King reigns and does not govern. Authoritarian and even stubborn, he expected to chose his ministers and truly preside over his council. 'I am the driver of this coach', he said, which was not very different from Louis XIII's remark about being 'owner of the shop'. He had a policy of his own, which was conservative and favoured peace; being against all flourishes, bold strokes and adventures, he wanted to be the Napoleon of peace and set at rest the thrones which had shivered over the July Revolution. 'The monarchy in accordance with the Charter,' he said, 'nothing more, nothing less.' And yet he agreed to amend that Charter, and in a slightly more liberal direction.

The new king's intentions were good, but he was in a false position. In the minds of the legitimists and of his own wife, he was a usurper; he had pilfered the throne from the Duke of Bordeaux, whose protector the royal family had made him. He had the simple-minded and modest ambition to marry off his sons to 'legitimate' princesses. Those who, like Chateaubriand, averred a romantic attachment to a dynasty which, after all, they never supported till the day it fell, had a fine chance to shower the Palais Royal with shame and scorn. As for the July fighters, the workmen, the republican students, the Bonapartist officers, they had revolted out of a spirit of adventure. In case of absolute necessity, they would have accepted a chauvinistic monarchy, but their reason for having produced the Three Glorious Days was to obtain glory, to tear up the 1815 treaties, to regain the country's natural boundaries. The mystics of July were growing sad — as happens after every revolution — at seeing the politicians busy getting or keeping jobs. The extremists were asking who had consulted the French on the choice of a King of the French — half of an already dissolved Chamber, which represented, when it was in full session, a hundred thousand voters, had transformed a lieutenant-general into a sovereign. By what right? Like the monarchists, the republicans viewed this likeable fellow as a usurper.

Who did support him? The July Monarchy in fact leaned upon a new oligarchy, that of the middle classes, that of the businessmen and consular judges, newly-rich bankers and industrialists, so proud of being invited to the palace and already eyeing the peerage. Of course the new regime was going to broaden the franchise, but the vote was not to be conferred on all citizens, or on all 'qualified' ones, meaning educated citizens with formal diplomas, or even on all the National Guardsmen — those citizen-soldiers who were the bulwark of the regime. In a word, class government — that was the notion of the so-called 'Resistance' party, which was in fact the party of the established order, of Guizot and Casimir Périer. This resistance was of a wholly conservative sort: resistance to change. It was under fire from the dissatisfied of the Left and of the Right. Thiers, one of the men who had wrought the 1830 revolution, inclined to adhere to the Resistance. Against the Resistance was aligned the 'Movement', reformist and liberal, under the leadership of Lafayette, Laffitte and Odilon Barrot, this last 'the most solemn of the uncertain and the most pensive of the empty-headed'. To the Right of both there were a few legitimists; to their Left, the hot-headed crowds of Paris; between them, the middle party, the everlasting Swamp, by turns powerless and all-powerful; above 'the Castle'; around them, the thirty million French who fed, enriched and defended France, but had no voice in the councils. This surely was an unstable equilibrium.

The regime's first days were troublesome. A people which has just witnessed the triumph of an uprising is tempted to turn to force every time it is discontented. Now the people of Paris are not readily contented; the July fighters had had all the demands, with none of the rewards, of victors. Charles X's ministers had been placed under arrest; the more violent demanded their lives, but General Daumesnil, a wooden-legged hero in command of the fortress of Vincennes, refused to hand them over to the mob. Ultimately the King and the Government succeeded in saving them, but not without hubbub in the streets. Passions continued red-hot; in reaction against the clericalism which had triumphed beyond bounds during Charles X's day, there appeared an aggressive anticlericalism. The church of Saint-Germain-l'Auxerrois was broken into and plundered, and the Archbishop's palace was pillaged. Even though Louis-Philippe had called upon the Movement party and Jacques Laffitte, a radical banker with a winning tongue, to form a Government, riots spattered Paris and a number of provincial cities with blood. Timidly Laffitte made a beginning of reform; for municipal elections, he added to the rolls those holding certain academic degrees, over and above those already having the franchise because they paid certain minimum taxes; for other elections, he lowered that minimum, but even though his measure doubled the electorate, it did not enfranchise the masses. No one was pleased with the Government: its prudence annoyed the Movement and its weakness incensed the Resistance. It was 'government by surrender'.

The conquest of Algeria, begun during the last days of Charles X's reign, continued gloriously; it displeased England, which was jealous of anything

HIPPOLYTE LECOMTE: THE BATTLE IN THE RUE DE ROHAN An episode of the July 1830 revolution. (*Musée Carnavalet.*)

happening in Africa and, to keep the British Government quiet, it was essential to avoid other conflicts with its policy.

The situation in Belgium, however, threatened to prove dangerous; the Belgians had revolted against the Dutch and asked the French for protection. Should annexation be attempted, thus restoring the frontiers of the Revolution? The King would thereby have gained prestige, but England had always stood out against this solution. Louis-Philippe had the courage and wisdom to arrange with England that Belgium should be made an independent nation and to refuse, on behalf of his second son, the Duke of Nemours, the crown the Belgians proffered him. A Coburg, Leopold I, became King of the Belgians and son-in-law to the King of the French. This policy of good sense kept France out of war, but a golden-mean regime, backed at once by the shopkeepers and the bankers, exasperated both the aristocrats and the proletariat. As was to be expected, however, the elections, which expressed the voice of a class and not of the country, indicated benign contentment with the provender.

Strengthened by this vote, the King called upon the Resistance, with Casimir Périer as its leader, to form a cabinet. A banker succeeded a banker, but Périer was as gruff as Laffitte was jolly. He induced a certain dread in his partisans as in his opponents. He selected a fighting cabinet. 'France', he said, 'has wanted royalty to be national; she has not wanted royalty to be powerless'. The country felt his iron hand, and the opposition cried out to heaven. There were riots which were soon quelled without special legislation. 'The general law must suffice for everything', remarked Casimir Périer. At the very moment when this prudent strength seemed about to triumph, the cholera, which, like other perils, M. Périer had fearlessly fought, finished him off (1832).

A new ministry (Soult, Thiers, Broglie, Guizot), as must happen to all golden-mean governments, continued at odds with both Right and Left. On the Right a legitimist insurrection seemed possible when the Duchess of Berry, mother of the young Duke of Bordeaux, landed in France and attempted to incite those loyal to the senior branch of the Bourbons to rebellion in the Vendée and elsewhere. She was arrested and imprisoned in the citadel of Blaye; but no sooner had the Government disposed of insurrection on the Right, than the funeral of a liberal general served as excuse for a republican uprising, which ended in the slaughter of the Cloître Saint-Merri and the rue Transnonain. In 1834, Lyons, and then again Paris, rose in arms; in 1835 and 1836, attempts were made against the King's person. Nevertheless, despite the violence of both oppositions, the July Monarchy continued to rule, partly thanks to the talents of such men as Thiers and Guizot, partly through corruption and favouritism. 'What is the Chamber?' people would ask. 'A great bazaar, where everyone barters his conscience for a job.' To honest minds, the scandalous holding of public office by elected deputies became as important a matter as electoral reform, for whoever is a dependant on power cannot control it.

It has been remarked that the July Monarchy's only problem was to know whether France should be governed by M. Thiers or by M. Guizot, and it is true that 'these two great ambitions attended by two great talents' represented the two policies of the regime. At first Thiers and Guizot served together, 'duumvirs' in the livery of order. Both of them were 'gentlemen', historians, gallant fellows, and in case of need they were able to work together, but their personal traits set them against each other. Guizot, a Protestant of ascetic habits and irreproachable private life, remained loyal to the doctrinaire party, its doctrine being conservatism based on the middle class and peace based on agreement between France and England. Thiers, who was from Marseilles, slight in stature, charming and sprightly, and who supplied Balzac with a model for his Rastignac, had married the daughter of his wealthy mistress, Madame Dosne, and the 'astuteness of this bourgeoise united to the southern craftiness' of Thiers had together pushed the man, before his fortieth birthday, into the French Academy and the premiership. Paris was amused by this little dwarf of a genius who believed himself to be a 'civilian Napoleon'; a current jest was that some day Thiers would have his statue on the Place Vendôme between the Emperor's legs. Yet Paris likewise admired Thiers when, with his furious energy, he completed the Arc de Triomphe, adorned the Place de la Concorde with an obelisk, proceeded on horseback at Bugeaud's side to suppress a riot and held England in check.

With stubborn constancy, Guizot remained faithful to the doctrinaires' essential ideas; Thiers, far less steadfast, broke with the Left after having served as its guiding light, relied for support on the mass of the politically inactive and flirted with the conservatives. He at first advocated a Continental policy directed against England, and then turned savagely

ANTOINE-LÉON MOREL FATIO: THE NAVAL ATTACK ON ALGIERS (Musée de Versailles.)

   In spite of the opposition of the British and of the liberals, 'the last conquest of the king' took place. Morel Fatio, a painter of sea-scapes, witnessed the naval bombardment carried out on July 3rd, 1830, by Vice-Admiral Baron Duperré. *La Bellone* fires on the English fort while General Count de Bourmont, after landing at Sidi-Ferruch and twice beating the Arabs, has taken up a position on the heights overlooking the town. The dey Hussein surrendered on the 5th, just when the assault was due to begin. The French finally succeeded, where so many others, including Charles V, had for centuries failed, in cleaning out this nest of pirates.

against Austria and Metternich when the latter rejected his request for an archduchess for the Duke of Orleans. As for Louis-Philippe, who was expert in the game of divide and rule, he watched 'with amused interest' the quarrel between the parliamentary leaders and took advantage of it to build up the sovereign's authority.

Towards 1838, the regime's position seemed fairly strong; it had lasted, and that was a great merit. It was backed by the mass of the peasants, because it afforded them peace, prosperity and good roads. Guizot had bettered primary education, and Thiers had done as much for the public monuments. Lastly the Algerian war had added to the prestige of the King's sons, since they had fought in it with distinction. The Duke of Orleans, heir to the throne, had the reputation of being a liberal, and those who wasted no love on the father could await with confidence the reign of the son.

On the debit side, the Carlists (legitimists) remained hostile, and the Bonapartists, cheered by the public acclaim which greeted the solemn return of the Emperor's ashes and by the sentimental rebirth of the Napoleonic legend fostered by poets and song writers, clung to their hopes. The Duke of Reichstadt (ex-King of Rome) was dead; the new pretender, son of Hortense and perhaps of Louis Bonaparte, a bold and romantic young man, was merely Napoleon's nephew; nevertheless the Bonaparte name was enough to afford him an unquestionable prestige: 'It is a great deal to be at once a national glory, a revolutionary pledge, and a principle of authority'. Twice, first at Strasbourg, then at Boulogne, Louis Napoleon tried to excite the French into revolt; after the second attempt, he was interned in the fort at Ham. The King wanted peace at any price; he put Guizot in Thiers's place, because, like him, Guizot loved peace and the English. Anglo-French friendship was back on a firm basis, and the two countries' sovereigns exchanged cordial visits. Thereupon the King was more bitterly attacked than ever; the bourgeoisie, which owed him everything, poked fun at him, and his love of peace passed for cowardice.

Louis-Philippe made no great effort to win affection. Thanks to the limited suffrage, he had the voters on his side, and thanks to subsidies and gifts, the Chamber. With Guizot, a minister after his own heart, he in fact wielded personal power. Guizot remained the embodiment of the middle way, wise, realistic, without any yearning for false grandeur and without the least streak of bombast. He

admired England and wanted to live with her in 'cordial understanding' but the French public, at that time violently anti-English, regarded any agreement as surrender. The case of Pritchard, a British missionary and consul, who had been arrested by French bluejackets at Tahiti because of advice he had given Queen Pomaré, and for whom England demanded an indemnity, very nearly led to a declaration of war. Firmly resolved not go to war over Queen Pomaré, the King and Guizot granted the Pritchard indemnity, and were accused of being arrant cowards. Dissatisfaction grew when England induced Guizot to make a white peace with the Sultan of Morocco; Marshal Bugeaud had just defeated the Moroccans at the Battle of Isly, and the English watched with anxiety France winning a more and more extensive grip on North Africa. The cabinet won with a majority of only eight votes, and the King asked Guizot to remain in power. Louis-Philippe had always been authoritarian; as he grew older, he became stubborn, and he was now seventy. His eldest son, the Duke of Orleans, had been killed in 1842 in a carriage accident, and his grandson, the Count of Paris, the heir to the throne, was only four. The King's second son, Nemours, who would probably be regent, was not a liberal; the dynasty's future no longer seemed quite so secure.

Germany and Italy had aspirations to unity, and Austria, that unity's principal obstacle, seemed to the liberals the most oppressive power on the Continent. The Italian revolutionaries appealed to France for help; Guizot and the King refused to become embroiled with Austria, and they were right, but under the bitter attacks of the opposition, they had recourse to badly chosen weapons of defence. Corruption was constantly on the increase. The Minister of Public Works sold a salt-mine concession for one hundred thousand francs, with a former minister of war acting as go-between. Actresses bargained for privileges with deputies, and the gossip sheets supplied the public with tales of scandal. Many Frenchmen were moved to feelings of disgust and sadness. Now the opposition was penetrating into circles which had hitherto seemed by their very nature conservative. Among the Catholics, who had been so keenly legitimist in Charles X's day, there was a growing liberal party the leaders of which — Lamennais, Montalembert and Lacordaire — wanted to bring clergy and people closer. Meanwhile, in its struggle with the university, the higher clergy was arousing anticlericalism. The bishops reproached the university for producing atheists; the lec-

◄ NICOLAS GOSSE: LOUIS-PHILIPPE I REFUSES THE BELGIAN CROWN ON BEHALF OF HIS SON THE DUKE OF NEMOURS The Belgian National Congress elected the Duke of Nemours as king, but his father, foreseeing international complications, refused the crown. The scene is the Palais-Royal, February 1831. (Musée de Versailles.)

FRANÇOIS-MARIUS GRANET: LOUIS-PHILIPPE I PLACES THE CARDINAL'S BIRETTA ON THE HEAD OF MONSIGNOR DE CHEVERUS It is the privilege of the Head of State to confer the biretta on newly-created cardinals resident in France. The scene is in the chapel of the Tuileries, March 1836. *Conservation du Musée de Versailles.*

tures of Michelet and Edgar Quinet at the university condemned the Jesuits and the Inquisition. On all sides there was bitterness and a desire for change.

In 1794, at the time of Thermidor, the country, weary of the Revolution's violence, had dreamed of a restoration; in 1845, weary of material corruption, it recalled only the revolutionaries' idealism. Thiers and Mignet had begun their historical rehabilitation: Lamartine's *Histoire des Girondins* completed it. Lamartine felt the revolution surging up and awaited it with cheerful anguish. The *Histoire des Girondins* was an enormous success; its revolutionary romanticism consoled its readers for the depths of Louis-Philippe's prosaic rule. Those were the days of reformist banquets at which, while the dessert was consumed, orators demanded universal suffrage; throughout the kingdom dinners and speeches multiplied. Through his hatred of Guizot, even Thiers was turning to the Left and hoped for an outcome which he none the less knew was perilous. A monarchist

opposition declared itself in favour of reform in order to avoid revolution; a socialist and republican opposition hoped that the agitation for reform would lead to revolution.

In February, 1848, Guizot forbade attendance at a reformist banquet in Paris, and Lamartine determined to go to the appointed place despite the ban: 'Were the Place de la Concorde deserted, were all the other deputies to shirk their duties, I should go to the banquet alone with my shadow behind me.' His shadow added nothing, for he could hardly have rid himself of it. But it was a poet's shadow and it was for poets that the French then felt they hungered. The other deputies did not go, but students and workers filled the Place de la Concorde and made a bonfire of the Tuileries' chairs (February 21st). On the twenty-second, processions filed through the streets crying, 'Down with Guizot! Long live Reform!' During the night a few barricades were thrown up in working-class quarters:

EUGÈNE LAMI: A CONCERT IN THE GALERIE DES GUISES AT EU Queen Victoria

were entertained at Eu by the Orleans family, September 1843. (*Musée de Versailles.*)

when the National Guardsmen were summoned, they too cried out, 'Long live Reform!' This middle-class hostility meant serious business for a middle-class regime. Now worried, the King suddenly became constitutional, dismissed Guizot and summoned a reformist, Molé; people thought that everything was settled, and the vast majority of the French rejoiced. But on the evening of the twenty-third, during the course of a demonstration in front of Guizot's house on the Boulevard des Capucines, one of the demonstrators let off a pistol and the soldiery answered by firing a salvo. Some twenty persons were killed, both men and women; five of the bodies, loaded on a cart, were hauled through the city surrounded by torches. The mob cried out for vengeance; Molé refused to form a Government; the King called in Thiers giving command of the army to Marshal Bugeaud, a man very unpopular with the Parisians. Tired and demoralized, the troops gave way. Thiers advised the King to retire to Saint-Cloud. But under his sons'

pressure, he abdicated in favour of his grandson the Count of Paris.

Here was what such men as Victor Hugo had hoped for, since they would have liked to save the throne and looked to great things from the regency of the young Duchess of Orleans, Helen of Mecklenburg, who was an intelligent and liberal princess. On the advice of her friends, the Duchess went to the Palais Bourbon with her two children; she was welcomed there by the deputies, but an armed mob broke into the hall. Ledru-Rollin, a socialist deputy, proposed the formation of a provisional Government and was seconded by Lamartine, who read a list of names which the people accepted by acclamation: Dupont de l'Eure, an elderly figurehead; Arago, a moderate scientist; Lamartine, poet; Ledru-Rollin, Marie, Crémieux, Garnier-Pagès.

In the meantime, at the Hôtel de Ville, the socialists were likewise forming a Government. The struggles between the Assembly and the Commune which had stained

[154]

FRANZ-XAVER WINTER-
HALTER: THE DUCHESS
OF ORLEANS AND THE
COUNT OF PARIS
The Protestant princess
Helen of Mecklenburg-
Schwerin with her eldest
son, Louis-Philippe of
Orleans, head of the
House of Orleans till his
death in 1894. *Conserva-
tion du Musée de Versailles*.

the First Republic with blood must at all costs be avoided. In haste the Palais Bourbon Government took in a few of the Hôtel de Ville men: Louis Blanc, Marrast, Flocon and the working man, Albert, a personage of mythical renown, dignified, quiet and moderate. The July Monarchy was gone. It had died for 'lack of *panache*'. Accustomed by the Revolution and the Empire to harvests of glory, France had found this regime — peace-loving to the point of complacency — both dull and ridiculous. The whole crew of journalists and pamphleteers had created in the public mind an image of a vulgar and ridiculous creature. Louis-Philippe had afforded France some of the happiest years in her history, but the French do not live on happiness. In 1848 Paris was reopening the path to adventures.

The Palais Bourbon Government had moved over to the Hôtel de Ville, but between the two groups and their papers there continued to be a deep fissure; the *National* men (Palais Bourbon) wanted a political revolution, the Republic, prompt elections and the tricolour; the *Réforme* men (Hôtel de Ville) demanded a social revolution, delayed elections (to gain time in which to carry out their plans before the conservative provinces could make themselves felt), and the red flag. Lamartine was the republicans' great man, Louis Blanc the socialists'; Ledru-Rollin wavered between the two. All three were men of goodwill, but without experience in public affairs. Agreement was reached on three points: freedom of the press with abolition of the stamp tax, freedom of assembly (which promoted a rebirth of clubs) and the right of every citizen to belong to the National Guard (which seemed to strip the bourgeoisie of any possibility of governing by armed force). The opening days were riotous; delegation after delegation invaded the Hôtel de Ville. Workmen armed with guns demanded the right to work and minimum wages. Lamartine, Minister of Foreign Affairs, replied to everyone in speeches which were harmonious, noble and flowing. To quiet the sovereigns, he promised that the French Republic would not spread propaganda abroad. To protect itself against the cries for vengeance, that sad aftermath of revolutions, the Government decreed the abolition of the death penalty for political offences; Lamartine himself helped Guizot to get across the frontier. The heads of the provisional Government were not cruel men; they were romantic and warmhearted; they wanted a France great and free; they believed in progress through brotherhood and science; but they knew nothing about the national economy and precious little about the French provinces. On April 9th they determined to hold elections open to universal suffrage. The enfranchised population suddenly swelled from two hundred and fifty thousand to nine million voters; it was a leap in the dark.

[156]

GONZAGUE PRIVAT: ALPHONSE DE LAMARTINE One of the greatest Romantic poets, he became embroiled in politics during the 1848 revolution, and influenced the adoption of the tricolour flag. *Conservation du Musée de Versailles.*

HENRI PHILIPPOTEAUX: THE DUKE OF ORLEANS SETS FREE TWO ARAB
PRISONERS (Musée de Versailles.)

Ferdinand-Philippe of Orleans twice participated in Algerian campaigns. This scene
occurred in March 1840. He was to be killed two years later in a street accident at Neuilly-
sur-Seine.

The extension of the franchise had frightened the bourgeois, but they were quickly reassured. In the elections of April 23rd, the masses appeared more conservative than had the qualified voters; in deciding upon universal suffrage, Paris had signed away its right to govern the country and had handed over that right to the provinces. The Palais Bourbon had triumphed over the Hôtel de Ville. With good grace or ill, men accepted the Republic; almost everywhere, peasants and gentry had together planted Liberty Trees; the National Guard (still a bourgeois organization) had attended in full regalia; and the village priest had blessed the poplar bedecked with ribbons. The July Monarchy, hated by both Right and Left, found none to defend it. 'So much the worse for them; they have richly deserved it', said the legitimists. The greater number of the nine hundred representatives were republicans and moderates; the advanced republicans had only a hundred seats. The French were willing to accept a political, not a social revolution.

The workers of Paris were discontented, not that they had this time been swindled of the Republic, but because they had been swindled of the *Sociale*. They had, however, won two measures: the creation of a 'Government Committee for Labour', which met at the Luxembourg under the chairmanship of Louis Blanc, talked a great deal and did little or nothing; and the national workshops. The latter, intended to give the unemployed some occupation and to prove the feasibility of a collective economy, had been organized by the Minister of Commerce, Marie de Saint-Georges, otherwise known as Marie, who opposed them; he had therefore taken great pains to make sure they would fail. The labourers in these shops were employed on perfectly useless earthworks. Unable to take any interest in such idle toil, they spent their time tossing pennies or founding political clubs which would soon want their Day. On May 15th, under the leadership of those two veterans of Paris uprisings, Barbès and Blanqui, they broke into the Palais Bourbon, declared the Assembly dissolved and proclaimed a socialist Government composed of Louis Blanc, Barbès, Blanqui and the workman, Albert. The legal Government, however, sounded a general alarm, the National Guardsmen from the prosperous quarters freed the Assembly, and Barbès and Albert were arrested at the Hôtel de Ville — thus putting an end to the first escapade. Thereupon it seemed urgent to do away with the national workshops, a breeding-ground for disturbances.

On June 21st, the workshops were disbanded and the workmen were urged to enlist in the army or find jobs outside Paris. It was most likely that so radical a step would bring about another riot; the people of Paris, deeply disappointed, exasperated at seeing their victory again frittered away, were going to try yet another Day; wittingly the Government took its chances.

For some time past, Cavaignac, the Minister of War, had had his battle plan against the 'Reds'. On June 23rd, some thousands of working people gathered before the Bastille column, knelt in remembrance of the first martyrs in 1789 and, crying out 'Liberty or death!', retired behind barricades and demanded the re-establishment of the national workshops. The Assembly declared a state of siege and gave plenary powers to General Cavaignac. He had available about twenty thousand regular army troops, the National Guard from the western parts of the city (well fed to the point of bursting) and the militia. After February 1848, however, the workmen had also been issued with National Guard weapons. The battle, the sorry battle, was fierce and lasted for four days; the army fought with discipline, the bourgeois National Guard with fury. The rioters slaughtered General Bréa, and the Archbishop of Paris, Monseigneur Affre, was killed by a bullet while trying to make a plea for civil peace. In all there were several thousand dead.

Cavaignac's victory was complete, and he demanded from the Government the most severe reprisals. Thousands of the insurgents were deported, in mass and without trial, the socialist party was broken, and its papers were suppressed. Here was a misguided fury to provoke other furies, a new trench of blood, but this time between the workers and the bourgeoisie. And Louis-Philippe, recalling that he had been overthrown by a few corpses, said bitterly: 'The Republic is lucky . . . it is able to fire upon the people.' Four months had sufficed to weave the shroud of the February Revolution.

The Assembly decreed that General Cavaignac had deserved well of the fatherland; rather had he deserved well of the bourgeoisie. He was a republican beyond reproach, and everyone thought that he would be elected President — that is, everyone except Lamartine, who thought he himself had a chance, and who insisted that the election should be by universal suffrage. Lamartine won his point, but he had not thought of excluding members of families that had reigned over France. Who were the possible candidates? In

FRANÇOIS BIARD: THE ABOLITION OF SLAVERY This symbolic painting shows the rejoicings occasioned by the National Assembly's decree of April 27th, 1848. Those who have been slaves are now to be citizens. *Conservation du Musée de Versailles.*

order to be elected by a parliamentary assembly to the presidency of the State, a man must have given proof of political capacity and assurances of loyalty to the regime; election by plebiscite requires only an extended popularity. Lamartine thought he possessed it; Cavaignac had it among the bourgeois, but not among the workers and peasants; a third candidate was looming on the horizon. He was Louis Napoleon Bonaparte. This son of Hortense de Beauharnais and (perhaps) of Louis Bonaparte, who had become imperial pretender upon the death of the Duke of Reichstadt, had never wavered in his faith in the powers of his magic name. In youth he had been liberal and even *carbonaro*; when his first vain attempts at a *coup d'état* had landed him in jail, he had written much and worked hard during his confinement. In London, where he had long dwelt, he had made friends such as Benjamin Disraeli and Lady Blessington; rich Britons and bankers from the city had helped him financially, gambling on his future. From the dawning of the February Days, a little group of faithfuls had tried to launch the new Bonaparte. Prudently and wisely he had shown himself little; he was waiting for 'illusions to fade', but in the June by-elections, he was the victor in four departments. He continued to keep very much in the shade, through skill, or lack of it, merely sputtering before the Assembly, and thus calming the members' fears.

When Louis Napoleon at last ventured to place himself in nomination for the presidency of the Republic, a united front of republicans and royalists should at once have been forged against this potential Caesar. But the royalist leaders, who constituted what was called the Committee of the Rue de Poitiers, knew that a royalist candidate had no immediate chance, and so they turned to Louis Napoleon who, being ready to make any promises because he was resolved to keep none, thus won the support of Thiers and his associates. 'He's a simpleton', they said; he was no such thing, however, and they were handing him the majority of France. That majority was in a mood for adventures; the peasants and the middle class had been dismayed by the events of June. Ever since the business of the workshops, labour had been sulking at the Republic; now it rediscovered deep in its heart an old background of Bonapartism, and knew that this new Bonaparte called himself a socialist. When the votes had been counted, Prince Louis Napoleon had five and a half million, Cavaignac a million and a half, Ledru-Rollin, the socialist candidate, three hundred and seventy thousand and Lamartine less than eight thousand.

But Louis Napoleon, silent and close-mouthed, still trod warily. He solemnly swore as an honourable man to respect the Constitution, formed a cabinet under the chairmanship of the everlasting Odilon Barrot, and undertook, by travelling about the country, to solidify his popularity. On May 13th, 1849, were held the elections for the Legislative Assembly which was to replace the Constituent Assembly. This time the 'reactionaries' won sweepingly over the moderate democrats and the 'Reds'. The rue de Poitiers had brought about the election of some four hundred and fifty deputies, almost all Orleanists and legitimists, with a handful of Bonapartists. Seemingly this meant the country's return to monarchy, yet since those loyal to the Count of Chambord, ex-Duke of Bordeaux, in the senior Bourbon line, could not reach an understanding with the faithful followers of the Count of Paris, in the junior line, the methodical dreamer in the Élysée Palace could quietly and cynically complete his plans. To make use of the monarchists to crush the Republic, and then to disarm the monarchists in order to impose the Empire, seemed a rash manœuvre, but to a man who has no one in his way, everything is easy. Thiers, confident, sure of his majority, of the rue de Poitiers and above all of himself, gave the President paternal advice: he urged 'democratic simplicity'. Louis Napoleon listened, thanked him and secretly had imperial liveries designed for the Élysée footmen.

The President had organized an expedition on behalf of the Pope against Mazzini's Roman Republic; demonstrators of the Left, aroused by a speech of Ledru-Rollin, marched upon the Palais Bourbon crying that the Constitution had been violated. A cavalry charge easily halted them, but the Assembly took advantage of this excuse to withdraw liberties that had been granted — freedom of press and assembly. Sick at heart, the people of Paris remained passive. A law on education, called the Falloux Law (the Count of Falloux was Minister of Public Instruction) set up a *de facto* alliance between the Church and the University (1850). Now the Church rallied to the party of order, which was really that of the established order, while the bourgeoisie, once Voltairean and liberal, now, because it had been afraid, was reverting to a political catholicism. Louis Napoleon and his royalist majority had succeeded in creating the Republic without the republicans. Now the task was to discard the monarchists.

During the 1850 long vacation, each party made preparations for the *coup d'état*. Thiers went to see the Orleans

ANGE TISSIER: AT AMBOISE, THE PRINCE-PRESIDENT SETS FREE ABD-EL-KADER The Emir was freed in
October 1852 and was to be a defender of the Christians in Syria whither he retired.
Conservation du Musée de Versailles.

princes at Claremont House; the legitimists called on the Count of Chambord at Wiesbaden. Meanwhile the Prince-President held military reviews, and the troops who cried 'Long live the Emperor!' were those most commended. The *coup d'état* technique is simple; in key posts you must have your own men. The Prince removed Odilon Barrot from the presidency of the Council, although the latter had a faithful majority in the Assembly. For Changarnier, a monarchist general who was sure to protect the Legislature, the Prince substituted General Magnan, who was wholly devoted to his person. During the sad debate which fol-

lowed, Thiers, who now realized the truth — but too late — said: 'The Empire is made'. The Prince-President, master of the machinery of power and aided by tried conspirators, could act now with less secrecy; who could stand in his way? Not the Assembly, which was unable to agree about anything. Not the army, for Louis Napoleon and his associates, who were far from being children, had taken their precautions in that department.

The strength of every army, and also the chink in its armour, is that it obeys orders; capture the source from which orders flow and you are master of the whole stream.

Louis Napoleon was sure of the commander of the troops, Magnan; he still needed a minister of war devoted to his service. He sent to Algeria for General de Saint-Arnaud, a man whose courage was as great as his scruples were few. There remained the Prefecture of Police, another post of command; the President installed there a man on whom he could rely, Maupas. Morny, the Prince's half-brother, a witty, charming and wholly amoral adventurer, was to be the leader of the conspiracy. By the autumn of 1851, all arrangements had been made and the *coup d'état* was in readiness. December 2nd, anniversary of Austerlitz and of the coronation, was, for the Bonapartists, the auspicious day above all others; it was chosen.

On the evening of December 1st, Louis Napoleon and Morny displayed the greatest calm; the Prince received guests at the Élysée and no emotion betrayed him. When the last of those invited had left, he opened the file labelled *Rubicon*. At dawn the troops occupied positions mastering all Paris. When the inhabitants of that city left their homes the next morning, they found two proclamations plastered on the walls; one was an appeal to the people announcing that the object of these activities was to foil the Assembly's treacherous plans, and the other was an appeal to the soldiery. Many of the representatives had been put under arrest; Thiers had shown so little heroism that he was set free the very next day — to the great indignation of the Bonapartists. Others still at liberty gathered together at the *Mairie* of the twentieth *arrondissement*; Hugo, Carnot, Arago, Jules Favre and Michel de Bourges set up a resistance committee. At the meeting-place of the Assembly, its president, Dupin, yielded without a struggle before a show of bayonets.

'We are in the right', said he, 'but these gentlemen have the power. Let us go.' A liberal and bourgeois opposition had taken shape on December 4th; it was beaten down, without serious strife, by General Magnan. In Paris there were three hundred and eighty persons killed, many by firing squads without a trial; in all France there were twenty-six thousand arrests. The regime was never able to cleanse itself of these bloodstained and tyrannical beginnings. Just as in the days of the White Terror, ultras asked the Prince to veil the Statues of Mercy and Pity, to be a man of bronze, 'unbending and just', and to 'journey across the age, the blade of repression in his hand'. Yet Morny's grandfather, Talleyrand, had already remarked to Louis Napoleon's uncle: 'Sire, you can do everything with bayonets except sit upon them.'

All who remained loyal to the Republic were brutally eliminated, and local vengeances came to repression's aid. The injustice and extent of this persecution, however, created a republican opposition; the writers in exile, such as Victor Hugo, waged a war on Louis Napoleon which weakened his position abroad and eventually did so in France. The democratic dictatorship of a Bonaparte became, for the second time, a provisional solution. It was confirmed by a plebiscite. There were seven million four hundred thousand yeas and six hundred and fifty thousand nays. A *Te Deum* was sung in Notre Dame Cathedral. 'The people who a month ago asserted that Louis Napoleon was a congenital idiot are now proclaiming him to be a great man.' Twenty years later these same people would once again find him an idiot, but twenty years constitute a life span for a regime. Thiers was right, the Empire was made.

IX

The Second Empire

(1852-1870)

THE Constitution of January 1852 created in fact, if not in name, a consul in the Bonapartist sense of the word, meaning a dictator. This 'president' had the sole right to make treaties and war; he proposed all legislation and appointed all officials; neither he nor his ministers were responsible to the Chambers. Three major bodies were to assist the President: the Council of State, which framed the laws; the Legislative Body which voted the laws; and the Senate, which was made up of one hundred and fifty members appointed for life by the President.

The emperor was already beginning to hatch out of the prince-presidential shell. Soon he found himself announcing: 'The burst of enthusiasm which has made itself felt throughout France in favour of restoring the Empire forces on the President the duty of consulting the Senate with regard to this matter.' The outcome of this consultation was a foregone conclusion; the Senate ordered a plebiscite on the re-establishment of the imperial dignity in the person of Louis Napoleon Bonaparte, and over seven million yeas made the Prince-President into the Emperor Napoleon III. The King of Rome had been Napoleon II. The only fear which might have held the French back would have been that of a fresh crop of Napoleonic wars, but Napoleon III had reassured them — 'The Empire means peace'. He would have sincerely liked to be a good tyrant; sadly enough, there are no good tyrants.

EDOUARD RIOU: THE OPENING OF THE SUEZ CANAL The opening of the canal by the Empress Eugénie on November 17th, 1869, was the culminating moment of Ferdinand de Lesseps' astonishing engineering feat.

At the time of his becoming emperor, Napoleon III was almost forty-five years old; he was a large, heavy man, not without dignity. His long moustache and goatee lent him a most novel appearance, in its day much imitated; his grey eyes seemed lustreless, without a spark, but on occasion they could flash like lightning. A cosmopolitan prince, he spoke with the cautious slowness of a man who is not very sure of his words. He was silent, a good listener, courteous and gentle mannered, and he possessed a curious charm which attracted women as much as it did men. Twenty years of conspiracies, schemes and captivity had packed his brain with a whole world of illusions. His projects were generous, but always confused, except in conspiracy, where he had displayed a kind of genius; his extraordinary career made him fatalistic and superstitious. In 1853, the Emperor married a young Spanish girl, Eugénie de Montijo, and it was a love match. With little confidence in the dynasty, the courts of Europe had not been lavish in their offers of princesses. When he announced his marriage, he reminded the French that Josephine herself had not been of royal lineage; he informed the Council of Ministers: 'I am not asking your advice, gentlemen; I am informing you of what I have decided to do.' Eugénie was startlingly beautiful, with red hair and blue eyes and shoulders transparently white. She knew very little, but knew that little in four languages and uttered it with fiery conviction. It was said of her that she began by being the futile woman and ended by being the fatal woman — a harsh witticism, but by and large a true one.

A son, the Prince Imperial, was born to her in 1856, and the mother's anxiety for the child's future often had a baneful influence over French policy. This family of imperial upstarts and its amateurish court gave neither France nor the rest of the world any feeling of security.

Well intentioned but poorly counselled, Napoleon III began at a disadvantage. Through disgust and discouragement the workers had remained passive. But with few exceptions, the country's best minds and the student population were never reconciled to the regime; the *coup d'état* was regarded as a crime. Rebuffed by those whom he would have liked to allure, the Emperor could rely only on the interests which had created him and seek social progress through material prosperity. In this he succeeded fairly well, but prosperity has never compensated for freedom.

The early days of the regime were rather brilliant. Napoleon III did everything he could to reassure the rest of Europe of his peaceful intentions. Not that he renounced his great forebear's ambitions; but he knew that he must remain on friendly terms with England, whose hatred had overthrown the First Empire. Now the British Government of that day was resolved to defend the Ottoman Empire against Russia; Napoleon III proposed an alliance against the Czar. The ensuing conflict meant to him a means of increasing his prestige by winning England to his cause, by appeasing the French liberals, enemies of autocratic Russia, and, finally, by pleasing the Catholics, since the excuse for French intervention was the protection of the Holy Places. The Crimean War (1854-1856) was far from easy, but ended in the fall of Sevastopol and a total Franco-British victory. The peace conference was held at Paris, thus confirming France's new-born prestige.

France's internal prosperity seemed to match her apparent success abroad. Napoleon III was sincerely concerned about the welfare of poor people; under his reign, charitable associations, day nurseries and mutual-aid societies grew in number. In 1864 he finally did away with the ban on workers' associations and acknowledged the right to strike. The conditions under which labour lived were still dreadful; the working day was twelve hours. Yet we must grant that France's financial position was excellent. Never before had the country grown rich so quickly. First the lower middle class and then the peasants acquired the habit of investing in securities, and by this means large-scale, corporate capitalism developed. Savings canalized by these banks paid for France's economic development; the State encouraged railway construction and transatlantic navigation companies were organized. Great public works were undertaken to beautify the city of Paris; that city's prefect, Haussmann, took on the task of supplying the capital with those broad avenues which the increased traffic made imperative. In 1855, a World's Fair attracted five million visitors.

Yet, in spite of the success of its prosperity policy, the Empire was not a stable regime; it lacked that mysterious virtue, legitimacy. The adventurer seemed successful, but he remained none the less an adventurer; a muzzled public opinion was not convinced. The newspapers were cautious and pro-Government; even private conversations were subject to police surveillance: 'Only the Government speaks, and no one believes what it says.' However a few writers, such as Sainte-Beuve, Mérimée and Nisard, had attached themselves to the regime, allured by the Empress and the Princess Matilda. As for the republicans, those who were

FRANZ XAVER WINTERHALTER: THE EMPRESS EUGÉNIE AND HER LADIES-IN-WAITING (Musée de la Malmaison.) *Photo Draeger*.

Winterhalter was in great demand as a court painter and was considered as the obvious successor to Sir Thomas Lawrence. He painted this harmonious group portrait in 1855. The Empress is surrounded by six ladies-in-waiting and two friends. In 1860, her suite was increased so as to include twelve ladies-in-waiting.

RÉGNIER after EUGÈNE GUÉRARD: THE QUAI AUX FLEURS This lithograph of the Second Empire features the flower market in the Ile de la Cité. (*Musée Carnavalet.*)

not living in exile sought refuge in seclusion. The requirement that every deputy should swear a personal oath to the Emperor kept out most of the republicans; between 1857 and 1863 the opposition in the Legislative Body consisted of only five members. In 1859 Napoleon III felt strong enough to grant a full and absolute amnesty; Victor Hugo and Louis Blanc refused it.

The whole opposition was weak, and the Emperor could have overlooked a handful of malcontents had he not alienated two powerful conservative groups which until that time had supported him. A new phase in imperial policy was precipitated by a plot organized by the Italian *carbonari*, who could not forgive the Emperor Napoleon III for having forgotten the commitments of their 'brother', Louis Napoleon Bonaparte. An assassination attempt by Orsini modified Napoleon III's Italian policy in the direction which the Italian patriot desired. The Emperor had a secret interview with Cavour, Minister of the King of Piedmont; it was

agreed that France would help the Italians to drive out the Austrians and, in return, would obtain Savoy and the County of Nice. This nationality policy seemed generous since France was going to help people of the same race, held apart by force, to unite; in fact it was fraught with danger. To establish new major States in Europe was to set up rivals. The Italian war began in 1859; Austria was defeated at Magenta and Solferino. All Italy, and especially the Romagna, rose against the Pope, whereupon the Empress and the French clerical party protested. Napoleon III temporized; and when Prussia took sides against Italy, he signed an armistice with Austria — thus alienating the Italians — and then advised the Pope to yield — which alienated the French clergy. Ultramontane and liberal Catholics, hitherto split, joined forces; the Emperor had lost the Church's support without having won Italy's friendship and had succeeded in dissatisfying both liberals and clericals.

[165]

A second cause of discontent was Napoleon III's free-trade policy, against which the French industrialists protested. A treaty with Great Britain which lowered all tariffs caused a general outcry from all French industry; the manufacturers thought they were ruined and cursed the Government. Thus under attack from both clericals and capitalists, Napoleon was inclined to draw nearer to the mass of the people and the republicans. So began that new regime which was called the Liberal Empire.

After 1860 the Emperor and the Empire were on the decline. The Emperor, worn out by sensual excesses, was beset by a chronic and painful bladder complaint. The Empire faced growing opposition, and Napoleon III yielded by stages: first, the Legislative Body obtained the right annually to vote an address in reply to the speech from the throne; then publication of the debates was authorized. The Union Libérale, a conservative parliamentary group, obtained two million votes in the election of 1863. Since the middle class's taste for parliamentarianism was reawakening, concessions were in order; in the new Legislative Body, Thiers was able to champion 'the necessary liberties'. Meanwhile, the Emperor had taken it into his head to revive his prestige by intervention in Mexico, where the financiers, who had risked some of their capital there, wanted to install a European emperor — Maximilian of Austria. But the Mexicans had no use for an emperor, least of all a European emperor. In 1865, the United States reaffirmed the Monroe Doctrine, which suffered no interference by European Powers on the American continent. Juarez, the Mexican patriot, seized the unfortunate Maximilian and had him shot. France, having suffered futile losses in this débâcle, was heartily weary of the Emperor's great notions.

Bismarck, however, with cynical genius, played on Napoleon III's illusions. His nationality policy had led him to accept, in contempt of the law, Prussia's annexation of the Danish provinces of Schleswig and Holstein. When in 1865 Bismarck announced that he was going to declare war against Austria and that, in return for French neutrality, he would gladly permit France to gain certain territorial compensations, once again Napoleon was seduced. But when Napoleon claimed his reward, he was outwitted. Nothing fails like failure. Disaster in Mexico and diplomatic defeats in Europe shifted the equilibrium of internal forces.

The 1869 elections reflected the disaffection of the French people; Gambetta, an eloquent young lawyer who had stood as an 'irreconcilable', became deputy for Belleville. The Emperor decided that he must surrender and amended the Constitution; henceforth the Legislative Body would, like the Emperor, be able to initiate laws. Meanwhile the Emperor was secretly bargaining with the middle party, and on January 2nd, 1870, Émile Ollivier was entrusted with the selection of a cabinet. Ollivier was more pliant, and also younger than Thiers, and this seemed fitting if there were to be a completely new deal. Yet the pessimists remarked that freedom would finally crown the structure 'at that moment when its foundations gave way', and Gambetta remained unreconciled. In conformity with the Empire's principles, these liberal reforms were submitted to a plebiscite in May 1870. There were about seven million yeas, and one and a half million nays; Paris and the large cities of the south were the only opposition citadels; all the country districts were in favour of the Empire. After the results had been made known, Gambetta sadly remarked: 'The Empire is stronger than ever.' Internally, this was true, but in foreign affairs all the storm warnings were out.

Bismarck had been deliberately seeking an excuse for war ever since 1866. The offer of the vacant Spanish throne to a Hohenzollern prince lit the fuse. Although the Hohenzollern candidacy was withdrawn to calm French fears for the balance of power, the Duke of Gramont, French Foreign Minister, had the absurd idea of demanding that William I of Prussia should forbid the Prince to reverse his decision. William's reply was in no way offensive, but in it Bismarck saw an opportunity to start the war he had wanted; he shortened the telegram which the King had forwarded him from Ems in order to keep him informed, thus giving it an abrupt and peremptory tone. Both Gramont and Ollivier charged at the red rag which Bismarck dangled before them. Before the Legislative Body Ollivier proclaimed war. Thiers alone protested; Ollivier replied that he accepted this responsibility 'with a light heart'. In the streets of Paris, the crowds cried out, 'Hurrah for the war! On to Berlin!' Never had an international cataclysm been set in motion on a flimsier excuse.

Germany had prepared for war. France had to improvise. Food, ammunition, ambulances — everything was lacking. This did not prevent Marshal Lebœuf from saying: 'We are ready, more than ready... Were the war to last a year, we should not have to buy so much as a button for a pair of leggings...' But the greatest German superiority lay in the quality of the men in command. The army leaders of the Second Empire were utterly ignorant of how to wage a war of movement. Moltke, a great general, had behind

HENRI BARON: AN EVENING AT THE TUILERIES The Second Empire had a reputation as a pleasure-loving era.
The ladies are here seen wearing crinolines.

him a man of genius, Bismarck. Napoleon III, who wanted to take active command of the army, left behind him in Paris only the unfortunate Empress and an unpopular Government. From the very beginning the campaign was disastrous. In two days the Germans had won two victories, had broken across the frontier and had invaded Alsace and Lorraine; excitement throughout the country reached so high a pitch that on August 12th the Emperor had to transfer command to Marshal Bazaine, of Mexican fame. Bazaine, weak and irresolute, retreated and let slip the last fleeting opportunities for victory, allowing the enemy to cut off the army of Lorraine at Metz. There remained the armies of Alsace and of Châlons, under MacMahon which were surrounded at Sedan on September 2nd, and surrendered. The war was barely a month old; it was lost and the Emperor was held captive. Shortly afterwards he sought asylum in England.

For the second time the Empire, a monarchy by popular vote, left France invaded and at the mercy of her enemies; for the second time a Bonapartist regime, lacking deep roots,

had been swept away in a few hours by the wind of defeat.

Literature in the Second Empire entered a twilight of the gods. Victor Hugo, who had not accepted the *coup d'état*, lived in exile until the end of the regime. Baudelaire, Flaubert found an escape in the creation of perfect forms. But the bulk of the bourgeoisie under the Second Empire found escape in pleasure. The whole world rushed to Paris to be entertained by all its sparkle and gaiety. And never had that country brought forth a more vigorous generation of critics, essayists and historians. Sainte-Beuve was the critical sovereign, and his Monday essays made and unmade reputations. During the days of the liberal Empire, reaction against romanticism produced realism. Maupassant and Daudet were realists, as was Zola, who likewise was one of the first to praise the realistic painters at a time when Courbet and Manet were acutely disturbing both public and critics.

The 1871 defeat reduced to silence those writers who had rallied to the Empire but it invigorated the best men and brought them back to reality.

[170]

◀ CLAUDE MONET: PICNIC ON THE GRASS Painted in 1866. *Photo Durand-Ruel.*

X

The Third Republic, and After

(1871-1946)

A GOVERNMENT survives serious military defeat only if it is both old and strong. The Second Empire was still bent on adventure, and Sedan killed it. On September 3rd, Jules Favre, in the name of the Left, moved for dethronement; on the fourth, Thiers suggested the naming of a Government Committee of National Defence. The deposition of Napoleon III and the dynasty was announced, but the mob clamoured for the republic. The Paris deputies formed the Government Committee of National Defence, with Jules Favre and Jules Simon representing the moderate bourgeoisie, Crémieux and Garnier-Pagès the memories of 1848 and Gambetta radicalism. Thiers preferred to await a regularly elected government, but he persuaded the Empire's Legislative Body to disperse without resistance; the Empress had already left the Tuileries. Crémieux was sent as a delegate to Tours to organize provincial resistance; General Trochu, in command of the Army of Paris, became head of the Government, which thus indicated its dedication to military resistance. On September 12th, the Government entrusted Thiers with a mission to London, Vienna and Saint Petersburg; he was to sound the attitude of the Powers towards France. Jules Favre met Bismarck at Ferrières to discuss an armistice with an eye to an election, but the provisional Government refused to accept the German conditions. On September 19th, Paris was surrounded.

At Tours a group of fine men did its best to recruit armies, but it lacked a leader. Suddenly, on October 7th, came the astounding news: 'Gambetta, having left Paris in a balloon, has arrived at Amiens and is hastening towards Tours.' Gambetta's selections were excellent. For the War Office he chose a young engineer, Charles de Freycinet, who worked wonders. Six hundred thousand men were placed under arms and organized in their respective units. Very shortly the Army of the Loire was in a condition to resume the offensive. The efforts of the Tours delegation failed, but for reasons unconnected with the activities of Gambetta and

his associates. On October 29th, 1870, Metz surrendered. At the same time Gambetta learned that Thiers' trip across Europe had been a total failure. If the delegation wanted to act, it must do so before the arrival of Prince Frederick Charles from Metz. Gambetta ordered the retaking of Orleans and won the day at Coulmiers. Here was a surprise for all Europe, a vast hope for France.

Had France then found support abroad, her heroic efforts would have saved her; in her isolation she was doomed. The Army of the Loire had to retreat and the Tours delegation had to withdraw to Bordeaux. In Paris the siege was becoming a heavy burden; the Parisians were eating dogs and rats and the animals in the zoo. Bombardment had begun. On January 18th, 1871, the German Empire was proclaimed at Versailles, in the Hall of Mirrors. Paris was as the end of her resources, and on January 28th an armistice was signed at Versailles between Jules Favre and Bismarck. A national Assembly was to meet at Bordeaux; there the strife between Jules Simon, who came as representative of the Paris government, and Gambetta was violent; Gambetta refused to forgive his colleagues for the nature of the armistice, and handed in his resignation. For the majority of the French, the man of the hour was Thiers who described Gambetta as a 'raving idiot'.

The elections of February 1871 were held without preparation. The country voted for the old monarchist candidates in order to cast its vote for peace. Out of six hundred and fifty deputies, four hundred were legitimists or Orleanists. The monarchist party, not wanting to saddle itself with the defeat, did not at once restore the monarchy. Hence the Assembly adjourned the question of the form of government, and appointed a 'head of the provisional government of the French Republic' who could be no one else but Monsieur Thiers. This little old fellow, with his conspicuous forelock, then possessed tremendous prestige. He had been elected by twenty-six departments. The peace negotiations

DIDIER and GUIAUD: GAMBETTA LEAVES PARIS BY BALLOON During the Siege of Paris, 1870-1871, contact with the rest of the country was maintained by means of balloons. Gambetta left for Tours to take command of the government's delegation, October 6th, 1870. In the background, the Butte Montmartre. (*Musée Carnavalet*.)

with Bismarck were painful; Thiers and Jules Favre succeeded in having the indemnity reduced by one milliard and saved Belfort, but could not prevent the annexation of Alsace and Lorraine.

One of the terms of the treaty of peace was a symbolic German entry into Paris; this triumphal march along the Champs Elysées (March 1st) was brief, but it sufficed to raise Parisian indignation to fever pitch. On March 18th revolution broke out in Paris. Its immediate cause was an attempt to take away from the National Guard the cannon which had been given them during the siege; the underlying cause was the old communal and Jacobin tradition. A central committee took charge of the uprising. Here was civil war, and Thiers was well aware of it; his strategy was to abandon Paris to the insurgents, to gather loyal forces outside the city and to attack only in full strength. He

himself withdrew his Government to Versailles. This plan brought him victory, but only after two months of terror for which both parties must be held responsible. Versailles lined up 'federated' prisoners before firing squads, whereupon the Commune seized hostages who were shot prior to the final defeat of the Commune.

Its defeat was inevitable because the provinces did not support the capital. Thiers, triumphant, showed a want of generosity; he allowed the slaughter of prisoners by the Versailles troops. Repression produced seventeen thousand dead plus arrests and deportations without number; no defeat in the war of 1870 cost France so many lives. From the days of the Commune dates the 'secession of the proletariat'. Thiers, however, emerged even stronger from this 'appalling victory'; he had shown that the Republic could subdue a revolution.

PIERRE-AUGUSTE RENOIR: A DANCE AT THE MOULIN DE LA GALETTE
(Musée du Jeu de Paume.) *Photo Giraudon*.

This painting, one of Renoir's best known, shows one of Paris' most popular rendezvous, in 1876. The wooden windmill of the Galette is still extant, the only survivor among a large number of windmills which used to line the Butte Montmartre. It dates from the XVIIth century. A member of the family which owned the mill was killed there while defending it against the Cossacks in 1814. The same family, Debray, started the ball which made the mill such a popular meeting-place for artists and writers.

A RECEPTION IN THE GREAT HALL OF THE ELYSÉE After the Tuileries was burnt down by the Commune rioters, the President took up residence at the Elysée Palace. This scene is of 1873. *Photo Viollet.*

The important thing now was to rid the country of the Germans. The final treaty had been signed at Frankfort on May 10th; there remained, to bring the occupation to a close, payment of the war indemnity. For his first loan, Thiers' obtained five milliard francs, the total sum required. Once again France astounded Europe by the speed of her recovery. By-elections took place in July, and the same electorate which in January 1871 had given a crushing majority to the royalists, on July 2nd of the same year elected only republicans. France severed herself from a class she distrusted; Gambetta became the head of an 'opportunist' party and supported Thiers. Their alliance enraged the Right. Thiers, who had the support of the opportunists, changed his title to that of President of the Republic. The excellence of his administration had added even more to Thiers' prestige; but because Thiers had done his job too well, the Assembly wanted to get along without him.

The monarchists decided to eliminate Thiers. In this manœuvre they had, from 1873 on, the support of the Bonapartists, who had lost their leadership with the death of Napoleon III. The monarchists had finally unearthed a leader, the Duke of Broglie, son of Louis-Philippe's minister and grandson of Madame de Staël. He challenged Thiers, and on May 24th, 1873, out-voted him. That same day, during an evening session, Marshal MacMahon was elected

President of the Republic. The monarchists planned to use this Marshal simply as a care-taker till the King's restoration.

The Duke of Broglie, now head of the government, was fully resolved to set up the monarchy and to do it legally. But there remained an obstacle — the Count of Chambord, posthumous son of the Duke of Berry. Believing that his only strength lay in the principle of legitimacy, he refused to come to terms with any assembly. The symbol to which he passionately clung was the white flag. Now all his partisans knew that the army would not accept this. Vainly did messenger after messenger seek him out; the Count was unwilling to be the 'legitimate king of the Revolution'. These handsome feelings cost him the throne.

The Bonapartists and republicans were delighted. 'None will deny', said Thiers, 'that the founder of the French Republic is *Monsieur le Comte de Chambord.*' There remained for the Right what the Duke of Broglie called the line of retreat: the continuance of Marshal MacMahon's powers by personal right. On November 19th, the term of the Marshal's personal mandate was fixed for seven years. There followed a period of confusion, during which continued the policy described as that 'of moral order', but which was neither moral nor conducive to order. It consisted in bullying the Left press and purging republican bureaucrats. For the firm establishment of the Republic, an alliance was needed bet-

[173]

ALFRED ROLL: A MINERS' STRIKE There were
innumerable labour troubles around 1880, the
workers living too often in inhuman conditions.
(Musée de Valenciennes.)
Cie des Arts Photographiques.

ween Gambetta and the moderate monarchists; Gambetta himself proposed this difficult union, and the constitutional law of 1875 founded the Third Republic. Thiers and the Duke of Broglie had finished their work; the future seemed to belong to Gambetta.

1876 was an election year; in the Senate the Right retained the majority, though it was smaller; the Chamber had a republican — but moderate — majority. The stumbling block was the anti-clericalism of the Left. After Jules Simon had agreed to one or two votes in the Chamber which ran counter to the Marshal's principles, on May 16th, 1877, that old soldier in effect cashiered the minister, and asked the Senate for the dissolution of the Chamber. The Left banded together for republican defence; by contrast the coalition of the Right was crumbling. In October 1877, despite shameless pressure by the Government, three hundred and twenty-six republicans were elected; they retained a majority of one hundred and nineteen votes. MacMahon, for his part, submitted, but against the grain.

The Republic of the dukes was dead; that of the republicans began under happy auspices. The country was prosperous. A balanced budget had been re-established from the proceeds of indirect taxes alone. At the Congress of Berlin, in 1878, Bismarck offered France Tunisia, not without the base ulterior motive of embroiling the French with Italy and drawing France's attention away from the Rhine. Bismarck, however, miscalculated, and through his stratagem consolidated France's colonial empire. The Republic grew ever stronger; the 1878 elections stripped the Right of its last citadel, its majority in the Senate. The Marshal's position was becoming too difficult, and he handed in his resignation. Jules Grévy, his successor at the Élysée, was a man of the upper middle class with liberal views. An old man of seventy-six, he was rather weary and suspicious of adventures. Gambetta had led the republicans in their victorious fight; Grévy should have offered him the premiership; but Grévy did not like Gambetta's impetuosity and he feared his prestige. He called in Waddington, and then Freycinet. Until that time religious and lay schools had competed on an equal footing; but now Jules Ferry, a doctrinaire of the Left, introduced an educational code whose famous Article VII deprived unauthorized congregations of the right to teach. This measure, by creating the 'godless school', drew upon him unrelenting wrath. In 1880 there were also established the first secondary schools for girls — a great novelty, since the teaching of young

women had been the last inviolate citadel of Catholicism. The conflict which thus set the Church against the State was unfortunate, since in France the Church was a powerful force; it retained spiritual strength, and by means of its missionaries, it had done more than the State to spread French culture throughout the world.

Gambetta remained at once the prodigy and the problem child of the Republic. After the 1881 elections, which confirmed the republican majority, Grévy finally decided to let Gambetta form a cabinet. The country expected that Gambetta's ministry, about which there had so long been talk, would be a great government 'of all the talents'. Nothing of the sort took place; one by one the great ones refused to participate. Gambetta finally formed a ministry consisting of clerks and personal friends; within a few weeks it was out of office and a few months later Gambetta died, at the age of forty-four. Of all crimes, pre-eminent ability is that which men least forgive.

In foreign affairs, the debate was between those who, like Ferry, sought to build a colonial empire, and those who, like Clemenceau, were obsessed by Germany and the Rhine. In 1885, when Ferry wanted to make Tonkin into a French colony, Clemenceau feverishly denounced him, had him voted out of office, trampled on his prostrate form and had the 'Tonkinese' booed in the streets of Paris. On that day, Ferry saw his political career ruined. These violent altercations created a spirit of anxiety and distrust which harmed the Republic and cleared the way for those who might be tempted to overthrow it. The 1885 elections proved calamitous to the republicans; they had succeeded in making themselves masters of the Republic. Would they succeed in remaining so?

The nation was ready for adventure, a tribute to chauvinism; all it lacked was an adventurer, and Freycinet unintentionally dug up one when he took General Boulanger into his cabinet as Minister of War. He was a youthful general of forty-nine, with an instinct for flashy self-advertisement, and he achieved great popularity. The League of Patriots, founded by Déroulède, clasped him to its bosom; Clemenceau and Rochefort, who had founded the Paris liberal weekly *La Lanterne*, gave him wholehearted support. Here was all that the crowds needed; Boulanger became their idol, 'Boulangism' a system of political philosophy, and 'La Boulange' a political party. The President and Parliament were disturbed, and appointed Boulanger to the command of the Thirteenth Corps at Clermont-

ALBERT-PIERRE DAWANT: THE RUSSIAN SOVEREIGNS AT BETHENY (Musée de Versailles.)

On September 21st, 1901, a review took place at the Betheny Camp of all the troops who had taken part in the great manœuvres of the east. Emile Loubet, President of the Republic (1899-1906) is here seen greeting Nicholas II Alexandrovitch, Emperor of All the Russias, and the Empress Alexandra Fyodorovna. A Cossack holds open the carriage door. Behind Loubet stand Waldeck-Rousseau, President of the Council, and Armand Fallières, President of the Senate, who was to be next President of the Republic.

Ferrand, thus forcing him to leave Paris. Basically a man of discipline, timid, he reported for his new duty.

Yet events were to afford him a fresh opportunity. In 1887 a republican scandal was uncovered; Daniel Wilson, President Grévy's son-in-law, had made use of his influence to traffic in the sale of posts and decorations. Grévy made the mistake of trying to defend Wilson, but finally he had to hand in his resignation. It was urgently necessary to elect a new president. Sadi Carnot, who possessed all the republican and middle-class virtues, was elected. Boulanger, however, won a seat in the Chamber. As against 'parliamentary corruption', the mob worshipped him. The Right supported him because it innocently hoped that he would beat down the Republic. The Boulange had become 'the union of the malcontents'. In January 1889 Boulanger was elected deputy for Paris. The crowd would have borne him to the Elysée, but by temporizing he gave the republicans time to pull themselves together. They took steps which alarmed Boulanger, and, fearing arrest, he took the train for Brussels. The bubble burst; Boulangism was finished.

The World Fair of 1889 was remarkable in more ways than one. It made it possible for thousands of foreign visitors to see with their own eyes how firmly established was the Republic, and it afforded them a lofty notion of France's genius. The success of the exhibition, and the country's justifiable pride finally led the most reasonable elements of the Right to rally round the regime. Moreover, an encyclical of Pope Leo XIII wisely drew the French Church and the Left towards each other and permitted the establishment of a Catholic republican party, which caused the parliamentary majority to shift towards the Centre. The Republic was becoming moderate.

The moment the French Republic appeared more stable, stronger and more tolerant, foreign friendships began to be cemented. Russia, perturbed at the formation of a Triple Alliance (Germany-Austria-Italy) was gradually drawing closer to France; between czarist Russia and republican France the ideological breach was broad, but the loans which Russia floated in France were well received. The French were no longer isolated.

In 1893 a financial scandal shook the columns of the Palais Bourbon. Ferdinand de Lesseps, who had pierced the Isthmus of Suez, had announced his intention of digging a canal across Panama, and the French public had backed him with its savings. But the task was far more burdensome than he had foreseen, and in order to muzzle criticism, the

Panama Company paid money to the newspapers, and bought votes in the Chamber. In 1892 the Rightist paper, *La Libre Parole*, saw a political weapon in this business and exploded the bombshell. Baron Reinach, who had acted as intermediary, committed suicide. A whole generation of public men was bespattered; Floquet, Clemenceau and a score of others were compromised and had for long years to withdraw from public life. The Republic was by circumstance forced back somewhat more to the Right. From 1893 to 1898 France was ruled by moderate ministers. But a socialist party was growing and it had remarkable leaders: a third crisis was to bring into office various of these elements of the Left.

This crisis was the Dreyfus Case, which began in 1894 and at first seemed merely a matter for the courts to settle. A memorandum found in the waste-paper basket of the German military attaché seemed to prove that a general-staff officer was acting treasonably. Suspicion fastened upon the Jewish Captain Alfred Dreyfus; he was condemned by a court-martial, stripped of his rank and shipped to Devil's Island. His family, who knew him to be innocent, investigated further and furnished proof of his innocence. The Prosecution then forged documents to prove his guilt. France split into two camps, for and against Dreyfus, and the Right made the mistake of identifying itself with the anti-Dreyfus group in order to defend the army and the Church, but, quite on the contrary, it compromised both by associating them with a bad cause. Déroulède wanted to try a *coup d'état*, in 1899, but he failed. So great was the scandal of the forgeries that a review of the trial was imperative. Loubet thought the moment opportune for crushing the enemies of the regime; he called in Waldeck-Rousseau, an opportunist, but brave. The whole Left joined forces around him. The Court of Appeals reversed the 1894 decision and remanded Dreyfus to the Rennes court-martial. This second decision found Dreyfus guilty but with extenuating circumstances. The decision enraged the Dreyfus faction. It was not until 1906 that the second decision was to be annulled by the Court of Appeal; Dreyfus was to be restored to his rank and then promoted and decorated.

Waldeck-Rousseau and his successor, Émile Combes, above all strove to prevent the recurrence of such offensives against the Republic. Unruly soldiers and rebellious monks had for several years dominated the Government; a law was voted to expel all those religious orders not 'authorized'. An over-zealous Minister of War had files prepared on all army officers by certain of their colleagues and encouraged tale-bearing. From this there resulted a dangerous uneasiness which would finally be healed in 1914 by the danger in which the country found itself. But, taking everything into account, the French Republic emerged from this third and most serious crisis with honour.

It is to the Third Republic's honour that it created a magnificent French colonial empire. Expeditions, led by men like Savorgnan de Brazza and Faidherbe, gave France Senegal and the Niger as far as Lake Chad, then Dahomey and Madagascar; Cochin-China, Annam and the Protectorate of Cambodia had been added to Tonkin in Indo-China. Several of these possessions had been won almost without the country's knowledge and despite parliamentary opposition. The development of a French empire created bad feeling between France and England. The sudden encounter of Major Marchand's expedition with General Kitchener's far more numerous force at Fashoda, a village in the Sudan, almost caused a war. But the Foreign Minister, Delcassé, had the courage to defend Anglo-French concord against hostile public opinion. In his labours for such a reconciliation Delcassé was abetted by King Edward VII, who was moved both by his sentimental affection for France, and by a legitimate fear of his nephew Emperor William II's ambitions. England wanted the winding up of any French claim on Egypt; France wanted to have a free hand in Morocco. On these foundations Delcassé and Lord Lansdowne built up the *Entente Cordiale*, and William II himself undertook to tighten these bands by landing at Tangier with an eye on Morocco. The 1906 international conference at Algeciras, however, recognized France's rights in Morocco; England supported France with all her weight.

From 1906 to 1914, it seemed as though France were living on two levels: that of patriotism and that of dissension. While France gathered a whole retinue of allies, the country's internal policy was unstable. Clemenceau, pro-English, had to share power with Caillaux, advocate of reconciliation with Germany. The latter, who was trying to introduce income tax in France, thus aroused against him the representatives of the Established Order; as for Clemenceau, opposed by aggressive socialists and a powerful General Confederation of Labour (C.G.T.), which stirred up a series of strikes extending as far as government employees, he wanted to re-establish the State's authority and thus drew upon himself the hatred of the extreme Left. In 1909 Clemenceau fell from power. Germany, more and more irritable and irri-

tating, provoked incident after incident (Agadir, Casablanca) and made Caillaux's policy impossible. Towards 1912 the country began to understand the immediacy of the threat. This was the reason for selecting as President of the Republic a patriotic Lorrainer and nationalist, Poincaré. Political uneasiness still engrossed all minds when suddenly there came the first thunder clap, giving notice of the great conflict (June 1914). A young Serb's successful attempt at Sarajevo against the life of the Austrian Archduke and heir-apparent at once struck the Germans as an excellent excuse for the war of liquidation which they believed inevitable. On July 18th, 1914, Austria declared war against Serbia. This unleashed an automatic sequence of mobilizations. Austria began it; then came Russia, then Germany, then France. The invasion of Belgium supplied the British Government with the emotional excuse necessary to win over public opinion. Very fortunately the 'holy union' of the French took place the moment mobilization was ordered. The country had been terribly divided, but in 1914, the French, confronting the enemy, forgot their own quarrels. They all felt that they were about to defend one of the loveliest and the happiest civilizations in all the world.

In France, the superimposed layers in the pyramid of power were now less clearly defined than in the days of the kings. The power of the oligarchy was mitigated by the activity of the provinces. Democratic and anti-clerical freemasonry was potent, and there the lower middle class counted for more than the upper. The opposition of the Church to the regime was less ardent and the separation of the Church from the State, while it had impoverished the priests, had also brought them closer to the people. The purchasing power of the masses remained inadequate, and wages were too low, but the position of working people had been improved and the working day had been shortened from twelve to ten hours. The majority of the population remained rural, but the split between country and city had grown less. In relation to the other great Powers, France in 1914 still seemed a country of handicrafts, of small businesses; but concentration was far advanced in banking and industry. The Third Republic's financial position had never been disastrous. Altogether, before the 1914 war, reasons for worry seemed few; the currency had long been stable, the French peasant and *petit bourgeois* bought Government securities, and each family planned the lives of its children from the cradle to the grave. The middle class, high and low, continued legalistic, economical and prudent.

PAUL JOBERT: THE RUSSIAN SQUADRON PAYS A VISIT TO TOULON The Russian flagship *Admiral Nakimov* puts
into the harbour, October 1893. (*Musée de Versailles.*)

The Third Republic furnished literary history with a list of brilliant names; immediately after the war of 1870, Taine and Renan, both overwhelmed by the defeat, laboured to supply France with moral goals. Anatole France was Renan's disciple as far as the graceful effortlessness of his style and his ironic scepticism were concerned; while Maurice Barrès was the inheritor of Chateaubriand's beautifully singing sentences. Zola and his followers had continued the line of Balzac. Among the poets a burning desire for escape first produced the Parnassians (Leconte de Lisle), then the symbolists (Mallarmé) and finally Paul Valéry, a great poet and writer of classic prose, whose work was to dominate his time. Charles Péguy was the very embodiment of the French people, a Christian socialist and patriot. One philosopher had a profound influence on French thought, literature and art: Henri Bergson probed the mechanism of the memory, the immediate data of consciousness, the wellsprings of morality and religion. His teaching was to inspire a French novelist as great as Balzac, Stendhal and Flaubert — Marcel Proust, who in 1913 published the first volume of his lengthy work, *A la Recherche du Temps Perdu*. In art a fine school of painters sought out the underlying reality beneath the stereotyped;

these were the impressionists — Monet, Renoir, Sisley, Pissaro. Manet and Degas, although differing greatly from the impressionists, like them breathed new life into French painting, as also did Cézanne, Seurat, Toulouse-Lautrec. At the same time, Fauré, Debussy, Ravel and Dukas thrust to the fore a new school of French music. In the sciences, Berthelot, Pasteur, Henri Poincaré, Hadamard and Painlevé had built for their country a position equalling that which it held in the arts, while Becquerel and Pierre and Marie Curie were already beginning the great discoveries of the atomic era.

France, in August 1914, was confident; the troops marched off singing the *Marseillaise*. The desire for *revanche* had been aroused ever since Germany had renewed her blackmail. Joffre's plan, which was offensive, involved an invasion of Alsace during the first days of the war, but the defeat of the French army at Charleroi opened to the Germans the road to Paris. In early September, Joffre saw the German army engaged on the Marne along the arc of a circle by the French army, and threatened on its left wing by the Paris garrison, which Gallieni had painstakingly prepared for such a manœuvre. He decided it was time to join battle. By every means at hand, even by requisitioning the taxicabs of Paris, Gallieni brought up his troops against the rear of the German army. Foch, halted in the marshes of Saint-Gond, dispatched his stirring telegram: 'My left is broken, my right is weakening; the situation is excellent: I am attacking.' Von Kluck, fearing he would be outflanked and cut off from his bases, drew back. Paris and France were saved. On both sides the troops dug trenches, protected by barbed wire. For months and years the opponents were to seek means to break through this barrier and resume a war of movement. Meanwhile the Austro-German armies had crushed Serbia, and Briand had effected at Salonika the opening of a new Eastern front.

In order to prevent the Germans from moving their reserves from one front to the other Joffre in 1916 won acceptance for the idea of a general Allied offensive. The Germans decided to forestall this, and made Verdun the key point of their attack, February 1916. Joffre entrusted the defence to General Pétain, who had in less than two years become commander of an army group. Pétain organized his supply trains, counter-attacked, and after assaults without number, the German attacks began to lose their force; the battle of Verdun was as costly to the Germans as the 1915 offensive had been to the Allies.

The countries which had taken sides with the Triple Entente — Italy (1915) and Rumania (1916) — found themselves in no better position than France. The year 1916 ended in deep discouragement for the Allies, and in 1917 serious mutinies broke out in sixteen army corps; Nivelle was replaced by Pétain, who undertook personally to visit many of the regiments, improved the soldiers' diet and re-established discipline with a minimum of severity. Allied disasters continued to pile up. The imperial Russian Government collapsed; Kerensky's pro-Allied Government was replaced by Lenin's, and in order to devote himself entirely to the internal revolution, Lenin negotiated an armistice with the Germans. The United States' decision to go to war on the Allied side meant the turning-point in the Allied fortunes. In France, all those who urged a compromise peace were subdued by Clemenceau; with the help of the forceful Georges Mandel, he rebuilt for France her spirit of Public Safety.

After Ludendorff's thrust towards Amiens, March 1918, an inter-Allied command was established which was entrusted to Foch, with Haig and Pétain both placed under his orders. Foch was a good strategist, intrepid, who believed victory possible and was resolved to win it. Allied power was on the increase. Already American divisions were arriving under General Pershing. Foch was daily strengthened by fresh reserves, whereas Ludendorff had none remaining to him. In July 1918 hope changed camps. Foch launched a counter-attack from Villers-Cotterêts, and pressed his attacks all along the line in an endlessly renewed series of jabs and surprises. Haig, Pétain and Pershing each in turn moved forward. In the East, also, the Salonika front was becoming active; Franchet d'Esperey was very soon to force the Bulgarians to sue for peace, opening the road to Vienna for the Allies. At the end of October, Turkey withdrew from the war. On November 4th, Austria capitulated. On November 11th, an armistice was signed at Rethondes, the Germans accepting all the conditions laid down by Foch.

It was a great victory for the Allies, and especially for France, which had exercised supreme command. The President of the United States and the Prime Ministers of Great Britain, Italy and Japan assembled in Paris to discuss with Clemenceau the future order of Europe. The decisions of the Paris Conference were based on nationality; and consequently the Treaty of Versailles left a strong Germany confronting a Balkanized Europe. German disarmament was sabotaged, and reparations were paid only at the beginning,

FRANÇOIS FLAMENG:
AIRCRAFT IN WORLD
WAR I A French mi-
litary airfield, Feb-
ruary 1918.
(*Musée de l'Armée.*)

and then with American money. Thus France, bled white by her terrific losses, once again found herself at grips with a Germany which had lost almost none of her war potential and which was to gird herself for a new war. It is true that France had finally won back Alsace and Lorraine, but on the essential point — security — she had no guarantee whatever.

There was great disillusionment in France, and deep discouragement. Clemenceau, the country's idol in 1918, was defeated in 1920 when he stood as candidate for the presidency of the Republic. Soon the socialist party was cut in two; the partisans of the dictatorship of the proletariat founded the French communist party; the others continued to back a unified socialist party with Léon Blum as its leader, a talented speaker and writer who abided by parliamentary discipline. The fears of the middle class were increased by an odious financial situation. To make Germany foot the bills for reconstruction and pensions soon seemed an insoluble problem. France had to find money or go bankrupt. Millerand had replaced Deschanel as President of the Republic, and in 1922 summoned Poincaré to the premiership; Poincaré tried to make Germany pay by occupying the Ruhr. But in the 1924 elections Millerand, who had supported Poincaré, was ousted by the Chamber. Power returned, as before 1914, to the radicals. Doumergue was elected President of the Republic; the Ruhr was evacuated; Caillaux, father of the income tax, became Minister of Finances. He crashed into the 'wall of money'. The radical party, then led by Édouard Herriot, found itself forced to waver between the socialists and the moderates, whose support it needed to secure loans. In 1926, when the country's credit was melting away, Poincaré had to be recalled, a new 'family lawyer', who brought the franc up to 20 per cent of its prewar value. In the 1928 elections, thanks to Poincaré's prestige, the moderate party triumphed. Tardieu, the political leader of this Chamber, left foreign affairs to Briand, the last hope in Europe for peace-loving and liberal men. Aristide Briand, a man of compromise and insight, had placed his skill and his eloquence at the service of the League of Nations. He succeeded in negotiating the Locarno Pact (1925) under which France, Germany, Poland, Italy and Great Britain mutually guaranteed one another against any aggression. Briand still hoped for direct reconciliation with Germany. In this he failed.

On the surface, nothing in France had changed. But in many minds the parliamentary system had suffered serious blows; the attacks against the institutions of the Third Republic came from both the Left and the Right. These redoubled in violence when the Stavisky Affair, which proved the corruption of some politicians and a few judges, came into the light of day. In Paris, disorders, at first sporadic, quickly turned into an uprising, and on February 6th, 1934, the Palais Bourbon was literally besieged by the mob; the troops had to open fire. The Third Republic was saved, first of all by the socialists who called a general strike, and then by President Lebrun's summoning his predecessor, Gaston Doumergue, whom he asked to form a ministry of reconciliation. In November 1934 Doumergue, under attack from all sides on account of his proposed reforms, had to step down.

Now these domestic divisions were all the more dangerous as the power and aggressiveness of the European fascist States increased; not only was Mussolini absolute master of Italy, but in Germany an anti-Semitic agitator, Adolf Hitler, had come to power in 1933. Hitler's bible, *Mein Kampf*, asserted that France's final destruction was his goal. Those who governed France hesitated to take any steps. In her hour of peril, France was unfortunately busier about her domestic politics than about foreign affairs. A victory of the Popular Front, in 1936, put Léon Blum in power. He was able to effect a few useful reforms, but like all Governments of the Left, ran up against the 'wall of money'. In Great Britain, the Chamberlain cabinet still hoped to appease Hitler. Hitler played upon this desire for peace, which he sensed was no less ardent in France. So the German armies, in March 1938, entered Austria, and in October of the same year, Czechoslovakia, without any hindrance from the democratic governments. On the contrary, at Munich (September 1938), Czechoslovakia was carved up with their blessing.

France and England had tried everything — and perhaps too much — to keep the peace; when, without declaration of war, Germany invaded Poland, England, then France addressed an ultimatum to Hitler, and on September 3rd, 1939, began the second world war. The issue was whether violence and cynicism or international law would dominate the world.

On the eve of war France lacked man-power and munitions. Some people placed their faith in the Maginot Line, a system of reinforced concrete structures which shut off the eastern frontier; this line was strong and was defended by crack troops, but it was not difficult to outflank it by crossing Luxembourg and Belgium. In the spring of 1940

THE FRENCH FIRST ARMY LANDS IN PROVENCE The landing took place on August 15th, 1944, under the command of General de Lattre de Tassigny. *Photo S. C. A.*

the Allies thought they would 'cut the iron route' by a Norwegian offensive; but in the light of German air superiority, the British cabinet judged the operation too risky, and Norway was abandoned. On May 10th, Germany violated the neutrality of Belgium, the Netherlands and Luxembourg. The German armoured divisions made for the North Sea to sever the Allied army group in Belgium from its bases. General Weygand, appointed Commander-in-Chief, gave orders to attack southward: to sever the German corridor, it was only necessary to make a thrust of some twenty-five miles. Weygand's manœuvre did not succeed because the flood of refugees brought the armies to a stand-still,

and because the First Army Group was in great disorder, being cut off from its supplies. The enemy's total mastery of the air made it impossible for a general command to function.

The French Government decided not to defend Paris, in order to save the city from destruction. Paul Reynaud handed in his resignation and President Lebrun called in Marshal Pétain, who asked for an armistice, which was signed June 22nd. Under the armistice, France was divided into two zones, one called 'free' into which the Germans at first did not penetrate, and the other called 'occupied', far greater in extent. The Government of the free zone established itself at Vichy. On July 10th, the National Assembly granted full powers to Marshal Pétain. Thus the Third Republic died. On June 18th General de Gaulle had issued his famous appeal from London to the 'Free French'.

From the signing of the armistice to the Allied landings, the French war drama was played on several planes. France could be liberated only by the establishment of an anti-German coalition and that coalition's victory; she was to be saved by the tenacity of England, by Russia's entrance into the war, by the intervention of the United States and by her own resistance elements working as a team with the Allies. On the internal level, the so-called Vichy Government was subject to constant enemy pressure. By way of internal resistance, a secret army and information network had been set up immediately after the armistice. Then there were the Free French, the first name given by General de Gaulle to his London organization. Having the British radio at his disposal, he heartened the French; and he kept French troops in the war alongside the English. In North Africa, the armistice had permitted the continued existence of a French army, which clandestinely preserved its weapons.

The Anglo-American landings in North Africa (November 1942); the part taken by the French army in the Libyan, Italian, French and German campaigns; the formation of a provisional Government of the French Republic — all these marked stages towards the liberation of France. In August 1944, the American armoured columns rolled towards Paris where, on the 26th, General de Gaulle made his entry. Hitler committed suicide, and in May, 1945, at Rheims, the enemy signed an unconditional surrender.

After the liberation, the Third Republic was not re-established; it was decided that the French Republic would be administered by a provisional Government under the presidency of General de Gaulle, that a Constituent Assembly would be chosen, and that the new Constitution would be ratified by a plebiscite. The balloting method whereby each *arrondissement* voted for a single representative was replaced by voting for a list, with proportional representation. The result was to promote the establishment of big parties. The elections showed that three great parties dominated the new France — the Communist party, the United Socialist party and a new party, called the Popular Republican Movement (M.R.P.), a Catholic organization. The problems to be solved were vast. The ravages of war had turned the country upside down.

The political equilibrium was not stable; from the very first months, conflict had arisen between General de Gaulle and the Constituent Assembly. Not that the General opposed the policy of planning and nationalization desired by the Communists and Socialists and accepted by the M.R.P. But the General, more concerned with France's greatness and her place in the world than with finance and economics, clashed with the Assembly on the question of military credits and handed in his resignation on January 21st, 1946. Meanwhile the proposed Constitution, calling for a single all-powerful chamber, was rejected by the electorate. The second Constituent Assembly revised the proposed Constitution in accordance with the desires of the electorate and created a Council of the Republic; in the second referendum the yeas carried it by a very small margin; the Fourth Republic was born.

Léon Blum set up an interim cabinet composed principally of Socialists. The Congress elected to the presidency for a seven-year term (January 16th, 1947) Vincent Auriol. Outside the Chambers, General de Gaulle urged revision of the Constitution, a presidential administration; and, in order to push this campaign, established the Rally of the French People.

XI

The Fourth Republic

(1947-1958)

THE Fourth Republic made its bow in circumstances of considerable difficulty, partly because it found itself faced by a situation which would have endangered any regime, partly because its Constitution was badly drafted. Those who created it had hesitated between a presidential form of government, modelled on that of the United States, and a government by Assembly. The result was a mixture of the worst features in both systems. The President of the Republic had power to nominate the President of the Council, whose *investiture*, however, had to be carried by a constitutional majority of the National Assembly (one-half of the total votes, *plus* one). Such an absolute majority was not easy to obtain. The first Ministry was a three-headed affair, consisting of the M.R.P. (*Mouvement Républicain Populaire*) or Catholic Republicans, the Socialists and the Communists. This alliance was a direct result of the Resistance, in which the three groups had worked hand in hand.

The end of the year 1947 saw a complete rupture between the Communists and the two other groups in the Government coalition. Up till then, the Communist party had supported the freezing of prices and wages. But now it made a complete turn round and gave its backing to a policy of wage-claims and strikes. A whole series of strikes, accompanied by violence, began in December. Gangs of miners moved about the Nord department, stopping trains and calling for the closing of factories. Very soon there were disturbances all over France. For a while it seemed not impossible that the Fourth Republic would be overturned. The Government, however, won the day. Léon Blum, the old and respected leader of the Socialist party, had advised the formation of a new group of parties, *La Troisième Force*, the object of which should be to rally 'all republicans, all who refuse to submit to the dictatorship of a political party, all who refuse to seek help against that danger in a system based on personal power'.

The task facing the Governments of the *Third Force* was beset with problems which soon became well-nigh insoluble. The successive Ministries were necessarily composed of disparate elements, and these were at odds on all the more important issues. The Socialist ministers were bound to support the demand for higher wages. The Radical ministers found themselves compelled to champion the rural sections of the community. It was more difficult in France than elsewhere to solve the housing problem, because the maintenance of rents at a very low level discouraged new building. But what party would have dared to shoulder the responsibility of decontrolling rents? The only way of driving this ill-assorted team without risking a spill was to see that it never moved forward at all. There has been much criticism of the 'stick-in-the-mud' methods of the first leaders of the Fourth Republic. That these should have existed at a time when there was so much to be done, was certainly regrettable: but as soon as any eager or authoritative President of the Council attempted to act, he was overthrown.

Nevertheless, there was a good deal of work going on behind the scenes. Frenchmen are always more ready to dilate upon the mistakes of their Governments than to praise their achievements. The programme of national rehabilitation, known as the Monnet Plan, assisted by American aid (the Marshall Plan) was to some extent realized. Those who criticize the Fourth Republic should remember that it had to grapple with problems caused by widespread destruction, and that the country found itself faced by the necessity of rebuilding roads, harbours, bridges, railway-tracks and stations. Not only did the new regime complete this tremendous labour of reconstruction; it provided France with electric power on a scale never before attempted, and equipped many factories with the most modern machinery. Between 1948 and 1953 the production of electricity, in terms of kilowatt-hours, moved from 23 to 42 milliards; the number of tons of motor fuel handled in French refineries, from

THE UNITED NATIONS ASSEMBLED IN PARIS, NOVEMBER 6TH, 1951 The Sixth General Assembly inaugurated at the Palais de Chaillot by M. Vincent Auriol, President of the French Republic. *Photo USIS.*

2,800,000 to 22 million; the deliveries of cement from 3,400,000 tons to 8 million. The motor-car industry increased prodigiously. To all of this the critics will reply that such results were wholly inadequate, that France has moved forward far more slowly than other countries. That is true; but conditions in France were more difficult than in other countries. The pre-war level, from which this new advance started, had been very low. The country had been subjected to enemy occupation. Above all, her population, after a long period of stagnation, had suddenly and rapidly increased. This increase will be of immense value in the years to come, but its immediate effect was to saddle the community with more children than it had ever prepared for. A gigantic effort was made to build new schools. All things considered, it is only fair to admit that the work of the Fourth Republic, in its early years, was not negative. Far from it.

As the 1951 elections approached, the Third Force found itself called upon to deal with a new problem, that of the electoral law. Prior to the war, Frenchmen had voted by the method of *scrutin d'arrondissement*, with two ballots. In 1946 a system of proportional representation had been tried. From a purely arithmetical point of view it seemed fair enough, but life is more than a calculation of figures and, in fact, proportional representation has never, anywhere in the world, produced majorities capable of carrying on a Government. It multiplies parties. It sows disorder. If, in 1951, it had been applied without modification in a France brimming over with discontent, the two great opposition parties, Communists and *Rassemblement*, would have together formed a majority. But, since they could never agree about anything, government would have become impossible. What actually happened was that a new method was devised: proportional representation *plus* 'alliances'. The parties were given the right to conclude alliances among themselves. In the Departments where such an alliance obtained more than 50 per cent of the votes, all the seats would go to the 'allied' lists. In the other Departments the rules of proportional representation would hold. According to the calculations of its authors, this electoral law would bring about a diminution in the seats won by Communists and Gaullists, and this was precisely what happened. The Communists polled the same total number of votes as at the previous elections, though they captured fewer seats. The Gaullists (R.P.F.) carried 121. The Conservatives, who now called themselves *Independents*, increased the number of their representatives.

It looked as though it would be easy to control an Assembly in which a Fourth Force, comprising the three groups of the former coalition with the addition of a few Independents, would have a comfortable majority. But almost immediately the dangerous question of the undenominational schools was unfortunately reopened. In itself it was quite enough to divide the M.R.P. (Catholic) from the Radicals and the Socialists. The Socialists found themselves flung back into the ranks of the opposition.

The financial position very quickly deteriorated. The deputies added enormously to public expenditure and resolutely refused to vote the taxes necessary to meet it. The country was importing more and more, exporting less and less. Edgar Faure, the President of the Council, had to warn Parliament that the country's reserves of gold and specie were scarcely sufficient to meet the requirements of three days' foreign payments. He demanded new taxes. The Assembly threw him out. Vincent Auriol next called upon Antoine Pinay, an industrialist from the provinces, to form a Government. He had already been a minister, and the President had been struck by his sound common sense. Pinay was accepted by the Assembly because he managed to get the support of a certain number of Gaullists who had grown sick of always voting with the Communists. He checked inflation by issuing a tax-free loan with a gold backing which was a great success. When, however, he proposed to raise the duty on alcohol, he, in his turn, was thrown out. The Assembly seemed to be incapable of resisting the pressure brought to bear upon it by vested interests. Since, too (as we shall see later), the war in Indo-China, and the fulfilment by France of certain international obligations, demanded credits on an enormous scale, the indebtedness of the country increased.

At the end of 1953, the Congress (the National Assembly and the Council of the Republic) met at Versailles for the purpose of electing a new President of the Republic. Monsieur Vincent Auriol had bestowed high prestige upon the office. For several difficult years he had seen to it that the country was never for long without a Government. In this task he had acquitted himself honourably. The election of the new President went on for several days, and only at the thirteenth ballot was Monsieur René Coty chosen. He was a senator from Normandy, a sturdy and patriotic man. He was to be brought up against worse difficulties than those faced by his predecessors, both at home and in the French Union.

DAM AND HYDRO-ELECTRIC STATION AT L'AIGLE One of France's best hydro-electric stations, on the Dordogne, with a maximum potential of four hundred million kilowatts an hour. *Photo Roubier*.

At the Brazzaville Conference of 1944, it was decided that the word *Empire* should no longer be used in speaking of the French territories situated beyond the frontiers of the mother country. From then on these territories were to be known as the French Union, and their inhabitants were given grounds for hoping that they would achieve, by successive stages, a position of independence *within* the French political system. The idea of an Empire had become unpopular for several reasons. (1) It seemed only right to grant to the native populations of lands which had furnished many soldiers to the French military effort, the right to take part in the government of their country. (2) Both America and Russia were waging a campaign against the concept of 'colonialism', and, by so doing, were arousing lively hopes of emancipation. (3) The non-European peoples, as a result of the early successes of the Japanese, and of the Allied recognition of the importance of China and the Arab nations, were becoming conscious of their strength.

But each country in the French Union needed special treatment. Algeria was regarded as forming an outlying part of France and came, for administrative purposes, under the Ministry of the Interior. Black Africa consisted of territories to which the vote had been granted, and which were looked after by the Ministry of Overseas Possessions. Morocco and Tunisia were Protectorates, the one with its Bey, the other with its Sultan, operating under the aegis of the Foreign Office. In Indo-China (or Viet-Nam) an Emperor, Bao-Dai, had been set on the throne by the French, though he was not recognized by the country at large. Laos and Cambodia were 'Associate States' as, indeed, was Indo-China. This latter country was to a great extent controlled by the Communists acting under the leadership of Ho-Chi-Min. Reforms had been promised to all these peoples, but successive home Governments, occupied exclusively with their own problems, had made little if any attempt to apply them. They did not begin seriously to consider the special difficulties of the French Union until an explosive situation had developed within its component parts.

A profound change had been brought about in North Africa by the formation of the Arab League, which now set about encouraging the nationalist movements in the different territories. The soil had been already well prepared. France had educated the younger generations, and taught them the love of liberty. Reforms which, had they been carried out earlier, might, perhaps, have satisfied the peoples of North Africa, were now regarded by them as inadequate.

A state of terrorism rapidly developed. Rebel bands (in Tunisia they were called the *Fellaghas*) endangered the safety of the colonists and of those Moslems who had remained loyal to France. Violence and assassinations brought repressive measures. Tempers rose on either side. In Morocco the French authorities believed that they could restore calm by removing the Sultan, Sidi Mohammed Ben Youssef, and replacing him by Ben Arafa. Events proved that this was a mistaken view. Disorders increased: outrages multiplied.

In Indo-China it might have been possible, in 1947 or 1948, to negotiate with Ho-Chi-Min, and any settlement with him would have been of far greater benefit to France than was the long and terrible war in the course of which she lost many brave soldiers, the pick of her officers and several milliards of francs which were urgently needed at home. It was easy to foresee that the ending of hostilities in Korea, by making available much of the war material supplied by China, would lead to a fresh flare-up in Indo-China. So long as General de Lattre de Tassigny was in command there, morale was kept at a high level, and Hanoi was saved. But he was a sick man and returned to Paris where he died. However, it would have been beyond even his ability to bring the war to a successful conclusion. Two-thirds of the country were controlled by the 'Viets' and, in the remaining third, their secret sympathizers were numerous. By fighting with the utmost heroism and at the cost of heavy losses, it was still possible for the French troops to gain ground, but only to lose it again almost at once as the result of infiltrations which no defensive system could keep out. Many statesmen began to realize how useless and dangerous this obstinate resistance was, but the Americans insisted that the struggle should go on. The disaster of Dien-Bien-Phu, where a French garrison of 12,000 first-rate soldiers was made prisoner by the Viets, put the whole of the Delta, and Hanoi, in peril. In spite of so much wasted heroism the game was lost.

The Indo-China affair brought about the fall of the Laniel Government. The President of the Republic chose Pierre Mendès-France to succeed him. The newcomer had a reputation for courage, not only in the military sense, but in the political as well. As one of General de Gaulle's Ministers in 1945, he had suggested to his leader a programme of austerity similar to the one which had brought financial salvation to Belgium. This plan was rejected, and he at once resigned, since he refused to administer a policy which was not his own. On June 17th, 1954, he delivered his

THE SS JEAN MERMOZ LAUNCHED AT SAINT-NAZAIRE
(*Photo Baudelaire.*)

investiture speech before the Assembly. 'A cease-fire in Indo-China must be arranged as soon as possible', he said. He declared that his Government would achieve this in four weeks. Either he would present the Assembly with the required solution on July 20th, or he would resign. He further announced that he would offer a scheme of economic reform, and a means of solving the problem of a European army; that he would pursue a liberal policy in North Africa; and, lastly, that his Ministry would be formed without any concern for arithmetic or party vetoes. He gained an astonishing majority — 320 non-Communists, plus 99 Communists. There were only 43 adverse votes. Critics abounded in the lobbies, but there was a general feeling abroad that the country needed rapid solutions, and even his secret adversaries dared not withhold their support.

A Conference was, at that moment, in session at Geneva. Delegates from China were present, and it was upon them that the issue of peace in Indo-China depended. Contact was at first established with them, and afterwards with the representatives of Viet-Min. On July 21st, a cease-fire agreement was signed. Thus ended a war which for years had been a wound from which the blood of France had drained. Parliament gave its approval and then adjourned for the holidays. A few days later, Mendès-France, accompanied by Marshal Juin, took 'plane for Tunis, saw the Bey and returned with a peace plan by which Tunis would be granted internal independence. It seemed as though a

second grave problem had been solved. The solution did not satisfy everybody, but it was widely supported on the ground that it seemed to be the least bad of many bad possibilities. Meanwhile, at the Ministry of Finance and Economic Affairs, Edgar Faure was putting the finishing touches to an eighteen months' plan which was to produce excellent results.

Only on one issue was France still deeply divided — the construction of a European community. Robert Schuman had succeeded in getting adopted, without much difficulty, his scheme for the creation of a European Coal and Steel Community, a supra-national organization with headquarters in Luxembourg. Many French 'Europeans' were hoping that the second stone in the European edifice would take the form of a European Defence Community (E.D.C.). It was scarcely to be expected that the rearmament of Germany should be greeted with much enthusiasm in a country which had been so frequently invaded by the Germans. But the advantage of E.D.C. was that it would integrate the new German army with a collective force. Mendès-France was of the opinion that E.D.C. would not be ratified by the French Parliament and, in any case, he was not himself very warmly in its favour. He left the Assembly free to decide, and E.D.C. was buried without a debate. The 'Europeans' were much incensed against him because of this check to their plans. He revived the scheme in a different form, asserted that he had always been a faithful adherent to the Atlantic Pact, and agreed that Germany should be admitted to membership of N.A.T.O. on condition that the British and Americans should leave their armed forces on the continent of Europe. Nevertheless, the supporters of E.D.C. remained disappointed and bitter.

The 'style' of the Mendès-France Government, the rapidity with which it reached decisions, had all the appearance of being popular in the country. It was less so in the Assembly, which had been brought to heel at a moment of great national disillusionment. Many of the deputies were grateful to the President of the Council for having presented them with solutions which they knew to be necessary though they themselves lacked the courage to press them. But in February 1955, a vote of confidence was taken on the Government's North African policy, and the Ministry was overturned. Monsieur Edgar Faure's investiture was carried by 369 votes to 210. There had been a modification in the Constitution. From now on a simple majority was held to be sufficient for investiture, and only those deputies who were actually present in the Chamber were entitled to vote on issues involving a question of confidence. The Faure Government encountered serious difficulties in Algeria, where bands of terrorists were a standing menace to isolated farms, to roads and even to towns. Till then, Algeria had been free from troubles. The situation quickly developed in an alarming manner, and reinforcements had to be sent. A large proportion of the French army was now in North Africa. In Morocco Edgar Faure reinstated the Sultan, Mohammed Ben Youssef, and by this measure restored a state of relative calm if not of complete peace. The Sultan showed great wisdom, and promised that the rights of the French settlers in Morocco should be respected. It was agreed that negotiations should be opened immediately after the elections, with a view to establishing Moroccan independence.

The elections were due to be held in June or July 1956. But by the terms of the Constitution the President of the Council was empowered to dissolve the Assembly if two successive Governments were defeated within eighteen months on issues of confidence voted on in due form. The Assembly gave Edgar Faure a minority vote, and he at once exercised his right to dissolve. The two Radical leaders, Mendès-France and Faure, were no longer on good terms. The Radical party found itself cut in two. The elections were advanced to January 2nd, 1956. The principal parties were as follows: the Communists; the Republican Front (Socialists and Mendès-Radicals); the Faurists (R.G.R.); the Right Centre (Pinay); the Social Republicans (former Gaullists whom the General had forbidden to make use of his name); and a new party, the Poujadists, which consisted of a number of small shop-keepers and craftsmen, who had at first presented their movement to the electorate as a defensive protest against taxation, though, in the course of the election campaign, they launched a violent demagogic attack. The results of the voting were surprising and disquieting. The Communists won 150 seats, and the Poujadists 52. This meant that in the new Assembly one-third of the members would be in declared hostility to the regime. The Social Republicans were reduced to a mere handful. Neither the Right Centre nor the Left Centre could command a majority. It was, therefore, a matter of great difficulty to form a strong Government. This was the more to be regretted since a number of urgent questions were awaiting solution.

First and foremost was the problem of Algeria, which was considerably more complex than that of Tunis or Morocco. These two countries possessed responsible sovereigns who could speak for them. Algeria had never been a nation. Such unity as it could boast had been entirely the work of France, and the colonist population was large and long-established. These colonists feared that, in an independent Algeria dominated by the *Front de Libération Nationale* (F.L.N.), a group of extremists and terrorists, they could be guaranteed no security. The F.L.N., for their part, would accept no solution short of complete independence. Guy Mollet, after a visit to Algiers, decided to fight and sent to Algeria over 400,000 men. It is to be hoped that a solution can be found which assures peaceful co-existence between the French and the Moslem communities.

Whatever the solution adopted for Algeria, the French Union, including Black Africa, must, sooner or later, become a federation of free states, maintaining with France strong political, economic and cultural links. The evolution of ideas, and the progress of the populations concerned, make impossible the continuance of a simple imperial regime. But we must not forget that the widespread improvements and the economic development of these territories have all been due to French initiative. It must be borne in mind, too, that the task is as yet far from being terminated, and that the continued collaboration between France and the African natives is still necessary. If such collaboration fails, then, either these countries of North Africa will relapse into poverty and